Poverty, Income Distribution and Well-Being in Asia During the Transition

Studies in Development Economics and Policy

General Editor: **Anthony Shorrocks**

UNU WORLD INSTITUTE FOR DEVELOPMENT ECONOMICS RESEARCH (UNU/WIDER) was established by the United Nations University as its first research and training centre and started work in Helsinki, Finland, in 1985. The purpose of the Institute is to undertake applied research and policy analysis on structural changes affecting the developing and transitional economies, to provide a forum for the advocacy of policies leading to robust, equitable and environmentally sustainable growth, and to promote capacity strengthening and training in the field of economic and social policy-making. Its work is carried out by staff researchers and visiting scholars in Helsinki and through networks of collaborating scholars and institutions around the world.

UNU World Institute for Development Economics Research (UNU/WIDER)
Katajanokanlaituri 6 B, FIN-00160 Helsinki, Finland

Titles include:

Aiguo Lu and Manuel F. Montes
POVERTY, INCOME DISTRIBUTION AND WELL-BEING IN ASIA DURING THE TRANSITION

E. Wayne Nafziger and Raimo Väyrynen
THE PREVENTION OF HUMANITARIAN EMERGENCIES

Studies in Development Economics and Policy
Series Standing Order ISBN 0–333–96424–1
(*outside North America only*)

You can receive future titles in this series as they are published by placing a standing order. Please contact your bookseller or, in case of difficulty, write to us at the address below with your name and address, the title of the series and the ISBN quoted above.

Customer Services Department, Macmillan Distribution Ltd, Houndmills, Basingstoke, Hampshire RG21 6XS, England

Poverty, Income Distribution and Well-Being in Asia During the Transition

Edited by

Aiguo Lu
Senior Fellow
Institute of World Economics and Politics
Chinese Academy of Social Sciences
Beijing

and

Manuel F. Montes
Program Officer for International Economic Policy
The Ford Foundation
New York

palgrave macmillan

in association with
The United Nations University/World Instutute for Development Economics Research (UNU/WIDER.)

First published 2002 by
PALGRAVE MACMILLAN
Houndmills, Basingstoke, Hampshire RG21 6XS and
175 Fifth Avenue, New York, N.Y. 10010
Companies and representatives throughout the world

PALGRAVE MACMILLAN is the global academic imprint of the Palgrave Macmillan division of St. Martin's Press, LLC and of Palgrave Macmillan Ltd. Macmillan® is a registered trademark in the United States, United Kingdom and other countries. Palgrave is a registered trademark in the European Union and other countries

ISBN 0-333-97026-8

This book is printed on paper suitable for recycling and made from fully managed and sustained forest sources.

A catalogue record for this book is available from the British Library.

Library of Congress Cataloging-in-Publication Data

Poverty, income distribution and well-being in Asia during the transition / edited by Aiguo Lu and Manuel F. Montes.
p. cm. – (Studies in development economics and policy)
Includes bibliographical references and index.
ISBN 0–333–97026–8 (cloth)
1. Asia–Economics conditions–1945- 2. Asia–Social conditions.
I. Lu, Aiguo. II. Montes, Manuel F. III. Series.

HC412 .P6595 2002
330.95–dc21

2001057529

10 9 8 7 6 5 4 3 2 1
11 10 09 08 07 06 05 04 03 02

Typeset by EXPO Holdings, Malaysia
Printed and bound in Great Britain by
Antony Rowe Ltd, Chippenham and Eastbourne

Contents

List of Tables and Figures

Tables

Figures

List of Contributors

Kathryn Anderson, Graduate Program in Economic Development, Vanderbilt University, Nashville TN, USA

Paul Glewwe, The World Bank, Washington, DC, USA

Karel Jansen, Institute of Social Studies, The Hague, The Netherlands and National University, Ho Chi Minh City, Vietnam

Doowon Lee, Economics Department, Yonsei University, Seoul, Korea

Sahiya Lhagva, Institute of Economics, Mongolian State University, Ulaanbaatar, Mongolia

Jennie Litvack, The World Bank, Washington, DC, USA

Aiguo Lu, Institute of World Economics and Politics, Chinese Academy of Social Sciences (CASS), Beijing, China

Manuel F. Montes, Program Officer, Human Rights and International Cooperation Unit, The Ford Foundation, New York, USA

Mamta Murthi, Research Fellow, Centre for History and Economics, King's College, Cambridge, UK

Richard Pomfret, Department of Economics, University of Adelaide, Australia

Menno Pradhan, Free University, The Netherlands

Kinnon Scott, The World Bank, Washington, DC, USA

Paolo Verme, London School of Economics, UK

Zhu Ling, Institute of Economics, Chinese Academy of Social Sciences (CASS), Beijing, China

Foreword

It is now generally recognized that in most of Eastern Europe and the Former Soviet Union the transition to the market economy has generated disappointing economic and social outcomes. In contrast, the 'Asian road to the market' has generally been seen as a model of success and the object of widespread admiration. So far, however, the human impact of such an approach has been analysed only tangentially, on the presumption that the positive growth experienced in most of the region generated favourable social results. By affecting visibly living conditions elsewhere in the region, the 'Asian crisis' further contributed to the neglect of the social impact of the transition in formerly socialist Asia.

This study aims at filling, if in part, such a gap and at debunking some of the most widespread impressions in this area. It does so by identifying the linkages between alternative transition models, public policies and household responses on the one side, and key welfare changes on the other. The study underscores that social outcomes have differed markedly across countries depending on the pattern of transition followed, that is, an 'Asian gradualist-model' (as in China and Vietnam), a 'Russian-type reform model' characterized by rapid liberalization and stabilization and severe output losses (as in Kazakhstan, the Kyrgyz Republic and Mongolia) or an 'unsustainable procrastinating approach' characterized by limited liberalization, slow stabilization, no structural reforms and contained output losses over the medium term (as in Turkmenistan and Uzbekistan).

But the study also shows that even in countries experiencing sustained growth, there have been unmistakable signs of deep social strain. Though gains were achieved in specific countries and sectors, there were also large increases in inequality, temporary or permanent regressions in health and education coverage, the emergence of a large floating migrant population (with the attendant spread of urban slums), the erosion of social cohesion and spread of anti-social activities. Such marked – and avoidable – increase in social stratification makes the deepening of reforms in the region (such as privatization of inefficient state-owned entreprises) more problematic. Finally, irrespective of whether growth remained positive or not, the Asian transition has brought with it an erosion in law and order, the spread of crime and corruption, and an increase in racial and ethnic tensions. As such – as the authors of the study note – these unwelcome effects question the social sustainability of the transition process itself.

This book appears at an appropriate moment, that is, when the reform process in the formerly planned economies of Asia is about to intensify. The book shows that – in spite of the enormous gains achieved in parts of the region – this process could be jeopardized if the past policy neglect of its social impact continues. Because of its timeliness, originality and clarity of exposure, the book is a must for the scholars and policy-makers dealing with the transition to the market economies in Asia. As such, I strongly recommend it to them as well as to the informed reader interested in economic and social change in this region.

UNU/WIDER gratefully acknowledges the financial contribution to the project by the United Nations Development Programme.

Giovanni Andrea Cornia
Director, UNU/WIDER

I Introduction

1
Well-Being During the Transition in Asia

Manuel F. Montes and Aiguo Lu

The transition processes in Asia have generally been declared to be models of success and the object of widespread celebration and admiration. The chapters in this volume evaluate the social and human impact of the Asian transition process, a subject that has so far only been analysed tangentially, on the presumption that positive growth rates must have had a positive impact on human welfare (World Bank 1996; Lavigne 1995). It is also important to recognize at the outset that not all Asian transitions have been associated with positive economic growth. Mongolia (ADB 1992) and the Central Asian Republics have seen drastic declines in output and employment.

Though there are indications of positive gains in a few countries and specific sectors, initial evidence from these economies points to significant increases in inequality, the erosion of social cohesion, and spread of anti-social activities. An analysis of the gains or deteriorations in human welfare and social cohesion in the Asian transition process is not just intellectual, but interrogates the meaning of the Asian story, whether successful or not, and throws light on the social sustainability of the process itself.[1]

What are the channels by which positive growth rates translate into higher standards of living for the general population? Through more private provision of basic goods and services? Through more widespread public services made possible by an improvement in public finances? Whether economic growth has been positive or not, have there been significant budget cuts in the provision of health, education and other social services, and does this explain better the growth in private services? Has the experience proven the private provision of basic goods and services to be socially efficient? Are the benefits of growth shared equitably by the population? More specifically: to what extent has growth or decline been dependent on increasing disparities in income and employment security? Can the unintended distortions of the reforms be corrected without jeopardizing the positive gains in growth and efficiency already achieved? Are there tradeoffs between transition reforms, equity and social welfare? If yes, are these unavoidable?

These are fundamental questions of development, which in this case are being raised in societies that are also undergoing widespread reassignments of property rights, employment arrangements, and the economic responsibilities of the private and the public sector.

Drèze and Sen (1989) distinguish between two types of successful development processes: (1) 'growth-mediated' and (2) 'support-led' processes. In 'growth-mediated' processes, the benefits of growth are broadly based and widely shared, while 'support-led' processes do not rely on growth but instead depend on high priority being given to providing social services. Pre-reform China and Sri Lanka, in spite of low per capita incomes, made enormous progress in promoting human development, approaching levels found in middle-income countries. Indices such as life expectancy at birth, infant mortality rates, women's status and literacy rates improved broadly and tremendously in these countries. The question of whether China's path was 'growth-mediated' or 'support-led' still requires resolving (Lu 1996). What is undeniable is that the nature of China's growth process has undergone a profound change and the question arises whether the gains in human development achieved in the past must now be sacrificed for faster economic growth.

Under the central planning system, achievements in human development in these countries were commonly greater than the level of economic development might have indicated. This pattern, however, no longer holds once the transition begins. Whether human development tends to suffer or not will depend not only on economic performance, but also on social policies. This research emphasizes the view that human welfare is the ultimate goal of transition, suggesting a need to move away from a one-sided focus on economic growth to a people-oriented approach.

There are at least two, or perhaps three, patterns of transition in Asia. These groupings are characterized by different initial conditions and contrasting processes of change.[2]

The first type of transition, best exemplified by China, has been led by state authorities and has involved a significant amount of experimentation/tentative reforms (Naughton 1995). The Chinese date the start of their transition from 1978, and Vietnam from 1986 with the launching of the *Doi Moi* programme at the Sixth Party Congress of the Communist Party. These reforms began with experimentation in the introduction of economic incentives, especially in the rural areas, by authorities worried about the need to improve supply responses. These transitions have been launched in economies with a larger proportion of output in agriculture and with a considerable degree of decentralization. A common feature of these transitions, in terms of outcome, is that economic growth rates have remained positive during the process of change.

Vietnam might reasonably be counted in this first group because of economic decentralization and the importance of agriculture. Yet it had a foreign trade pattern that was highly integrated into the Council for Mutual Economic Assistance (CMEA). These transitions have enjoyed significant amounts of foreign direct investment flows. In terms of policy approach, the Vietnamese, unlike the Chinese, removed price controls quickly and, in 1989, carried out a drastic macroeconomic stabilization programme.

The second model of transition emerged in 1989 in economies with a greater degree of Soviet-style[3] control of output and pattern of production/trade. These transitions share with the European transitions (and contrast with the Asian transition of the first type) the experience of drastic political change, even though the governments that have emerged continue to enjoy considerable political authority. In terms of initial conditions, these economies had higher per capita incomes and a larger dependence on an industrial sector, much of which would be made obsolete by price reform.

We count Mongolia, Kazakhstan and the Kyrgyz Republic in the second type. All of these economies undertook rapid price reform and achieved rapid macroeconomic stabilization. These economies incurred cumulative declines in economic activity in the order of 50 per cent between 1989 and 1995, though Mongolia's relatively smaller cumulative output loss of about 12 per cent is understandable in terms of its smaller industrial sector.

Turkmenistan and Uzbekistan possibly represent a third pattern of transition, which shares the initial conditions and rapid price reform with the second type but differs in the slower macroeconomic approach to stabilization, as a result of which cumulative output losses in these two economies have been about half those in the other Central Asian Republics. If the proposition is true that one can only delay macroeconomic adjustment but not reduce the amount of adjustment, then this third type is only a 'lagged version' of the second type.

All of these transitions, be they associated with positive growth or not, have involved privatization, wage liberalization and the reform of the social safety net.

The transition in Central and Eastern European countries has also witnessed large-scale and widespread deterioration in social conditions (UNICEF 1993, 1994, 1995; Milanovic 1998). The worsening in social development indicators has been commonly viewed as an inevitable consequence of the severe economic decline. The concurrence of the two processes seems to have provided strong support for this simple causality. One view is that social policies matter, but, compared with the severe impact of economic decline, the role of social policies is considered derivative or of secondary importance in the determination of welfare changes.

Before the transition to the market the centrally planned economies had demonstrated notable success in improving social conditions beyond what would have been expected at their per capita income levels. This raises doubts about the actual relationship between the economic and social changes during the transition. Moreover, if economic recession was indeed the main determinant of the deterioration in social conditions, is it the case that the economic growth in the more successful transitional economies has been automatically followed by rising living standards and improved human development? And if not, why not?

Studies of the welfare situation in the Asian transition economies (ATEs) are far less comprehensive than those undertaken on the Central and Eastern European countries (CEECs). This is at least partly due to the lack of systematic, reliable and comparable data. This study faces similar problems. It is based on existing studies, information and data, which are published by various sources and rely on different methods. As a result, cross-country comparisons using the available figures will not be highly reliable, but will be highly indicative of the larger picture of socioeconomic development in these countries.

Asian transition economies in this chapter refers to those Asian countries which were under a central planning system and which began to reform this system through the introduction of market mechanisms at various times, mostly since the late 1970s. These countries in this volume include China, Mongolia, Vietnam, and the Central Asian Republics of Kazakhstan, the Kyrgyz Republic, Uzbekistan and Turkmenistan. Mention needs to be made of the special treatment of North Korea. At the end of 2001, the Democratic People's Republic of Korea has yet to implement reform measures that would indicate an obvious shift towards socioeconomic transition.

This definition of the ATEs immediately makes it clear that there is no single, so-called 'Asian model', even if the basis were only post-reform economic performance. On many other counts, the ATEs are far from being homogeneous, for there is a great diversity, for example, in initial conditions both economically and in the social welfare system, in reform approaches, policy sequences, social consequences and so forth, not to mention the great differences in culture, geopolitics and history. In many respects, the diversity is greater among the ATEs than it is among the Central and Eastern European countries.

In terms of transitional strategies and performances, the Central Asian Republics and Mongolia appear to be closer to the European transition model rather than the 'Asian model', although these countries are located in Asia. However, this does not pose a problem in the current effort, since a definition of transition models is not the goal here.

On the other hand, in addition to geographical location, the ATEs do share some common socioeconomic features which set them apart from the European transitions. For example, the ATEs were and still are among the lower-income countries, for which development remains as crucial an issue as market transition.

1.1 The pre-reform economies and welfare and social policies

Compared with the European transition economies, the ATEs are poor or relatively poor developing countries. At the onset of reforms, income levels in most of the ATEs were generally lower than those in the transitional economies in Europe (Table 1.1).

Table 1.1 Per capita GNP of the ATEs before the reforms, current US$

1978		1990	
China	230	Kazakhstan	2600
Vietnam	170	Kyrgyz Republic	1570
		Turkmenistan	1690
		Uzbekistan	1340
		Mongolia	780

Sources: Figures for Central Asia from Pomfret (1995), chapter 4; for the remaining countries, from World Bank (1980), pp. 110–11, and Mongolia estimated from the data in ADB (1992).

The figures are indicative of the presence of two groups. The East Asian group, which includes China and Vietnam, was among the poorest in the world in the late 1970s, at the time when China formally embarked on the road to reform. In the case of Vietnam, no radical improvement in per capita GNP took place between the late 1970s and the mid-1980s, when economic reforms were officially undertaken. The per capita income in these countries continues to be unquestionably lower than in other countries of interest. The Central Asian Republics and Mongolia were not as poor. On the eve of the transition, they ranked as low-to-middle-income countries. Among them, Mongolia was the poorest, as shown by the above figures, but its per capita GNP may actually have been lower still. For example, estimates put forward by others place the per capita GNP of Mongolia in the range of US$522 to US$880 in the late 1980s (see Kim 1996). In the early 1990s, when radical changes began to sweep the entire former Soviet bloc, the per capita GNP of Central Asia, with the exception of Kazakhstan, remained lower than that of all transitional economies in Central and Eastern Europe.

However, compared with most market economies at similar income levels, social development indicators pointed to a relatively good performance in all the ATEs before the transition. Because of the low or relatively low income levels, the pre-reform ATEs faced resource constraints in welfare provision. Especially in the poorest ATEs, per capita calorie intake, the access to consumer goods and quality housing, the consumption of public utilities and so on were low, and a relatively large proportion of the populations were poor. However, considering the available resources, people in the ATEs enjoyed a large amount of social protection. Poverty was widespread, but the income gap remained relatively narrow. Other important social development indicators, such as life expectancy and educational attainment, were generally more positive among the ATEs than they were in market economies with the same or even considerably higher per capita incomes.

China, the largest centrally planned economy among the ATEs, made considerable progress in social development in the first three decades after 1949. Measured by social indicators such as life expectancy, infant mortality and educational attainment, China forged way ahead of most market economies at similar income levels and surpassed a number of countries with per capita incomes many times greater. 'Analyses of anthropometric data and morbidity patterns confirm that China has achieved a remarkable transition in health and nutrition' (Drèze and Sen 1989: 204). Many of the social indicators for China reached the average levels for middle-income countries. For instance, life expectancy at birth increased from less than 40 years at the beginning of the 1950s to approximately 65 years in 1978.

In the 1980s, the GNP per capita in Vietnam was lower than that in China in the late 1970s. Because of the country's overall poverty, there were chronic food shortages, and the population suffered from widespread malnutrition. The incidence of malnutrition, particularly as reflected in the height-for-age and weight-for-height indicators for children, confirms that the most serious health problem in Vietnam was the lack of adequate amounts of food (John Mellor Associates 1993; Fforde and de Vylder 1996). The level of well-being, as measured by calorie intake, consumption of goods, access to safe water and so forth, was low. However, indicators show that the health situation in the country had improved significantly during the decades since independence. Life expectancy reportedly rose from 42 years in 1960 to 59 years in 1983, and the infant mortality rate declined from 165 per 1000 live births in 1960 to somewhere between 35 and 64 in the mid-1980s. The people in Vietnam were living longer than were people in countries such as Algeria, Brazil, Iran and Peru, all of which had per capita incomes more than ten times greater than that of Vietnam (Fforde and de Vylder 1996: 234). Overall, the social development in Vietnam before the reforms was more like that in a middle-income country (for example, the Philippines) than that in a low-income country (see Table 1.2).

Table 1.2 Economic and social indicators for Vietnam

Indicator	*Value*
Population (millions)	70.9
GDP per capita (US$)	220
Life expectancy at birth (years)	63
Infant mortality (per 1000 live births)	39
Adult literacy (%)	88
Urban population (%)	20
Population growth rate (%)	2.0

Sources: UN, World Bank and Asian Development Bank data for the most recent year (1990 for literacy, 1991 for mortality and life expectancy at birth and 1993 for other statistics) from Pomfret (1996), p. 61.

Mongolia, too, fared quite well in terms of social development, although the gap between the social development indicators and per capita income was not so wide. Before the transition, its per capita income ranked Mongolia among the lower-middle-income countries. Because of serious measurement problems, the size of Mongolia's GDP may have been overestimated (Pomfret 1996: 79). But even if Mongolia were classified as a lower-middle-income country, its human development record was quite favourable (Table 1.3).

Under the central planning system, Mongolia achieved significant improvements in the quality of life of its people. As Table 1.3 shows, the major social indicators were not only better than the average for all countries in the world, but they were also better than the average for the developed countries in some areas. Mongolia's achievement in education was especially pronounced and was far better than that of China. Eighty-nine per cent of all students had completed the eighth grade; 50 per cent had completed the tenth grade, and 16 per cent of the workforce had received higher education. With a per capita GDP that was not particularly high, Mongolia achieved a literacy rate of 97 per cent among the population above ten years of age. In 1990, it had 88.8 medical personnel and 119.5 hospital beds per 10 000 population. The nutritional standards were adequate and comparable with those in middle-income countries. Infant mortality (60.6 per 1000 live

Table 1.3 Human development indices

Indices	*Mongolia*	*All countries*	*LDC*	*DC*
Life expectancy at birth (1990)	62.5	62.8	50.7	65.5
Daily calories in % of requirement (1984–86)	116	107	89	113
Access to safe water in % of population (1985–88)	65	62	34	–
Primary and secondary school enrolment, % (1986–88)	95	70	41	78
Mean years of schooling (1980)	6.0	3.5	1.4	5.4
Female/male ratio in school enrolments (1980)	90	53	40	66
Female/male ratio in labour force (1988)	83	52	46	57
Per capita GNP (US$, 1988)	880	710	230	3 410

Note: LDC = least developed countries; DC = developed countries.

Source: UNDP (1991), cited in Kim (1996), p. 316.

births) and maternal mortality (1.44 per 1000 live births) were high, but there had been substantial progress over the years (MRIM 1994, cited in Abeywickrama 1996: 27).

Although within the USSR they were the poorest republics, the Central Asian Republics had far higher per capita incomes than did the rest of the ATEs. For instance, if one sets per capita income in the USSR at 100, then the respective index in 1988 was 93 for Kazakhstan, 62 for Uzbekistan, 71 for Turkmenistan, and 72 for the Kyrgyz Republic (IMF et al. 1991: 231). Poverty in Central Asia was more pronounced compared to the USSR average. It was reported that in Uzbekistan, significant numbers of people were living in poverty during the Soviet era. According to a 1989 household survey, about 44 per cent of the population were living below the official Soviet poverty line, of which 16 per cent subsisted on incomes less than two-thirds of the value of the line.

However, compared to the East Asian transition economies, not to mention neighbouring countries such as Afghanistan, the Central Asian Republics had reached higher standards of human development (Table 1.4). Life expectancy had improved steadily. In Uzbekistan, for instance, life expectancy had risen since the 1970s from 67.3 to 69.8 years, running counter to the downward trend in Russia from 67 to 64 years over the same period. Infant mortality continued to improve, from 47 per 1000 live births in 1975 to 34.6 in 1990 and then to 26 in 1994. However, serious problems, such as high maternal mortality, persisted. In particular, the literacy rates and the levels of education were very high, largely as the result of the Soviet education and healthcare systems.

The experiences of the ATEs under the central planning system indicate that there was an obvious gap between economic level and social development that was clearly in favour of the latter. The degree of this general 'imbalance' may be roughly measured through a comparison of

Table 1.4 Human development indicators, Central Asia, 1990

Country	*Life expectancy*	*Adult literacy rate*	*Mean years of schooling*
Kazakhstan	68.8	93.0	5.0
Turkmenistan	66.4	93.0	5.0
Uzbekistan	69.5	93.0	5.0
Kyrgyz Republic	68.8	93.0	5.0

Source: UNDP (1993), pp. 135–6.

a country's ranking in the world in terms of economic development and its ranking in terms of social development. For example, at the end of the pre-reform period, China ranked as the 22nd poorest country in the world (World Bank 1980: 110–11), but, measured according to human development index (HDI) values in 1980, it ranked as the 51st country from the bottom in terms of human development. In addition, China was among the dozen or so countries in the world that moved from the low human development group in 1960 to the medium human development group in 1980.

For the discrepancy between per capita income and human development in other ATEs, the following information from the UNDP human development index provides a fairly comprehensive picture (Table 1.5).

The pre-transition discrepancy between income levels and social development was particularly pronounced for East Asian transitional economies. As in other centrally planned economies, the relatively good social development records in the ATEs were an outcome, first of all, of the official ideology, which emphasized that human development based on equitable income and welfare distribution was a development priority. Second, there was a strong support system and government policies to buttress the official commitment to social development. Education and health services were significantly better than in most other countries at similar income levels. Welfare systems were supported by nationwide institutional establishments, which not only functioned as agents to carry out welfare programmes, but also oversaw the relatively equal coverage of education, healthcare and other social services.

The progress in social development in the ATEs was achieved largely through state-sponsored social welfare measures. There were essentially two types of state-sponsored welfare provision: the Soviet type and the

Table 1.5 The GNP rank and the HDI rank of six countries

Country	*GNP rank*	*HDI rank*	*HDI rank minus GNP rank*
Vietnam	16	62	40 (1987)
Mongolia	96	100	4 (1990)
Kazakhstan	53	54	1 (1990)
Kyrgyz Republic	81	83	2 (1990)
Uzbekistan	68	80	12 (1990)
Turkmenistan	51	66	15 (1990)

Sources: UNDP (1990, 1993).

East Asian type. The Central Asian Republics were constituent parts of the Soviet Union, and welfare provision before independence was therefore a function of the overall Soviet welfare system. In the Soviet economies, full employment was largely guaranteed; education and healthcare services were free; lifetime pensions were granted to all employed persons, and women were offered virtually equal opportunities in employment. These provisions served as the foundation for the remarkable attainments in human development.

For the relatively low-income region of central Asia, resources from outside the region within the USSR played an important role in supporting this comprehensive welfare system. Although net inter-republic resource flows in the Former Soviet Union are difficult to disentangle, the Central Asian Republics are likely to have been net beneficiaries of the resource redistribution among the republics (Pomfret 1996: 91). Largely because of extensive state employment and the provision of various social benefits through enterprises and farms during the Soviet era, a sense of security was enjoyed by people in Central Asia. On the eve of the economic transition, these republics inherited a fairly well-developed Soviet system of social insurance and assorted social assistance measures.

Mongolia was known as the '16th republic' of the USSR because of its close political relations and high degree of economic integration in the Soviet system. Mongolia possessed a welfare system similar to that of the Soviet Republics, in which education and healthcare services were run by the state and provided free. Privately owned housing did not exist. Urban housing was owned and allocated by the state, and rural housing belonged to cooperatives. Utilities (electricity, heating and so on) were furnished with zero marginal charges. Public transport and food were heavily subsidized.

In the poorer East Asian transitional economies, the role of the state in welfare provision was not as comprehensive as it was in Central Asia and Mongolia. While the state normally took full responsibility for the welfare of employees in the state sector, the larger part of the population outside the state sector, that is, the rural population, was left out of state provision. Rural populations had to rely mainly on local resources and rural institutions, that is, the collective or cooperative organizations, for welfare support. Rural collective frameworks, such as the commune system in China and the agricultural cooperatives in Vietnam, were responsible for the satisfaction of the basic needs of their members through the mechanism of the sharing of resources within their respective administrative boundaries. Admittedly, welfare coverage in the non-state sector was poorer in both quantity and quality than it was in the state sector, and this commonly resulted in less favourable welfare conditions among rural populations.

None the less, it ought to be remembered that the availability of the collectively sponsored welfare services, even at low coverage, made a great difference among low-income rural populations. Precisely because of the development of this organizational mechanism, the East Asian transitional economies were able to perform well in the area of human development, despite the agrarian nature of these societies before the reforms.

Unlike the Soviet type, the East Asian type of welfare provision, which combined direct provision by the state with collective sponsorship, worked to a great extent in a decentralized manner. The differences in access to resources between urban and rural areas, as well as among rural localities, contributed to the high degree of regional variation in social development. Nevertheless, judged by performance, the East Asian planned economies did relatively well in the utilization of natural and organizational resources to improve the well-being of their populations.

Despite these achievements, both the Soviet type and the East Asian type of welfare provision were not without problems. In general, the most serious and common problem was the severe resource constraint, which could not be relaxed as significantly as expected because of the inadequate economic growth. This was particularly true in the East Asian transitional economies, in which living standards remained low, and the efforts to eliminate widespread poverty were met with great difficulties. Given their resources, an important issue for Mongolia and Central Asia was the sustainability of the relatively comprehensive welfare coverage. This problem became more urgent and obvious after independence, when Soviet subsidies dried up as the result of the collapse of the USSR at the same time that inefficiencies and budget pressure were growing.

For all or some of the ATEs, the potential for further improvements in welfare was also limited because of such factors as inefficiencies in resource utilization, the lack of universal coverage, and the bureaucratization of welfare institutions. One of the basic lessons is that the relatively egalitarian income distribution and relatively advanced welfare services in the ATEs under the central planning system offset to a great extent the negative welfare impact of the relative economic backwardness of these countries, but could not be substitutes for the lack of dynamic economic growth.

1.2 Macroeconomic patterns of transition

The onset of the economic transition in the ATEs varied from country to country, as did the first initiatives in the new economic course. China was the pace-setter, inaugurating economic reform in 1978. Following a few years of spontaneous 'fence-breaking' and the relaxation of central control over the economy, Vietnam began official reform programmes in 1986.

In 1991, more than a decade after China's first reforms, strong external shocks were largely responsible for opening the way to a more radical economic transition in Central Asia and Mongolia. The sweeping changes in and the ultimate collapse of the Soviet Union left these countries no alternative but to modify immediately the economic and political structures so closely associated with the Soviet system.

For the East Asian transitional economies, the push for change came mainly from within. The accumulated problems of central planning, which resulted in the stagnation of income and less-than-satisfactory economic growth, propelled governments to adopt gradual yet far-reaching economic reforms.

The ATEs took diverse approaches towards reform, ranging from the so-called 'gradualism' or 'incrementalism' in China to the drastic 'revolution' in countries such as Mongolia. Transition is not merely a matter of economic change. In Central Asia and Mongolia, in particular, because of the sudden external shocks generated by the disintegration of the USSR, economic transition has had to proceed hand in hand with the reorganization of the state. The East Asian transitional economies, on the other hand, have managed to maintain political stability while pursuing reform. In all the ATEs the sociopolitical situation has been crucial in the formulation of transition strategies and in limiting the policy options available to governments.

1.2.1 Overall economic growth

With regard to economic performance, marked differences exist between the East Asian transitional economies on the one hand and Central Asia and Mongolia on the other (Table 1.6).[4]

The East Asian pattern of economic performance involves a combination of transformation and growth. China and Vietnam have witnessed the acceleration of economic growth since the early years of reform. In the nearly two decades since its first reforms, China has registered a tremendous 9 per cent annual growth rate. Vietnam has had a

Table 1.6 Estimates of real GDP growth rate, 1985–95, and per capita GNP, 1994

		GDP growth rate (%)			*GNP per capita*
Country	*1985–92 average**	*1993*	*1994*	*1995*	*1994 (US$)*
China	9.6	13.5	11.8	10.2	530
Vietnam	4.9	8.1	8.8	9.5	190
Mongolia	0.8	–3.0	2.3	6.3	340
Kazakhstan	–14.9	–12.9	–25.4	–8.9	1100
Kyrgyz Republic	–15.9	–15.6	–26.5	–6.2	610
Uzbekistan	–6.1	–2.3	–3.4	–2.7	950

*Refers to 1986–92 for the Lao PDR and Vietnam and to 1992 for Kazakhstan, the Kyrgyz Republic and Uzbekistan.

Source: ADB (1996), p. 204.

slower start, but in the first half of the 1990s the GDP growth rate reached 8–9 per cent in that country.

Meanwhile, in Central Asia and, somewhat less applicably, Mongolia, radical transition measures have led to severe economic contraction, and there has been a substantial erosion in GDP and standards of living during the initial stages of the transition. The extent of economic decline has varied. The output drop in Central Asia has been generally milder than that in the former USSR as a whole, while it has been less dramatic in Uzbekistan and Mongolia than in the Kyrgyz Republic and Turkmenistan. In particular, in 1992, as inter-republic trade in the Former Soviet Union diminished, output began to fall more rapidly in all the newly independent Central Asian Republics (Pomfret 1996).

GDP growth has made a significant difference to the material lives of people. In the transitional economies exhibiting positive economic growth, as average income has risen, the quality of life has improved. Poverty has been reduced substantially in both China and Vietnam. The chronic hunger faced by a large proportion of the people living in the high population density regions in the north of Vietnam has eased.

On the other hand, because of the drop in GNP, income per head in the Central Asian Republics and Mongolia has decreased, and the negative effect has become quite evident in changes in the profile of diets. Expenditure on bakery goods and vegetables has remained stable, but the consumption of meat and especially dairy products has fallen. There was a significant change in the structure of diets in Central Asia beginning in 1992, when starchy foods came to account for two-thirds of caloric intake, while the protein component of diets declined sharply. In Turkmenistan, the consumption of dairy products during the first three quarters of 1992 was only about two-thirds of that of the comparable period in 1991 (Pomfret 1995).

1.3 Policy patterns in the transition

Without having to ascribe an overall purposiveness to the transition effort in each country, one can consider the different patterns into which the approaches to transition have fallen. These patterns have arisen because all transition economy policy-makers have had to face the same issues.

1.3.1 Macroeconomic transition

Transition processes have typically been launched in the context of fragile macroeconomic stability, uncompetitive domestic costs of production *vis-à-vis* foreign-produced goods, and tax systems heavily dependent on profit transfers from state enterprises (Montes and Van Arkadie 1995). For Vietnam and Mongolia, the hazards of macroeconomic imbalance were magnified by their dependence on the CMEA economies.

As in other economies, macroeconomic instability has meant inflation or increases in unemployment or both. For the Soviet-style Asian transition in particular, such as in Mongolia, rapid reform has been applied and the danger is that these economies might have been nudged unintentionally toward a 'low-growth equilibrium trap'. The advantage of the Chinese-style transition has been the maintenance of employment in the state-owned enterprises (and the associated social support programmes), at the cost of possibly wasted public funds.

The presence of a preponderant agriculture sector in the Asian transitions has turned out to have important welfare implications by permitting some leeway for more generous macroeconomic stances in at least two ways (Montes 1995). First, freeing incentives in this sector has seen an increase in output in the sector that has helped to keep the cost of wage goods down, counteracting the transition's inflationary tendencies. Vietnam moved into rice export production and attained the position of number two rice-exporting country one and a half years after restrictions on foreign sales of rice were removed, an unmistakable indication of a supply response that appears unprecedented in comparison with the non-Asian transitions. Second, a preponderant agricultural sector is associated with a relatively unmonetized economy, something that is particularly true of a large country such as China, but less so in the case of a smaller, more open country such as Vietnam. As marketization proceeded, the corresponding increases in the demand for money provided monetary authorities with the room for money creation at a smaller inflationary/balance-of-payments impact.

All the Asian transitions, including those under socialist leadership, have moved at a breathtaking pace in freeing the mechanisms of price setting and internal trade. In the initial period, increases in the prices of wage goods have imposed a drop in family living standards. The extent to which the loss in real family incomes has been made up for by subsequent growth requires further analysis. The impact of continuing inflation on family income and on the capacity of health and educational systems to maintain historical rates of real provision also needs to be analysed.

1.3.2 Microeconomic transition

In considering the impact of microeconomic policies, it is necessary to evaluate the differential welfare impact of these policies in different regions, especially in China. Regions that have had the benefit of greater external trade and foreign investment have also reaped the advantage of access to inputs and financing through which the hypothesized supply response to microeconomic reforms can take place. More remote and less economically diversified regions or those that are adjacent to slower-growing and less open economies (a case that probably applies very well to the Central Asian Republics but also applies to parts of China and Vietnam) suffer from poorer possibilities of microeconomic response to the overall reform process. These areas could actually be victims, in terms of their loss of internal markets where goods used to be exported and through the higher costs of production inputs. These policies can have long-lasting impacts on employment prospects to the extent that these microeconomic changes render existing production methods obsolete and uncompetitive while the resources for responding to new price vectors remain meagre.

The previous emphasis on 'regional development', which in the planning period used to mean development of poorer areas for social and national defence reasons, has been weakened, if not abandoned. This has meant reductions in investment and infrastructural expenditures and reduced employment and welfare in inland and historically poor areas.

1.3.3 Privatization

In the Chinese-style transition process, privatization has focused on removing barriers to entry (Naughton 1995) and enterprise responsibility reform (Jefferson and Rawski 1994), instead of the widespread sale of state assets to private agents. This has protected employment and the welfare provisions tied to employment at state enterprises at the cost of continuing state subsidies for unprofitable enterprises. The impact of the national programme of progressively reducing these subsidies on welfare provision needs to be monitored.

Privatization in Kazakhstan and the Kyrgyz Republic proceeded along Soviet lines, with a strong element of privatization in the work collective ('insider privatization'). It appears that Turkmenistan and Uzbekistan have made only rather limited movements toward privatization. In the 'Soviet-style' privatization, insiders are motivated to protect their employment (at the cost of progressively declining incomes for workers, if the enterprise is not competitive).

The welfare impact of trends toward 'privatization' in the provision of education, healthcare and other social services also needs to be looked into. One example is in the provision of medicines. These privatization trends are occurring both consciously (as a result of policy change or ideology) and unconsciously (due to cost pressures, the impact of changing income distribution, and the increasing presence of foreign company employees in the economy).

1.3.4 Labour markets

The process of privatization has certainly had a profound impact on labour markets, labour security, family income and access to public support services. The Asian transition economies that are growing have seen large changes in the level and distribution of employment, with significant increases in the extent of private employment and employment in export-oriented enterprises.

While typically employment in these newer sectors has been at higher wages, such employment has also been at the expense of loss of access to enterprise-provided public support services, except where these are made available through family units, and certain family members have continued in public employment. The East Asian approach of providing these benefits through enterprises and work units is the principal explanation. Asian economies, even before the central planning period, have had limited experience of nationally based social welfare programmes (Hussain and Stern 1992), or perhaps these programmes have always been quite small.

A key challenge which must be addressed in the Asian transition is that of ensuring that such support programmes continue to be available. Given the limited tradition in national public provision, one possible approach would be mandated benefits provided by all enterprises, an approach that has its own inefficiencies and is vulnerable to the creation of gaps in coverage. Asian transitions need to address this issue because the rigidity of access to benefits also makes the labour markets themselves relatively rigid, to the extent that qualified employees are reluctant to move out of enterprises because of loss of access to healthcare, education and housing benefits.

It is critical to understand the impact of the changes in the types of incomes families are receiving in both urban and rural areas. Milanovic (1998) identifies labour-market-based wage inequality as an important determinant of differences in income during the transition in Europe. It is important to ask: are the same mechanisms at work in Asia? Is wage income increasing in the rural areas, and are these incomes extremely unevenly distributed? What are the reasons, if any, that wage incomes are highly unequal? What is happening to public works schemes, labour training programmes and wage subsidies (if any)? What is happening to the minimum wage and wage-setting regulations?

The substantial role of agriculture in the Asian transition raises specific issues in analysing the impact of transition on labour markets. One aspect is the phenomenon of migration. Another aspect is the question of access to income-earning assets (even though this element is also important in urban areas). It is important to find out what has been the policy and the performance with regard to transferring income-earning assets to the actual manager of the resource. Reforms in agriculture in China started with the so-called 'responsibility system'. To what extent have the same reforms been implemented in the other Asian transitions and what is their impact on family income? Have formal credit markets begun to assist smallholders and entrepreneurs to increase their production?

1.4 Measuring the welfare impact of transition

In order to introduce the evaluation criteria implicit in the studies in this volume, we conclude this introductory essay with a consideration what we see as the 'ideal' means by which one might measure the welfare impact of the transition (or of development, for that matter).

The word 'ideal' speaks to the fact that in many cases these concepts cannot be operationalized, or even if they might be, the information does not exist.

We start from the position that the possession of commodities is far from being an adequate measure of human welfare. There are other equally (if not more) important factors which affect well-being. We propose a set of five types of indicators which need to be taken into account in the assessment of welfare change in each country. The set of indicators proposed here proceeds from earlier work carried out in European transition economies (UNICEF 1993, 1994, 1995; Cornia et al. 1996).

These five general types of indicators are the following:

1. *Opulence indicators*. These are mainly economic indicators concerning the changes of material well-being of the population. The most common is per capita income. Others include the actual possession of durable commodities, the availability of food, housing, and so on. At the national level distribution is as important an indicator of the well-being of the population as is these goods' overall availability. Other measures in this class include the incidence of poverty.

   It will be advantageous to broaden opulence-related measures beyond per capita income. Measures of changes in the diet and possession of durable goods are particularly valuable since they track not only income improvement but also accessibility to the benefits of growth. Measures of savings and the quality and size of housing are also important measures in this regard.
2. *Capability-based indicators*. These indicators are meant to measure how people actually function in society. Life expectancy, mortality and morbidity are all crucial to the quality of human life. 'The dead cannot do much' (Sen 1995), and the sick and weak do less than healthy citizens. Access to long life and health also depends on improved nutrition and medical care. In addition to living long and healthy lives, the fulfilment of human lives in modern society increasingly depends on educational attainment, skills and knowledge.

   For capability-based indicators, a comparison between pre-reform and post-reform trends in life expectancy, mortality and morbidity (and other similar indicators) can provide useful indications of the long-term impact of the reform process. It is also important to assess whether the gaps in these indicators between rural and urban areas and across gender are widening or declining. Changes in these indicators also indicate how the healthcare and educational systems are holding up under the pressures of marketization. Are budget pressures reducing the coverage of the system? Is the public sector losing personnel because of the increasing availability of better-paying positions in the private sector for doctors, nurses and teachers? (Desai 1992). Pressures on public budgets and marketization will also affect performance with regard to education and literacy indicators.

3. *Demographic-based measures.* Marriage, divorce and fertility rates reflect expectations and perceptions about the future. This has been demonstrated in the case of European transitional economies, where demographic crises have exploded in distressed economies (Cornia and Paniccià 1996). It will be interesting to apply the same kind of measurement to the Asian transition economies, where both positive and negative patterns of growth have been witnessed. Understanding the demographic trends will throw light on how families and communities are perceiving the movement toward the market.

   Perceptions about current and expected welfare change can affect decisions to marry, divorce, or have children. In Russia and in most of Central and Eastern European countries, marriage and birth rates declined in 1989–95, the first years of the transition. Are these kinds of dynamics being reproduced in the Asian transitions where family and community traditions are different and where the income dynamics have been far more positive? There are, also, some intervening variables, such as the state policy of limiting births and the increasing cultural acceptance of cohabitation (as opposed to marriage). The interpretation of possible increases in the divorce rate also has to be undertaken very subtly, since it too might indicate greater economic independence on the part of women as market-created opportunities increase.

4. *Human ecology indicators.* The social and natural environment under which people conduct their daily life is crucial to their physical and mental well-being. One can classify the types of indicators in this group into (a) social cohesion and (b) protection indicators and human environment indicators. Both fast and negative economic growth can worsen environmental indicators of human ecology.

   The social environment includes the circumstances of personal safety, that is, the right to live peacefully without abrupt disruption or constant threat by violence and crimes. A dignified life with self-respect and confidence is also associated with other aspects of social environment such as corruption.

Changes in the incidence of crime and threats to personal security are a key aspect of the environment. Are the apparent increases in crime in the transition economies a result of 'glasnost' in statistics or is marketization proceeding to break down social relationships that used to obstruct the commission of crimes? The rising incidence of corruption in transition economies has become a journalistic staple, even though in an international comparison of corruption, market economies normally earn top marks. We have included this indicator as a measure of the security of individuals to transact their economic activities reliably and an indicator of the existence of limits to the authority of public officials. One possible measure is the number of corruption cases brought before the courts.

The fifth group of indicators, those of social stratification to be explained below are an important subset of 'opulence-based' indicators, but are put in a separate category to highlight important changes that are occurring with regard to the social hierarchy and mechanisms of exclusion.

5. *Measures of social stratification.* The welfare of a given country also has to be viewed in terms of how widely the gains or losses are spread among the population. Measures of social stratification can indicate the degree to which individuals and subgroups of the population (by gender, location, ethnic groups, skill level, age group, and so on) are being excluded from the gains/losses in the overall economic performance of the society. These can also point to the sources of social conflict, interregional tensions and individual alienation. Indeed, it can even be argued that an excessive increase in social stratification in societies with a long tradition of egalitarianism may give rise to a collapse of the overall reform effort.

   The role that marketization, whether accompanied by economic growth or not, is playing in providing the context for the marginalization of certain segments of the population is a key concern of this project. Migrant workers face problems with regard to safe housing, labour protection, work safety and medical coverage. This involves a breakdown in social protection. To the extent that these 'floating populations' became a permanent social feature and 'a way of life', these groups have been marginalized. Greater social stratification can also be related to the rise in illegal activities, including drug-dealing and prostitution.

One important aspect of social stratification concerns changes in the status of women during the transition process. Are any gains that women have achieved during the socialist period being maintained or are they being lost? In the pre-reform period, employment rates of women tended to be very high; however, market pressures on state enterprises have induced large bouts of retrenchment and the incidence on women workers has tended to be higher. On the positive side, marketization has increased the number of positions available in the private sector and increased the social mobility of many women.

Our hope is that this analysis of the welfare impact of transition will indicate the extent to which transition, as it has been actually practised so far, is sustainable. There is no need to belabour the awareness that public authorities in China and elsewhere have expressed with regard to problems of migration, increasing poverty and crime, and eroding social cohesion. The findings in this volume indicate the extent to which present patterns of transition are 'socially sustainable' and the possibilities of modifying the pattern based on the analysis.

Notes

1. On economic grounds alone, Cornia (1994, p. 585), in comparing the Chinese transition with the Eastern European pattern, suggests that many elements of the Chinese approach have been characterized by their 'self-reinforcing nature', that is, that the 'results of initial reforms generated pressures for the subsequent introduction of other reforms'. In contrast, many of the liberalization-dependent approaches implemented in Europe have themselves endangered economic stability, requiring additional stabilization measures and thereby raising issues of the optimal 'sequencing' of policy reforms. This proposed research is more concerned with the social aspects of sustainability.
2. ILO/EASTMAT (1996) suggests that there are four variables that can be used to categorize Asian transitions: (1) the structure of the economy at the start of the transition; (2) the extent and duration of controls during the central planning period; (3) the degree of integration with the CMEA system; and (4) extent of the pre-reform crisis in terms of macroeconomic stability.
3. It is of course well known that in Europe, reforms in Hungary were initiated in 1968, attempted in Czechoslovakia in 1967 when they were interdicted, and initiated much later in Poland in 1981. The former Yugoslavia abandoned formal planning in the 1950s.
4. See also the data on the growth of GDP in selected ATEs during the transition period in ADB (1996), Figure 2, p. 20.

References

Abeywickrama, K. L. (1996), 'The Marketization of Mongolia', *Monthly Review*, March, pp. 25–33.

ADB (Asian Development Bank) (1992), *Mongolia: A Centrally Planned Economy in Transition*, New York: Oxford University Press.

ADB (Asian Development Bank) (1996), *Annual Report, 1995*, Manila: Asian Development Bank.

Cornia, Giovanni Andrea (1994), 'Income Distribution, Poverty and Welfare in Transitional Economies: A Comparison Between Eastern Europe and China', *Journal of International Development*, Vol. 6, No. 5.

Cornia, Giovanni Andrea and Renato Paniccià (1996), 'The Transition's Population Crisis: An Econometric Investigation of Nuptiality, Fertility, and Mortality in Severely Distressed Economies', *MOCT-MOST*, Vol. 6, pp. 95–129.

Cornia, Giovanni Andrea, Gaspar Fajth and Renato Paniccià (1996), 'Fancy Models and Hard Facts: Children and Youth during the Transition to a Market Economy', in Alessandro Pio (ed.), *From Adjustment to Growth: The Role of Human Capital and the Informal Sector*, Milan: E.G.E.A. S.p.A. Milano, pp. 199–236.

Desai, Meghnad (1992), 'Is there Life after Mahalanobis? The Political Economy of India's New Economic Policy', *Indian Economic Review*, Special Issue in Memory of Sukhamoy Chakravarty, Vol. 27 (1992), pp. 155–64.

Drèze, Jean, and Amartya Sen (1989), *Hunger and Public Action*, Oxford: Clarendon Press.

Fforde, Adam, and Stefan de Vylder (1996), *From Plan to Market, The Economic Transition in Vietnam*, Boulder, CO: Westview Press.

Hussain, A. and N. Stern (1992), 'Economic Reforms and Public Finance in China', *Public Finance,* 47 (suppl.), The Hague/Koenigstein: Foundation Journal of Public Finance.

ILO/EASTMAT (1996), 'Transitions, the Asian Way: Growth, Employment, Equity', Bangkok: East Asia Multidisciplinary Advisory Team, Regional Office for Asia and the Pacific, International Labour Office (27 February).

IMF, World Bank, OECD, EBRD (1991), *A Study of the Soviet Economy*, Vol. 1. Paris: IMF, World Bank, OECD, EBRD.

Jefferson, Gary H. and Thomas Rawski (1994), 'Enterprise Reform in China', *Journal of Economic Perspectives* (Spring).

John Mellor Associates (1993), *Agricultural Policy Notes*, Vol. 2, No. 1.

Kim, Young C. (1996), 'Mongolia', pp. 295–425 in Pradumna B. Rana and Naved Hamid (eds) (1996a), *From Centrally Planned to Market Economies: The Asian Approach*, Vol. 2, *People's Republic of China and Mongolia*. Hong Kong: Oxford University Press.

Lavigne, Marie (1995), *The Economics of Transition from Socialist Economy to Market Economy*, New York: St. Martin's Press – now Palgrave.

Lu Aiguo (1996), 'Welfare Changes in China during the Economic Reforms', *Research for Action*, No. 26, Helsinki: UNU/WIDER.

Milanovic, Branko (1998), *Income, Inequality and Poverty during the Transition from Planned to Market Economy*, Washington, DC: World Bank.

Montes, Manuel F. (1995), 'Vietnam's Macroeconomic Transition', *Journal of Asian Economics*, Vol. 6, No. 3, pp. 351–66.

Montes, Manuel F. and Brian Van Arkadie (1995), 'Is There an Asian Approach to Macroeconomic Management in the Process of Transition?', in Manuel F. Montes, Romeo A. Reyes and Somsak Tambunlertchai (eds), *Macroeconomic Management in Southeast Asia's Transitional Economies*, Kuala Lumpur: Asian and Pacific Development Centre.

MRIM (1994), 'Economic Update: Mongolia, 1993', Ulaanbaatar: Market Research Institute of Mongolia, Ministry of Trade and Industry.

Naughton, Barry (1995), *Growing out of the Plan: Chinese Economic Reform, 1978–1993*, Cambridge: Cambridge University Press.

Pomfret, Richard (1995), *The Economies of Central Asia*, Princeton, NJ: Princeton University Press.

Pomfret, Richard (1996), *Asian Economies in Transition: Reforming Centrally Planned Economies*, Cheltenham, UK and Brookfield, USA: Edward Elgar.

Sen, Amartya (1995), 'Mortality as an Indicator of Economic Success and Failure', *Innocenti Lectures*, UNICEF, Florence, Italy.

UNDP (1990), *Human Development Report 1990*, New York: Oxford University Press.

UNDP (1991), *Human Development Report 1991*, New York: Oxford University Press.

UNDP (1993), *Human Development Report 1993*, New York: Oxford University Press.

UNDP (1994), *Human Development Report 1994*, New York: Oxford University Press.

UNICEF (1993), *Public Policy and Social Conditions, Economies in Transition Studies*, No. 1, Florence: UNICEF International Child Development Centre.

UNICEF (1994), *Crisis in Mortality, Health and Nutrition, Economies in Transition Studies*, No. 2. Florence: UNICEF International Child Development Centre.

UNICEF (1995), *Poverty, Children and Policy: Responses for a Brighter Future, Economies in Transition Studies*, No. 3. Florence: UNICEF International Child Development Centre.

World Bank (1980), *World Development Report, 1980*, New York: Oxford University Press.

World Bank (1996), *From Plan to Market: World Development Report, 1996*, New York: Oxford University Press.

II Welfare Trends in Key Sectors

2
Provision of Healthcare and Education in Transitional Asia: Key Issues and Lessons from Vietnam

Paul Glewwe and Jennie Litvack[1]

2.1 Introduction

Since 1980, almost all the countries that had operated planned economies have introduced market systems. This transition has affected the lives of nearly 1.7 billion people, and the countries involved are often called 'transition economies'. The experience in Eastern Europe and the Former Soviet Union is quite different from that in East Asia. In particular, the former countries suffered from sharp drops in real income, while the latter generally experienced substantial economic growth.

Economic growth can reduce poverty and improve living standards, but these outcomes are not necessarily automatic. The impact of growth on living standards depends on (1) how the benefits of growth are distributed, and (2) whether growth supports social services. Thus an important issue for Asian transitional economies is the extent to which economic growth has reduced poverty and raised living standards.

This chapter focuses on two aspects of living standards: health and education. Specifically, it analyses how the switch from a planned to a market economy among the Asian transitional economies affected health and education services and, ultimately, the health and education of the population. After framing the issues and examining recent trends in these countries, the chapter focuses on the case of Vietnam, where there are ample data for an in-depth examination.

2.2 The impact of transition on health and education: an analytical framework

The health status and education level of any country's citizens are determined by the amount and quality of health and education services, and by the use individuals make of those services. In a market economy, both public revenues and household income can affect the quantity and quality of services, and the extent to which they are used. Most countries subsidize these services. One justification for subsidies is that many of these services have 'positive externalities' (their marginal social benefit exceeds their marginal private benefit). Health and education services that are not fully subsidized must be financed, at least in part, by the households using those services. Wealthier countries typically have more government resources to subsidize these services, and individuals in those countries are, on average, more able to pay for them. Thus economic growth permits both public and private financing to expand, which should increase the quantity, and quality, of health and education services. However, for growth to improve health and education outcomes, growing public revenues must be transferred to these sectors, and the public and private sector roles must be successfully coordinated.

The Asian transitional economies, particularly those in East Asia, began their transitions to the market at very low income levels. Yet most had already made impressive progress in public health (for example, high life expectancy) and education (for example, high literacy) despite their low incomes. This reflects their commitments to basic healthcare and education (see World Bank 1996a). Thus their market-oriented reforms began with a strong human resource base.

The East Asian transitional economies are particularly interesting given their recent economic growth. They had strong social service delivery before transition, so that the governments' reduced role in service delivery after the transition could have jeopardized access. Yet rapid economic growth raised per capita government budgets and household incomes. The net result of these two phenomena needs further exploration.

Before examining the experience of the Asian transitional economies in health and education, a general framework is presented to organize the discussion.

In general, the most important determinants of individuals' health and education outcomes are: (1) income levels; (2) prices of health and education services; (3) the time costs of using those services; (4) the quality of those services; (5) the value households and individuals place on their health and education outcomes, independent of any remunerative benefits; (6) the economic returns to health and education; and (7) government requirements to use health and education services. Changes in education and health outcomes, whether due to the transition to the market or any other cause, come about by changing these determinants. For example, increased public expenditures on healthcare and education can reduce prices and time costs and increase the quality of services, which will encourage use of those services. While much of this is self-explanatory, a brief review is useful.

Household income clearly affects health and education outcomes in market economies because many services require fees. Even in planned economies, income matters since not all services are free, or even if they are there may be transportation or other costs to using them. Consequently, health and education outcomes are almost always higher for wealthier people.

Higher prices – with service quality held constant – reduce the use of health and education services, and thus lower healthcare and education outcomes. That is, the demand for healthcare and education is sensitive to price, and the poor are more price sensitive than the better off (Gertler and van der Gaag 1990). Holding prices constant, increased quality of health and education services should increase their utilization, and thus improve health and education outcomes. When prices and quality change simultaneously, the net result is ambiguous. In some cases, improved quality can more than offset increased prices, so that utilization of services increases; Litvack and Bodart (1993) document this in a controlled experiment on health services in Cameroon. In fact, that study showed that use of rural health centres by the poor increased more than use by wealthier groups when user fees were introduced and revenues were used to improve quality, even though the poor were more sensitive to prices. This indicates that the *quality-adjusted price* declined (despite higher fees), and this increased the demand for healthcare, particularly among the poor. Thus prices and quality must be considered together when assessing pricing policies.

Another cost of health and education services is the time lost by their use. Individuals using these services lose wages or self-employment income, or forego other activities; the higher their wages, or hourly income, the more expensive it is to use them. As economic growth raises wages, the indirect costs of obtaining services increase, which could reduce their utilization, although this effect is probably outweighed by the general income effect discussed above.

The value that individuals place on health and education also determines the use of services and, ultimately, health and education outcomes. Values are not easily changed by government policies, but information and awareness campaigns could alter people's values.[2] People also value health and education in terms of income. If economic growth increases returns to investments in education, the demand for education services, and the overall level of education, should increase. Finally, governments may require use of education and health services, and changing these requirements during the transition to a market economy could change the use of those services.

Consider now how the transition from planning to a market economy affects these determinants of the use of health and education services. First, economic reforms affect households' incomes. As explained in the next section, the experience of Central Asia has mirrored that of Eastern Europe and the Former Soviet Union; incomes declined substantially. In contrast, economic reforms in East Asia have raised average incomes; in these economies most households were engaged in agricultural rather than industrial activities, so that economic liberalization benefited the rural population through higher prices paid for their products.

The second mechanism by which the transition to the market affects health and education outcomes is through prices paid for health and education services. In general, increased prices are more likely if the transition leads to economic contraction, because governments have fewer resources to subsidize prices.[3] In countries where the transition increased economic growth there is less pressure to increase prices, yet the move toward the market generally implies shifting public expenditures toward services with public-good characteristics, and increased prices for health and education services whose benefits are largely private. Thus, in both growing and contracting transition economies, many healthcare and education prices increase.

The transition to a market economy may affect the time costs of using health and education services in several ways. Some public providers may close, increasing transportation costs for part of the population. Yet private suppliers may fill some existing gaps, lowering transportation costs. In addition, wages and income from self-employment will change; rising incomes will increase time costs, but this negative effect on use of services may be outweighed by the general income effect. A final aspect is that privatization of state firms may result in employees not being compensated for time spent obtaining healthcare. For example, in rural areas the previous agricultural cooperative system workers who took time off to obtain healthcare did not lose income, but in a market economy rural households are self-employed, so that time spent obtaining healthcare reduces income.

A fourth way in which the transition to the market may affect the use of health and education services is through changes in service quality due to changes in public expenditures on those sectors, and to changes in government priorities for different services within each sector. In countries experiencing economic contraction, shrinking government budgets may reduce quality dramatically, while in countries enjoying substantial growth governments can often improve quality. Finally, allowing private providers to offer services could increase quality, but almost certainly at a higher price.

It is unclear whether switching to a market economy will change the value that individuals place on health and education. Information campaigns need not be altered by this switch, although an economic contraction can reduce government funding for them. However, a strong sense of public welfare may have led socialist countries to emphasize public health and basic literacy in previous years, and the switch to a market economy may distract from this commitment. Economic changes may also increase the financial benefits of health and education, particularly the latter. Socialist economies often compressed wage differences to promote equity, but these policies also reduced private incentives to invest in education. Removing restrictions on wages could increase demand for education if rapid economic growth occurs *and* that growth increases the return to education in the labour market.

Finally, some socialist governments required use of education services and, to a lesser extent, basic health services. Removing or softening such requirements may reduce their acquisition by individuals.

An important lesson from this discussion is that the success of the new market economy in generating growth will have major implications for health and education outcomes. If incomes decline, so will public and household resources for health and education. Government budget constraints will generally increase prices and reduce quality, lowering the use of services and, ultimately, outcomes. In contrast, increased income will allow households to purchase health and education services in the private market, and will also enable governments – should they so choose – to subsidize at least some services, and maintain or improve their quality. Thus the interesting question is: for those transition economies that experienced substantial growth, how have health and education outcomes changed?

While economic growth is key, there are other factors. Indeed, additional public and private expenditures on health and education may not improve outcomes; health status or educational attainment may deteriorate if governments do not coordinate and rationalize the provision of public and private services. Governments must decide whether they should provide, or at least subsidize, specific health and education services. They must also regulate private providers of these services. Economic growth is thus an opportunity to improve social service delivery. Yet the appropriate role for the government is often unclear. Defining that role, and developing the capacity to execute it, are challenges for transition economies in Asia and around the world.

This section has provided a framework for analysing the impact of the transition from a planned to a market economy on health and education outcomes. The following section briefly examines the experience in the Central and East Asian economies.

2.3 Health and education trends in Asian transition economies

Of the nine Asian transitional economies, four are nations that became independent when the Soviet Union dissolved in 1991: Kazakhstan, the Kyrgyz Republic, Turkmenistan and Uzbekistan. A fifth, Mongolia, has an economic heritage similar to those of these four countries. These are the five Central Asian transitional economies. There are four East or Southeast Asian transitional economies: China, Cambodia, Laos and Vietnam. The transition in the five Central Asian Republics began about 1990. The transition began at different times in East Asia: about 1980 in China, around 1986 in Laos and Vietnam, and about 1989 in Cambodia.

All five Central Asian transitional countries grew steadily from 1980 to about 1989, after which GDP per capita faltered and then rapidly declined in the early 1990s. In Mongolia, the downward trend bottomed out in 1993, and GDP per capita has since modestly increased. Among the other Central Asian economies, Uzbekistan's downward slide was the least steep, but in 1996 it was still falling. The other three Central Asian economies experienced steeper declines in GDP per capita in the 1990s, but these declines appear to have bottomed out by 1995. However, their GDP per capita in 1996 was about one half of the levels prevailing when the transition began in 1990.

Incomes declined substantially in these five Central Asian countries. The discussion of the previous section implies no improvements in health and education outcomes in these countries, and declines are quite plausible. Data on both are fairly sketchy. Table 2.1 provides estimates of infant mortality rates for all five countries from 1985 to 1995, and secondary school enrolment rates for Mongolia.

Infant mortality declined in the four former Soviet countries in the late 1980s, but this progress halted in the early 1990s, when these countries began their transition to the market. Kazakhstan, the Kyrgyz Republic and Uzbekistan all fit this general pattern. Uzbekistan shows some improvement beginning in 1993, but Kazakhstan and the Kyrgyz Republic showed virtually no change in infant morality from 1990 to 1995. The Turkmenistan data show a large drop in infant mortality from 1989 to 1990; this may reflect overestimation in 1989 (the 1989 figure is even higher than that for 1985). Yet Turkmenistan also shows no improvement in infant mortality rates. Overall, in these four former Soviet Republics the lack of reduction in infant mortality rates in the early 1990s reflects their dismal economic performance. In principle, better health policies could have made public health expenditures more effective, but the lack of improvement suggests no major successes along these lines. These data support the hypothesis that the switch from a planned to a market economy in these countries led to stagnation in health outcomes. Unfortunately, there are no reliable data on education outcomes over this time period.

Trends in health outcomes for Mongolia are unclear due to missing data,[4] yet data on education outcomes span a sizeable length of time. Its secondary school gross enrolment rate was 91 per cent in 1989, when the economy began to falter. This rate dropped steadily until it reached 78 per cent in 1993, after which it increased, albeit modestly. Overall, secondary school enrolment closely followed patterns in GDP per capita, which suggests that Mongolia's education outcomes echoed the income decline that accompanied its transition to the market.

Overall, the health and education performances in the five Central Asian transition economies are sobering. Decreasing incomes halted past progress in reducing infant mortality, and in the one country with education data income reductions led to lower school enrolment. While sobering, this performance is not surprising given the discussion in Section 2.2. The more interesting question is what happened in the four East Asian economies, which is addressed in the remainder of this section.

China's economic growth since adopting market reforms around 1980 has been phenomenal – an average annual growth rate of 10 per cent yielded a real GDP per capita in 1996 nearly four times higher than in 1980. Vietnam displayed the next highest performance – in the

Table 2.1 Trends in health and education outcomes in Central Asian transition economies

	Infant mortality (per 1000 live births)					*Secondary school enrolment (%)*
Year	*Kazakstan*	*Kyrgyz Republic*	*Mongolia*	*Turkmenistan*	*Uzbekistan*	*Mongolia*
1985	30	42	–	52	45	92
1986	–	–	–	–	–	–
1987	–	–	68	–	–	–
1988	–	–	–	–	–	–
1989	26	32	–	55	38	91
1990	26	30	–	45	35	86
1991	27	30	–	47	36	–
1992	26	32	60	44	37	80
1993	28	32	55	46	32	78
1994	27	29	53	46	28	82
1995	27	30	55	46	30	–

Source: World Bank Database.

ten years since the reforms were adopted in 1986, average annual growth rates of 8 per cent raised real GDP per capita 60 per cent by 1996. Laos's performance was less spectacular, but its 26 per cent increase in real GDP per capita over ten years outperforms most developing nations.

The enviable economic growth of these East Asian transition economies contrasts sharply with the transition experiences of Central Asia, suggesting that their experience with health and education may also differ. Table 2.2 presents the evidence. In the early years of China's transition, infant mortality rates were roughly steady, but by the early 1990s they had declined substantially relative to the mid-1980s rates.[5] Lack of progress in the 1980s may reflect public spending priorities; while the government's health budget grew considerably faster than GDP, resources for public health measures declined, while investment in tertiary hospital services rose (World Bank 1992). Secondary school enrolment data, although patchy in the 1980s, show a steady increase from 1985 through the 1990s.

Laos and Vietnam both show steady declines in infant mortality in the 1980s and early 1990s. However, the secondary school enrolment data are troubling. Laos shows little change throughout the period, and Vietnam experienced a decline from 1985 to 1992, followed by increases only in 1993 and 1994.

To summarize, the three East Asian economies performed very well in terms of economic growth. They also have reduced infant mortality, although the decline in China took several years to appear. Secondary school enrolment patterns are less clear. China showed a clear improvement, Laos stagnated and Vietnam experienced a decline.

The main lesson of this section is that a transition from a planned to a market economy will generally lead to poor health and education outcomes if incomes fall during the transition, as in the five Central Asian transition economies. If the transition leads to economic growth, as in the three East Asian transition economies, social indicators often improve, but not always.

Taken together, the data for Asian transition economies show an association between economic growth and infant mortality. This is seen in Figure 2.1,[6] which shows a simple regression where the change in the infant mortality rates is regressed on GDP growth and a constant. However, there is substantial variation around this trend. China's infant mortality reduction is lower than expected given its economic growth, while Uzbekistan did much better than expected. Clearly, there is more to improving social indicators than simply raising economic growth. Yet drawing further generalizations across

Table 2.2 Trends in health and education outcomes in East Asian transition economies

	Infant mortality per 1000 live births			*Secondary school enrolment (%)*		
Year	*China*	*Laos*	*Vietnam*	*China*	*Laos*	*Vietnam*
1982	39	122	53	–	–	–
1983	41	–	–	–	–	–
1984	38	–	–	–	–	–
1985	37	–	–	39	23	43
1986	–	–	–	–	–	–
1987	38	110	47	–	–	–
1988	–	–	–	–	–	–
1989	–	–	–	46	25	35
1990	–	–	–	48	–	33
1991	31	–	–	51	22	–
1992	31	97	44	54	24	32
1993	31	95	43	55	25	35
1994	30	92	42	52	–	41
1995	34	90	41		–	–

Source: World Bank Database.

Figure 2.1 GDP growth and changes in infant mortality rates (%)

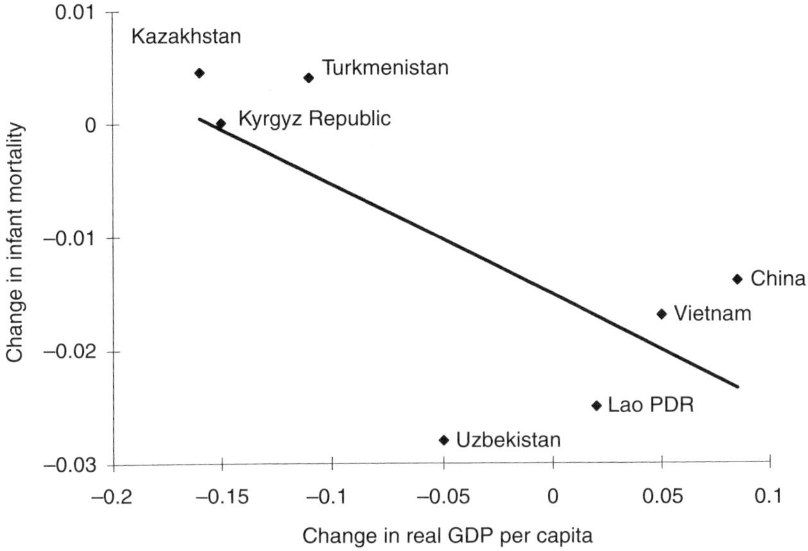

Notes: The time period for each country is from the year the transition began – 1990 in Central Asian Countries, 1980 in China, 1986 in Vietnam and Loas, and 1989 in Cambodia – until 1995. For Laos and Vietnam, the infant mortality data are from 1987 because there are no data for 1986.
Source: World Bank Database and IMF International Financial Statistics, various years.

this diverse set of countries is difficult. The remainder of this chapter will examine Vietnam in detail. Vietnam is of interest because its economic performance has been excellent, but its progress in health and education is mixed. Fortunately, a large amount of data has been collected and analysed in recent years, which will enrich the discussion.

2.4 Vietnam's *Doi Moi* reform programme

Vietnam began its economic reforms in 1986. Over the next ten years its system for delivering social services changed dramatically. While the overall impact appears generally positive, the distributional impacts must be studied to see whether certain groups are being left behind and, if so, whether corrective actions can ensure access to basic social services.

2.4.1 Historical background

The modern history of social service provision in Vietnam is complex, reflecting the extreme challenges and changes Vietnam experienced in the twentieth century. During the colonial period, before Vietnam's partition in 1954, provision of healthcare and formal education was quite limited. The government provided no healthcare for peasant households, and only limited care to plantation labour. Public schooling covered only a small, élite group of Vietnamese. Non-government schools were organized throughout the country, but few poor families could afford them. Therefore, serious health problems were endemic and illiteracy was widespread.

In 1945, Ho Chi Minh launched a literacy campaign, and by 1954 private schools in the North were incorporated into a free public education system (World Bank 1996b). Similarly, a widespread system of government healthcare was established. Major efforts to mobilize the population and disseminate information on health and education rapidly improved health and education status in the North. Before unification in 1975, social service provision in the South was much less developed, which led to lower health status (higher infant mortality and stunting rates) and lower adult literacy in the South (Aduki 1995).

Health and literacy efforts in the South expanded after 1975, but the weakness of agricultural cooperatives, which provided local finance, impeded these efforts. Still, farmers had incentives to produce because they were not (*de facto*) obliged to sell to the state; thus household incomes were higher. In the North, agricultural cooperatives still served a useful role in the 1970s and early 1980s, providing local funding for essential health and education services. However, since peasant families in the North had to follow government plans and sell their agricultural products to state agencies at low prices, they had little incentive to produce, which led to low household income and low agricultural output (Aduki 1995). Thus, before the *Doi Moi* policies were adopted in 1986 there was an inverse relationship between household income and social welfare indicators, with Northerners earning less while enjoying better health and education, and Southerners having higher incomes but lower health and education status.

2.4.2 Economic reforms

The Vietnamese economy's poor performance in the late 1970s and early 1980s led to a series of economic reforms that provided incentives to households. After the 1986 Sixth Party Congress, Decision Number 10 in 1988 formalized family-based production and dismantled the agricultural cooperatives. When Vietnam's chief benefactor, the Soviet Union, collapsed in 1991, Vietnam pragmatically decided to open up to the world. In the 1990s, Vietnam adopted policies that stabilized its economy and led to rapid growth.[7] By 1993, Vietnam was the world's third largest rice exporter (compared to importing rice in the 1980s), had an inflation rate below 10 per cent (compared to triple-digit inflation in the 1980s), and real economic growth was 8 per cent per year. In the mid-1990s, the economy remained stable and growth increased to 9.5 per cent (in 1995). Poverty dropped from about 75–80 per cent of the population in 1983 to about 55 per cent in 1993 (Dollar and Litvack 1998).

2.4.3 Reforms in social services

Before *Doi Moi*, education and healthcare were provided exclusively by the government. The central government financed all education and healthcare except primary education and basic health services, which were financed from cooperative funds or household contributions. Since most social services were not provided through state enterprises, their provision was not affected by the closure of 6000 non-viable state enterprises between 1989 and 1992.

Major reforms in the health sector included introducing user fees, legalizing private provision of health services and deregulating drug sales (Decision Number 45 in 1989). Since cooperatives no longer existed and thus could not finance basic social services, Decision Number 123 provided central funding of three health workers per commune. Reforms in the education sector encouraged private sector expansion through 'semi-public' and 'people-founded' institutions and permitted public institutions (except primary schools) to charge for tuition. Another source of funds for basic health services and primary education was 'voluntary contributions' (generally, a flat fee for each adult) by households (World Bank 1996b). Meanwhile, public expenditures for health and education increased, both in absolute terms and as a percentage of government spending. Thus the social sectors benefited both from aggregate growth (which increased public revenues) and from government commitment to these sectors.

The provision of other basic services, such as potable water, irrigation and roads, also improved during the economic reforms. Between 1991 and 1994, access to safe drinking water in rural areas increased from under 15 per cent of the population to over 35 per cent, and was expected to reach 65 per cent by the year 2000 (World Bank et al. 1996). Financial support for this is primarily from UNICEF, which committed large resources to Vietnam during its transition. The government is aware that sustained improvements in rural water supply require household contributions for operation and maintenance costs. This policy is feasible in most areas because incomes have risen and the demand for safe water is high. Water-borne diseases are the primary cause of morbidity in Vietnam, and the transition to the market implies that missed work due to illness has become increasingly costly for households. Thus paying for improved water supply not only directly improves welfare, it also increases household income.

Provision of irrigation services also changed during the economic reforms. Cooperatives had previously funded these services, but more recently local water management companies have been established that rely on user fees for operation and maintenance.

The rest of this chapter focuses on provision of health and education services. How have the reforms affected health and education outcomes? This question is addressed first for health (Section 2.5), and then for education (Section 2.6).

2.5 The impact of Vietnam's reforms on health services and outcomes

Section 2.2 presented seven pathways by which market-oriented economic reforms can affect health and education outcomes. This section discusses how Vietnam's *Doi Moi* reforms affected health outcomes via all seven pathways.

2.5.1 Income effects

Section 2.3 described Vietnam's recent economic growth, which has averaged 8 per cent per year since 1986. Clearly, average household incomes are much higher, but how has this growth been distributed among different regions and, ultimately, different households? In particular, have any groups been left out of the growth process? These questions are important because households are now expected to finance much of the social services they use.

Vietnam's transition to the market began in 1986 with a relatively equitable distribution of resources. Before the cooperatives were dismantled, commune land was distributed to households in a remarkably equitable way, particularly in the North (Van de Walle 1998). Moreover, the 1992–93 Vietnam Living Standards Survey (VNLSS) documented a relatively equitable distribution of consumption expenditures, with a Gini coefficient of 0.34.[8]

Has inequality changed since 1986? Economic growth has varied across Vietnam's seven regions, and between urban and rural areas, but all regions had positive per capita growth. More specifically, real GDP grew fastest in the southeast, at about 16 per cent, and lowest in the Mekong Delta, at 4 per cent. Growth in the other regions ranged from 7 to 9 per cent (Dollar and Litvack 1998). Analysis of inequality in Vietnam shows far more inequality within regions than between them (Dollar and Glewwe 1998). Thus variation in regional growth rates has not yet brought large increases in regional inequality. However, little is known about changes in inequality within regions, and the distribution of income may have become more unequal over time due to increased variation within regions.

Some observers have speculated that *Doi Moi* policies resulted in the 'rich getting richer and the poor getting poorer'. Yet the incidence of poverty dropped from about 80 per cent of the population in 1983 to about 55 per cent in 1992, and if growth remains high, rapid poverty reduction should continue, though the pace will depend on changes in inequality (Dollar and Litvack 1998). The government of Vietnam recently estimated that the percentage of poor households declined by 2 percentage points each year since 1992 (HEPR 1996). Therefore, there is no evidence that 'the poor are getting poorer'. Yet it is possible that inequality is increasing, that is, the rich are much richer while the poor are only a little less poor. Unfortunately, this cannot be checked with existing data.

While a substantial percentage of the population has escaped poverty in recent years, some poor groups may not be benefiting from the growth process. The Vietnamese government recognizes this, and has identified five factors that prevent some households from benefiting from *Doi Moi* (see HEPR 1996): (1) isolation (physical, social, communication); (2) excessive risk (disasters, health, investment); (3) inadequate access to productive resources (land, credit, skills); (4) lack of sustainability; and (5) inadequate participation (in economy, planning, decision-making). The poorest groups in Vietnam include non-diversified farmers, people with little education and several ethnic minorities.[9]

In summary, Vietnam's rapid economic growth has substantially increased households' incomes, enabling them to purchase health and education services formerly provided without charge by the state. This growth has been broad-based, reaching all seven regions, and both urban and rural areas. Thus most, and perhaps almost all, Vietnamese households are better able to pay for health and education services than they were before 1986. Yet some caution is in order. Although regional disparities currently account for little of overall inequality, persistent differences in regional growth rates may increase inequality.

2.5.2 Price effects

The change from a planned to a market economy generally involves shifting at least some healthcare costs to users of health services. Prices of commonly used medicines and medical services before and after the *Doi Moi* policies would be useful information for analysing the input of those policies. Unfortunately, very few price data are available.

Before the *Doi Moi* policies, no private sector existed, and virtually all healthcare was provided without charge. In 1989, privately provided health care was legalized, with prices largely unregulated. User fees were introduced at public facilities, with low fees for basic services and higher fees for specialized care.[10] Despite low consultation fees, private expenditures at public facilities can be high, especially for the poor. The 1992–93 VNLSS shows an average out-of-pocket expenditure for visiting a public commune health centre of 31 000 dong (about US$3), virtually all of which was for drugs. The average cost for a public hospital patient is 321 000 dong (about US$30), with more than 90 per cent for drugs. For the poorest 20 per cent of the population, visiting a commune health centre costs about 8 per cent of their annual non-food consumption. The figure for hospital outpatient visits is around 26 per cent (World Bank 1995). Multivariate analysis indicates that prices particularly affect the choice between seeing a private provider or self-medicating. In Vietnam, over 70 per cent of the poorest quintile choose to self-medicate, compared to 54 per cent among the wealthiest quintile (Gertler and Litvack 1998).

Perhaps the biggest change in healthcare pricing under *Doi Moi* policies is that drugs are no longer subsidized. Today, most drugs are purchased from private sellers either directly or through the public health centre as an intermediary.

Government healthcare spending is currently about 1 per cent of Vietnam's GDP, but total health expenditures are much higher because private healthcare expenditures have skyrocketed to 6–7 per cent of GDP. Eighty per cent of household healthcare expenditures is for drugs, an unusually high percentage. Even the poorest households spend large amounts of money on drugs.

A final aspect of healthcare prices is the Vietnam Health Insurance (VHI) programme, established in 1992. This programme is mandatory for current and retired civil servants, state enterprise employees, and employees of large private enterprises. Insurance is co-financed by employers and employees. VHI plans to expand insurance coverage to another 40 per cent of the population through voluntary insurance for farmers, small business workers and other self-employed individuals.

This expansion is currently being piloted in selected areas. For further details, see Behrman et al. (1996).

In summary, Vietnam's *Doi Moi* programme has increased the price of some health services, but others are still partially subsidized. Drug prices are no longer subsidized, and thus have increased substantially. Despite these increases, most people, even the poor, appear willing to pay. The new insurance scheme, VHI, provides an additional healthcare subsidy, but coverage is low. Overall, the switch to a market-based system appears not to have prevented the population from purchasing health services, though the quality of care may have been affected.

2.5.3 Time costs

A third determinant of the use of health services, and ultimately of health outcomes, is the time costs of using them. Time costs are an important determinant of the use of health facilities. As incomes have risen in Vietnam, time away from work to seek medical care entails a higher cost. Perhaps more important, for many rural households time spent getting healthcare now reduces income; under the previous agricultural cooperative system incomes were unaffected if a worker took time off to obtain medical care, but today self-employed farmers bear the full cost of time spent seeking care.

These negative effects on the use of health services may be ameliorated by opposing effects. The appearance of numerous private drug vendors may have reduced distances (and thus travel time), and obtaining medicine from public facilities may take less time because their medicine stocks have increased. Similarly, better staffing has probably reduced waiting times to see medical personnel; an example from Ha Tinh province is given below. Finally, since illness may reduce worker productivity, the cost of *not* seeking medical care has also risen since the transition.

2.5.4 Quality

The fourth way in which Vietnam's *Doi Moi* reforms may have changed healthcare services is by changing their quality. Unfortunately, Vietnam has few reliable data on quality of healthcare services. In general, the quality of care at hospitals exceeds the quality at commune health centres because the former have better equipment, and patients see doctors rather than nurses. This implies that rural residents receive relatively low-quality care because while 94 per cent live in communes with commune health centres, only 7 per cent live close to hospitals (Gertler and Litvack 1998). Since the cost of providing hospital services is significantly higher than the costs of providing commune health centres, urban residents, who are typically wealthier, benefit disproportionately from public subsidies to hospitals.

One important aspect of healthcare quality that may be overlooked is the heavy reliance on self-medication without consulting a healthcare provider. This is particularly prevalent among the poorest 20 per cent of the population, of whom 70 per cent resort to self-treatment for new health problems (Gertler and Litvack 1998). It is not clear whether high drug expenditures are necessary or even desirable for people who self-treat, since incorrect diagnoses may result in inefficient or even harmful use of medicines.

The VHI system also has implications for quality. It reimburses hospitals and other health facilities using set fees for various services. In principle, inadequate cost recovery from insurance payments can make healthcare providers reluctant to treat insured patients, and can reduce the quality of services. This appears to have happened in Vietnam: despite provision of 'free care' under VHI, many civil servants in urban areas use private practitioners to obtain better attention and higher-quality care (Behrman et al. 1996).

Perhaps the best way to examine overall changes in the quality of public sector services is to examine trends in public health expenditures. Although no time-series data exist on total healthcare expenditures, there are data on recurrent expenditures. Since *Doi Moi* was introduced in 1986, recurrent health expenditures have been protected, even during fiscally tight 1990–91. From 1989 to 1995, the share of total recurrent expenditures devoted to health increased, so that recurrent real health expenditures per capita doubled (World Bank 1996c). Since the number of public health facilities did not dramatically expand, this suggests that the quality of these services increased. However, this is difficult to verify; the impact of higher public spending on healthcare quality depends on subsectoral allocations, for which there are almost no reliable data. Also, healthcare quality varies greatly across regions, provinces, and so on. (World Bank 1996c). In summary, Vietnam's spending trends suggest that healthcare quality increased under *Doi Moi*, but it is unclear whether the improvement is substantial or only marginal. It is also possible that quality declined for some regions or population groups, but this cannot be checked with the data available.

2.5.5 Other determinants of use of health services

The other three determinants of households' use of health services were the value they place on health for its own sake, the financial benefits of better health, and government regulations requiring use of healthcare services. Controlling for income, there is little reason to think that the value households place on health has changed because of *Doi Moi* policies. The impact of health on income may be stronger – for example, now self-employed farmers lose income if poor health reduces working hours – but this effect may not be very large since people value health for its own sake. Finally, there were few government regulations requiring use of healthcare in Vietnam, and probably no recent changes in them. Thus, these last three factors have probably not changed appreciably since the *Doi Moi* policies were adopted.

2.5.6 Case study: Ha Tinh province

The discussion so far has focused on several different impacts of *Doi Moi* policies on healthcare services, but it has not calculated an overall effect, nor related this to health outcomes. The information at hand is insufficient to determine what services would be available if public and private expenditures were lowered to previous levels and private providers did not exist. However, a case study done in Ha Tinh province by OXFAM-UK-Ireland, a non-governmental organization with considerable experience in Vietnam, provides some insights.

The OXFAM case study of Ha Tinh considers the period from 1990 to 1995. Commune health centre utilization rates dropped between 1990 and 1992, but rose in 1993 and have been increasing ever since. The households interviewed prefer the current healthcare system to the previous one. For middle-income and well-off families, availability of health services and medicines has increased. For all groups in this poor district, treatment at commune health centres is still free, but now health staff are more accessible. Drugs are now available, albeit at a price; the study concludes that the poor's access to some treatments and drugs has improved. For serious illnesses, however, the situation is mixed. Because district hospital services are no longer free, the poor may be excluded from sophisticated medicine and treatment (OXFAM 1996). Another analysis of the impact of *Doi Moi* on healthcare reaches similar conclusions, cautioning that people in remote areas may not benefit from the new health sector policies and may suffer from reduced government entitlements (Aduki 1995).

In summary, healthcare services in Vietnam appear to be generally better today than before the *Doi Moi* policies were adopted. Higher incomes enable most people to purchase health services, despite higher prices. Quality has probably increased, although data on this are scarce. Other factors probably played little role. Finally, the steadily declining infant mortality since 1986 suggests that the net effect of *Doi Moi* on health has been positive.

However, two issues warrant government attention. First, specific efforts are required to ensure access to people with very low incomes, such as residents of remote areas and individuals requiring referral to district hospitals. Second, during China's transition to the market several healthcare issues arose that may apply to Vietnam, including: (a) an increasing share of health spending on hospital care and treatment services, rather than on prevention and health maintenance; (b) new equipment purchases and construction with little attention to financing future recurrent costs, which could strain future funding for disease prevention programmes; and (c) a high proportion of health expenditures devoted to drug consumption, which suggests changes in the drug industry on how drugs are priced and doctors and hospitals are paid (World Bank 1992).

2.6 The impact of Vietnam's reforms on education services and outcomes

This section examines how the provision of education, and ultimately educational outcomes, has been affected by the *Doi Moi* policies Vietnam adopted in the late 1980s. Figure 2.2 presents time-series data on two important educational outcomes, primary and secondary school enrolment rates. Overall, primary school enrolment has been remarkably stable, but secondary school enrolment declined soon after the adoption of *Doi Moi* policies and recovered only recently. These trends are useful summary indicators, but much more can be learned about what has happened in recent years. This section will examine the pathways by which *Doi Moi* policies may have caused these trends.

2.6.1 Income effects

The first pathway by which policies affect education outcomes is income growth. As explained above, Vietnam began with a relatively equitable distribution of income, and all seven regions have experienced economic growth since the late 1980s, although some more than others. Thus one would expect improved education outcomes from higher real per capita income. Yet Figure 2.2 shows that secondary school enrolment initially faltered, which suggests countervailing effects from one or more of the other six pathways. The remainder of this section examines these other pathways in detail.

Figure 2.2 School enrolment rates in Vietnam

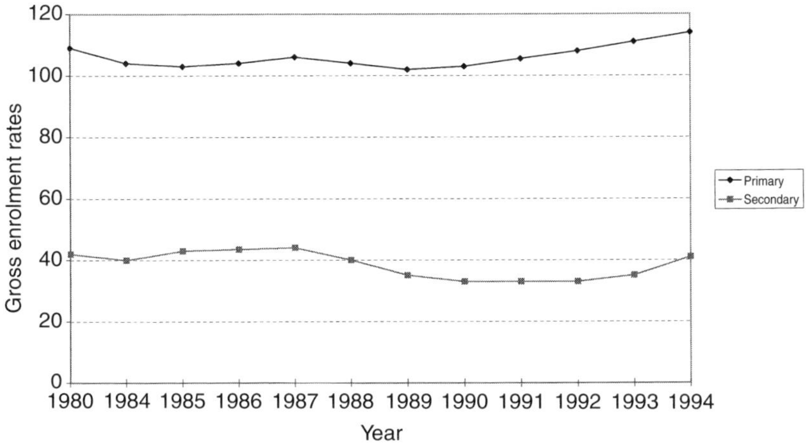

Source: UNESCO Statistical Yearbook, various years.

2.6.2 Price effects[11]

Changes in pricing policies can also affect education services, and ultimately outcomes. Households face two 'prices' for education services: official user fees and various contributions and payments. Before the *Doi Moi* policies, no tuition fees existed at any level of education. Other fees were often imposed, but they were probably minimal since people's incomes were so low. Instead, education was usually financed at the commune level, using income from the operation of agricultural cooperatives.

The *Doi Moi* reforms significantly changed education pricing policies. Although there are still no primary school tuition fees, tuition is now collected at higher levels of education. These fees are generally higher in urban than in rural areas. In both urban and rural areas, annual fees range between VND 18 000 and VND 45 000 in lower secondary schools and between VND 45 000 and VND 63 000 in upper secondary schools.[12] To reduce the burden of these fees, partial or full exemptions exist for certain students, such as children of war invalids, orphans, certain ethnic minorities, residents of remote mountainous areas and children of government workers.

Public post-secondary education tuition ranges from VND 40 000 to VND 100 000 per month, plus fees for matriculation, examinations, boarding and graduation. Again, certain students are granted either full exemptions (war invalids, orphans, and those with outstanding academic achievements) or 50 per cent reductions (certain ethnic minorities and children of government employees and soldiers).

In fact, these official fees provide an incomplete picture. A household survey conducted in 1996 reveals that official fees represent only a small portion of the household expenditures on public education. Even in primary school, where no tuition fees exist, household expenditures are substantial. In urban areas, each public primary school student pays, on average, about VND 261 000 (about US$24), and in rural areas they pay almost VND 105 000 (about US$10). These payments for primary school include school improvement fees, parent association fees, insurance, textbooks, supplies and materials, tutoring, and meals away from home (GSO and ADB 1996).

Household expenditures for secondary school are also much higher than the official fees, on average five to six times higher. In urban areas, a year of schooling costs about VND 488 000 (US$44) for lower secondary and VND 788 000 (US$72) for upper secondary school. The figures for rural areas are VND 203 000 (US$18) and VND 503 000 (US$46) for lower and upper secondary school, respectively (GSO and ADB 1996). To provide some perspective, per capita annual household expenditure in 1996 was VND 1.4 million (rural residents) and VND 2.4 million (urban residents). Thus for a typical rural family of five, annual household expenditures were VND 7 million, so that primary school costs 1.5 per cent of annual expenditures. Analogous costs for lower and upper secondary school are 2.9 per cent and 7.2 per cent, respectively. For a typical urban household of four, the analogous figures are 2.7 per cent (primary), 5.1 per cent (lower secondary) and 8.2 per cent (upper secondary). Of course, these percentages are much higher for poorer families.

Higher education also requires payments well beyond official tuition costs. In 1995 average annual fees were about VND 420 000 (GSO and ADB 1996). Other costs (books, transportation and room and board) more than doubled household costs, amounting to well over 10 per cent of a rural household's annual expenditures and about 10 per cent of urban household expenditures.

In summary, prices for education can be substantial, especially at the secondary and post-secondary levels. However, Glewwe and Jacoby (1998) argue that increased prices may not be the main cause of reductions in secondary school enrolment in the late 1980s. That study will be presented below, after a review of other factors that determine the use of educational services.

2.6.3 Time costs

Another determinant of school enrolment, and ultimately of years of schooling, is the time costs of attending school. School attendance requires much more time than using health services, so changes in time costs may significantly alter school attendance and enrolment. Because incomes have increased in Vietnam, this pathway may be particularly important. However, the key effect is probably not generally higher income, but the fact that the previous agricultural cooperative system did not closely link household incomes to the time household members spent working. In contrast, the current family farming system implies that farm households bear the full cost of the time their children spend in school, since they are not available to work on the family's farm. This time in school effect probably outweighs other time effects. For example, travel time is probably unchanged because very few private schools have appeared recently in Vietnam.

The substantial drop in secondary school enrolment after the *Doi Moi* policies began in 1986 supports the hypothesis that switching from agricultural cooperatives to family farms greatly raised rural households' incentives to remove their children from school to have them work on the family farm. Indeed, Glewwe and Jacoby (1998) show that declines in secondary school enrolments were primarily a rural phenomenon, and coincided with a dramatic increase in labour force participation among secondary school age children. Whether this was the main cause of the decline in secondary school enrolment is discussed further below. At this point we simply note that there may be a close connection.

2.6.4 Quality

As with health, there is virtually no information on changes in school quality under *Doi Moi* policies. Private schools, while no longer prohibited, are relatively rare, enrolling only 2–4 per cent of primary and secondary school students (see Glewwe and Patrinos 1998). Thus changes in quality are primarily changes in public school quality.

One way to approximate changes in school quality is by examining public expenditures for education and training. Such expenditures rose from 1.9 to 3.5 per cent of GDP from 1991 to 1994. Since GDP rose quickly during this period, real per student expenditures more than doubled from VND 21 866 to VND 47 931. Thirty per cent of these expenditures went to primary education, followed closely by secondary education (27 per cent), higher education (13 per cent), and vocational training (11 per cent). Between 1991 and 1994, primary education's share of the education budget declined by about 10 percentage points, and secondary's share increased by a similar amount. Higher education and vocational training's share also declined while 'other expenditures' (largely administration) increased (see World Bank 1996b). This increased expenditure suggests that, on average, school quality increased in the early 1990s.[13] This may explain, at least partially, the increase in secondary school enrolment that began in 1993.

2.6.5 Other determinants of school enrolment and attainment

The other three determinants of households' use of education services are the value they place on education, the contribution of education to income, and government school attendance requirements. As with health, there is little reason to think that *Doi Moi* policies have altered the value households place on education for its own sake, yet the other two factors may have been affected.

Consider the relationship between education and income. Before the *Doi Moi* reforms, Vietnam, like many socialist countries, set wages to reduce inequality among workers with different skills. Thus the economic returns to education were lower than they would be in a market system. While government employees' wages may still reflect wage compression under *Doi Moi* policies, private sector workers now earn whatever the market will bear for their educational background. Thus education may have become more attractive financially, which should increase school attainment.

Finally, there are government school attendance requirements. Before *Doi Moi*, no official regulation required children to attend school, but it was strongly encouraged. In 1991, a law was instituted requiring primary school attendance. However, apparently this law is not strictly enforced, and thus it probably has not significantly affected school enrolment in Vietnam.

2.6.6 Econometric analysis of the determinants of school attainment

Glewwe and Jacoby (1998) recently investigated the determinants of primary and secondary school enrolment in Vietnam. Using current and retrospective data from the 1992–93 VNLSS, they draw several tentative conclusions regarding Vietnam's school enrolment trends. First, they find no evidence that increased prices of schooling had any effect. Specifically, the decline in secondary enrolment preceded the 1989 increase in school fees, the increased cost of primary schooling had no apparent effect on primary school enrolment, and regression analysis showed only weak evidence of price effects on school enrolment and completion.

The study also investigated whether switching to family-based farming reduced secondary school enrolment. The time-series evidence supports this hypothesis; labour force participation jumped dramatically among secondary school age children in the late 1980s. Moreover, while there is evidence that primary schooling makes farmers more productive, there is no evidence that secondary education has any effect. Finally, secondary school enrolment declined much more in rural than in urban areas.

Glewwe and Jacoby also examined school quality and school enrolment. Both time series and cross-sectional analysis suggest that quality played a role, but other evidence is inconsistent with this hypothesis, and the school quality data are incomplete. Thus there is only weak evidence that changes in school quality significantly affected school enrolment trends in Vietnam.

2.6.7 Case study: Ha Tinh province

Further insights on the effect of *Doi Moi* policies come from the case study of Ha Tinh province by OXFAM (1996), which analyses three time periods. During the 'post-war, pre *Doi-Moi* period of discouragement', the early to mid-1980s, education in Ha Tinh was free, but teacher compensation stagnated, educational materials were scarce, and young people and their parents saw few returns to education.

In the period immediately following the *Doi Moi* reforms, the '1990–92 shock', Soviet aid vanished and macroeconomic imbalances led to severe stabilization and adjustment measures. Decollectivization of agriculture provided new income opportunities, but the social services that collectives had provided disappeared. Households increased production to cover costs previously paid by the state. Parents removed their children from school and put them to work, in part because of short-term needs for basic necessities. This is consistent with the analysis of Glewwe and Jacoby (1998). High dropout rates and lower teaching quality characterized this period.

The period since 1993 is called the 'post-*Doi Moi* adjustment' period. School enrolments rose as parents placed greater priority on long-term needs and benefits. Financial security increased as households adjusted to an economy without collectives. At the same time, due to higher tax revenues, teacher salaries and teaching quality increased (OXFAM 1996).

This case study of Ha Tinh province is fairly consistent with the evidence presented above. *Doi Moi* policies raised school fees and the opportunity (time) costs of schooling, and the disappearance of Soviet aid may have reduced school quality. All of these factors reduced school attendance, particularly secondary enrolment. However, steadily rising income increased the demand for education, both directly and indirectly by generating tax revenue to improve school quality. Thus, despite an initial decline immediately following the *Doi Moi* reforms, access to education has recently improved. However, there is still much room for improvement, particularly regarding school quality.

2.7 Conclusions and lessons from Vietnam

Several lessons emerge from this study of health and education outcomes in Asian transitional economies. First, protecting and improving health and education outcomes depend heavily on the success of economic reforms in raising incomes. Strong economic growth, as in China, Laos and Vietnam, makes it much easier for governments to finance improvements in publicly provided services, and for households to contribute through user fees. Yet although higher incomes provide opportunities for progress, governments must consider how to combine effectively both public and private finance and provision of health and education services, and where to allocate scarce government resources.

Second, the initial structure of the economy can determine the impact of policy changes on the provision of health and education services. The nature and sequencing of 'market-oriented reforms' appropriate for any country depend on specific country circumstances. In Vietnam, the dissolution of thousands of state enterprises had little effect on social sector delivery systems. However, the dismantling of agricultural cooperatives did seriously undercut local sources of financing for health and education.

Third, when adopting market-oriented reforms, some small-scale experimentation is useful: if an experiment fails the government must quickly stop it, or at least minimize its negative effects. One example is Vietnam's provision of health services. When the dismantling of agricultural cooperatives left rural communes unable to finance basic health services, the central government provided funds for three health workers per commune. In general, pilot-testing proposed policies allows governments to scrap bad policies and improve good ones.

Fourth, after the initial reforms, governments must develop medium- and long-run plans for blending public and private health and education services. Governments must both provide public services and create an enabling environment for private provision. A clear definition of the government's role is extremely important during the transition to determine when public revenues should be used and when private sector funds and initiatives should provide specific health and education services.

Finally, it is almost inevitable that some groups will face barriers that prevent them from taking advantage of market-oriented policy reforms. The government must identify and monitor vulnerable groups. Careful analytical work, using household surveys and other information, is extremely important. The alternative is to let political agendas and anecdotal experience guide national policy, which will eventually lead to policy failures that endanger the health and educational prospects of millions of citizens.

Notes

1. We would like to thank Kathryn Anderson, Branko Milanovic and Dominique van de Walle for comments, Sulekha Patel for locating data, and Dan Levy for research assistance. The findings, interpretations and conclusions expressed in this chapter are entirely those of the authors. They do not necessarily represent the views of the World Bank, its executive directors, or the countries they represent.
2. Another example of values being changed by government policy is female education; more educated girls may, when they become parents, place greater emphasis on their children's education.
3. Quality of services may also decline, in order to minimize price increases.
4. Mongolia's GDP per capita declined from 1990 to 1993, but infant mortality data are only available in 1987 and then from 1992 to 1995.
5. The 1995 figure shows an increase, but this may reflect a different data source. Even if accurate, this rate of 34 is still lower than the 1980s rates.
6. Two Asian transition economies are missing: there are no infant mortality data for Mongolia in 1990, and there are no infant mortality data for Cambodia in 1989.
7. For a full description of macroeconomic performance and policy reforms, see World Bank (1993) and Dollar and Litvack (1998).
8. For a full description of poverty and inequality in Vietnam, see World Bank (1995).
9. Interestingly, female-headed households were not poorer than male-headed households. Indeed, they were somewhat better off (see World Bank 1995). Although gender does not appear to determine poverty at the household level, *within* households women may be worse off than men.

10. In general, fees at commune health centres remain very modest and are often waived. Required payments are higher for hospital outpatients and highest for hospital inpatients.
11. This section draws on World Bank (1996b).
12. These figures refer to data collected in 1996, when one US dollar was worth about 10 500 Vietnamese dong.
13. School quality could have declined in certain regions or among certain socioeconomic groups, but this cannot be checked with the available data.

References

Aduki (1995), 'Poverty in Vietnam', Aduki Pty Ltd, Canberra, Australia.

Behrman, Jere, Jim Knowles and McInnes (1996), 'The Demand for Health Insurance in Vietnam', Abt Associates Inc.

Dollar, David and Paul Glewwe (1998), 'Poverty and Inequality in Vietnam', in D. Dollar, P. Glewwe and J. Litvack (eds), *Household Welfare and Vietnam's Transition to a Market Economy*, Washington, DC: World Bank.

Dollar, David and Jennie Litvack (1998), 'Macroeconomic Reform and Poverty Reduction', in D. Dollar, P. Glewwe and J. Litvack (eds), *Household Welfare and Vietnam's Transition to a Market Economy*, Washington, DC: World Bank.

Gertler, Paul and Jennie Litvack (1998), 'Access to Healthcare During Transition', in D. Dollar, P. Glewwe and J. Litvack (eds), *Household Welfare and Vietnam's Transition to a Market Economy*, Washington, DC: World Bank.

Gertler, Paul and Jacques van der Gaag (1990), *The Willingness to Pay for Medical Care in Developing Countries*, Baltimore, MD: Johns Hopkins University Press.

Glewwe, Paul and Hanan Jacoby (1998), 'School Enrolment and Completion: An Investigation of Recent Trends', in D. Dollar, P. Glewwe and J. Litvack (eds), *Household Welfare and Vietnam's Transition to a Market Economy*, Washington, DC: World Bank.

Glewwe, Paul and Harry Patrinos (1998), 'The Role of the Private Sector in Education in Vietnam: Evidence from the Vietnam Living Standards Survey', *Living Standards Measurement Study Working Paper* No. 132, World Bank, Washington, DC.

GSO and ADB (1996), 'Vietnam Social Sector Financing Survey', General Statistical Office and Asian Development Bank, Hanoi.

HEPR (1996), 'National Programme for Hunger Eradication and Poverty Reduction in Vietnam', draft document, Ministry of Planning and Investment, Government of Vietnam, Hanoi.

Litvack, Jennie and Claude Bodart (1993), 'User Fees Plus Quality Equals Improved Access to Healthcare: Results from a Field Experiment in Cameroon', *Social Science and Medicine*, Vol. 37, No. 3.

OXFAM (1996), 'Report on the Financing and Delivery of Basic Services at the Commune Level in Hy Anh, Ha Tinh, Vietnam', Hanoi.

Van de Walle, Dominique (1998), 'Safety Nets in an Emerging Market Economy', in J. Litvack and D. Rondinelli (eds), 'From Economic Transition to Social Transformation: Institution Building in Vietnam', typescript.

World Bank (1992), 'China: Long-Term Issues and Options in the Health Transition', Washington, DC.

World Bank (1993), 'Vietnam: Transition to the Market', Washington, DC.
World Bank (1995), 'Vietnam: Poverty Assessment and Strategy', Washington, DC.
World Bank (1996a), *World Development Report*, Washington, DC.
World Bank (1996b), 'Vietnam: Education Financing Sector Study', Washington, DC.
World Bank (1996c), 'Vietnam: Fiscal Decentralization and Delivery of Rural Services', Washington, DC.
World Bank, Asian Development Bank, FAO, UNDP and NGO Water Resources Group (1996), 'Vietnam: Water Resources Sector Review', Washington, DC.

3
Labour Markets in Asian Transition Economies

Aiguo Lu and Paolo Verme

3.1 Introduction

Transition from central planning to a market economy in Asian countries has invariably changed the pattern of employment. In all these countries, employment and wage levels have become increasingly determined by labour supply and demand and the market has been replacing central planning and administrative control as the key mechanism for labour allocation. Open unemployment emerged everywhere, indicating a radical departure from the socialist practice of full employment. Changes in the employment structure have been related to the process of privatization, restructuring and transitional reforms. As employment was the main or the only source of income for an increasing share of the population, the impact of labour market changes on people's well-being during the transition has been most significant. This chapter examines some of the major characteristics of those changes in Asian Transitional Economies (ATEs), and explores the impact of government policies on the performance of the emerging labour market.

ATEs are composed of countries with diverse socioeconomic conditions and transition experiences. This suggests that there cannot be a single, 'Asian pattern' of labour market transformation. However, ATEs do share some experiences as well as face similar challenges. For instance, compared with the Central and Eastern European countries (CEECs) and Russia, ATEs are in general less industrialized, with a larger share of the population employed in agriculture. Therefore, alongside the process of transition, these countries faced developmental issues. In countries such as China, creating wage employment for the large pool of rural labour represents a task no less pressing than to restructure the existing waged workforce.

This chapter is divided into six sections. The second examines labour market developments. The third focuses on unemployment, the fourth looks at wages and the fifth gives an overview of policy and institutional responses. A few final remarks will conclude the chapter.

3.2 Labour market developments

The pre-transition socialist legacy of employment can be characterized by full employment, low wage differentials and relatively equitable income distribution, high labour participation rates, including women, widespread government restrictions on labour mobility and wages, underemployment and low levels of output per worker. Transition to the market implied labour market restructuring and a reallocation of labour across economic sectors, across regions and from the state to the private sector. As a rule, labour market changes have followed economic reforms and macroeconomic developments, and the socialist characteristics of employment have been fading away, leaving the way clear for more dynamic, less stable and predictable labour markets.

3.2.1 Economic performance and employment

With regard to the relationship between growth, employment and productivity in Central and Eastern Europe (CEE) and the Commonwealth of Independent States (CIS), the literature has identified two paths of labour market adjustment during transition (World Bank 1996; Allison and Ringold 1996). The first path is characterized by output decline followed by a comparable employment decline which has prevented productivity from falling. This pattern is most common in the CEECs. Employment growth has resumed only in recent years and in a few of these countries. The second path is represented by the CIS countries, where employment decline has been relatively small, despite large drops in output. Instead of large-scale labour shedding, firms have retained their workforce, paying lower real wages, building wage arrears, putting workers on extended leave, reducing working hours and/or reducing benefits. This path has resulted in a decline in productivity.

In Asia, the CIS path is exemplified by the Central Asian Republics (CARs) where output slumped, employment declined relatively little or increased and productivity plummeted. In other countries, transition followed a radically different path. Reforms in countries such as China and Vietnam have been accompanied by a combination of GDP, employment and productivity growth. This is a distinct third transitional path (see Table 3.1).

Table 3.1 GDP, employment and productivity, 1995 as % of 1989 (unless specified)

Country	*GDP*	*Employment*	*Productivity*
Kazakhstan	57	82	70
Kyrgyz Republic	53	95	56
Turkmenistan	63	111	57
Uzbekistan	84	111	76
Mongolia	84	104	81
Vietnam	155	119	130
China (1985 as % of 1979)	174	122	143
Eastern Europe and Baltic countries*	74	81	91
CIS states average*	50	92	54

*Unweighted average.

Sources: EBRD (1997) p. 115; for Asian non-CIS economies, World Bank (1996) p. 173; World Bank (1995), pp. 173, 207; EIU (1997a), p. 53, and ADB (1997).

While the CARs preferred to bear the cost of the output decline within enterprises, China and Vietnam faced a quite different problem. Output and productivity have been growing faster than employment and in both countries labour supply remained in excess of demand. Thus one characteristic that all ATEs share is that they face tremendous pressure to create jobs irrespective of economic performance.

3.2.2 The reallocation of labour

The transitional period entailed for all ATEs a substantial reallocation of labour which took mainly three interrelated forms: a reallocation from the state to the private sector which occurs by definition in transition; a reallocation across economic sectors, and a reallocation across geographical areas. These three aspects of labour reallocation assumed different features in different countries. Two broad paths can be identified in Asia, one for the CARs and one for China and Vietnam (see Table 3.2).

The share of employment in state-owned entities in China and Vietnam was much lower than the corresponding share in the CARs at the outset of reforms. This is the main reason why privatization programmes became such an important aspect of reforms in Central Asia. China and Vietnam, with a large share of employment outside the state sector, did not have to go through this process on the same scale.

Table 3.2 Share of employment in state-owned entities

CARs	*1990*	*1996*
Kazakhstan	86.6	34.6
Kyrgyz Republic	73.3	27.7
Turkmenistan	57.3	46.7
Uzbekistan	65.4	30
China	*1978*	*1994*
	18.6	18.2
Vietnam	*1980*	*1995*
	15.3	8.6

Sources: CIS-Stat (1998), *China Statistical Yearbook* (1995), Jansen (Chapter 6, this volume).

Instead, they initiated the transition through a change in the pattern of incentives and regulations, limiting privatization to parts of the industrial and urban sector. This consideration explains why the CARs show such a decline in state employment while with respect to China and Vietnam only the latter shows a significant decline, though from a small proportion of total employment.

Consequently, the process of enterprise restructuring carried a smaller weight for the well-being of the whole economy in China or Vietnam than it did in the CARs. In the CARs, a successful transition became reliant on successful restructuring of privatized enterprises, while in China and Vietnam agricultural households had the potential to increase output and productivity from the start. China implemented reforms in the agricultural sector and in certain areas, first determining a growth base which became instrumental for supporting further reforms. The CARs, instead, dismantled the state sector before creating the conditions for growth in some specified economic sector or geographical areas. The rationale in this case was that the processes of privatization, liberalization of prices and trade and stabilization measures would have been sufficient conditions to create growth poles, especially in the new private sector.

In China up until 1994, the share of the state sector in total employment remained stable. This indicates that state sector employment continued to expand, while the overall non-farm jobs were growing. But the ability of the state sector to absorb labour declined as compared to other sectors. In 1985–90, the state sector provided about 70 per cent of all new jobs. By 1993 it provided only 9 per cent of new urban employment. The engine of employment growth moved to non-state sectors, particularly to Township and Villages Enterprises (TVEs), where employment grew ten times faster than in the public sector. However, employment growth in TVEs has not been fed by redundant state and urban workers but almost entirely by the rural labour force.

In Vietnam, state employment was cut considerably at the early stage of reforms and the labour force in state-owned enterprises (SOEs) declined both in number and as a proportion of total employment. Employment grew faster in non-state sectors, especially in entities of private and mixed ownership. Between 1988 and 1991, private sector employment increased 2.7-fold (Jamal 1996).

In the CARs, the private sector also expanded at a fast rate but as a product of privatization rather than genuine creation of new private jobs. Countries such as Turkmenistan, which privatized less and where employment was maintained or increased, did so by expanding state services rather than production. In Kazakhstan or the Kyrgyz Republic, where privatization has been a deeper process and where employment has declined, a substantial increase in employment occurred only in trade and catering activities in the form of self-employment. On closer inspection, self-employment is mainly represented by petty trade or individuals involved in marketing products of their own home production. This signals an expansion of subsistence activities rather than value-added production. In Kazakhstan, despite the increase in employment in trade and catering, real output in this sector has declined (CSAK 1997).

In all countries considered, the sectors' composition of employment changed during the transition. Again the starting-point is significantly different between the CARs and China and Vietnam, the latter two countries having a much larger share of the labour force employed in agriculture before and after the reforms. In the CARs, the share of the agricultural sector increased at the expense of the industrial sector while services have been stable, decreased or increased. In all the CARs, this meant a real growth of the number of employed people in agriculture, except for Kazakhstan.[1] In China, instead, the industrial and services sectors expanded their share at the expense of agriculture because these sectors grew faster (see Table 3.3).

In Mongolia, agriculture's share in the labour force fell below 50 per cent by 1976, and the agricultural workforce declined not only in relation to total employment but also in absolute terms. This trend was interrupted after 1990. Squeezed by industrial decline, the labour force turned to the services sector. As saturation in services employment occurred, people began to return to the farms. Privatization of

Table 3.3 Employment shares by economic sector

Country	Industry and construction 1991	Industry and construction 1996	Agriculture, forestry and fishing 1991	Agriculture, forestry and fishing 1996	Services and others 1991	Services and others 1996
Kazakhstan	31.3	21.0	22.1	23.0	46.6	56.0
Kyrgyz Republic	27.9	14.6	32.7	45.9	39.4	39.5
Turkmenistan	20.8	18.5	41.9	45.6	37.3	35.9
Uzbekistan	24.0	19.2	39.3	40.1	36.7	40.7
Mongolia	16.6	13.2	34.5	45.2	48.9	41.6
	1980	*1995*	*1980*	*1995*	*1980*	*1995*
China	14.0	22.9	74.0	52.9	12.0	24.2
Vietnam	15.1	12.7	70.0	66.2	14.9	21.1

Sources: CIS-Stat (1998), Jansen (Chapter 6, this volume), ADB (1997), World Bank (1995).

agriculture facilitated this reverse migration and by 1996 almost half of employment was again employed in agriculture.

In Vietnam, between 1988 and 1991, over 1 million workers (equivalent to around 20 per cent of the urban labour force) were retrenched from SOEs and government services (Jamal 1996). Many turned to the countryside, where the cooperative sector was being dismantled. However, most new employment was actually created in the services sector, especially in trade outside state commerce. Greater dislocation took place in the north of the country because of the concentration of SOEs, government departments and heavy industry, all of which contracted in the aftermath of reforms.

The reallocation of labour also entailed a geographical dislocation of workers. In China and Vietnam this migration took the path of a rural–urban and centre–coastal migration given the emerging opportunities in the urban industrial sector and the establishment of special economic zones. In the CARs this internal migration has been much weaker and sometimes took the opposite path: urban–rural. However, the most relevant migration of workers has been the emigration of ethnic Slavs towards Russia and Europe, given the poor labour market conditions and the existing discriminatory norms in the post-independence period.

The two transitional paths embodied by the two groups of ATEs feature major differences not only in respect of output, employment and productivity but also in relation to the different forces which shaped the reallocation of labour. While CARs seem to face a process of de-industrialization, China and Vietnam have been able to expand production in most sectors. However, and despite the exceptional growth experienced by China and Vietnam, both groups of countries are now confronted with an open labour surplus.

3.3 Unemployment

During the reforms, the advent of open unemployment marked the end of the socialist version of full employment. Strictly speaking, unemployment is not an entirely novel phenomenon in these countries. Although job security was an essential component of central planning, labour underutilization was reflected in overstaffing or labour hoarding and much of the employment was unproductive. Nevertheless, while full employment in central planning systems had serious shortcomings, it served as a foundation for the particular distribution pattern of low, but highly equitable and guaranteed, income and welfare. Open unemployment in the reform era presents a new challenge.

3.3.1 Main features

According to unemployment data, which became available only after the reforms, unemployment in ATEs has been on the rise in all countries.

There are good reasons to believe that the real unemployment rates are likely to be higher, if not substantially higher, than registered unemployment. A number of factors affect the accuracy of the official unemployment statistics, most notably the incomplete registration of unemployment. In the CARs, where household surveys are available, unemployment rate estimates made by the central statistical offices are two to four times registered figures (Table 3.4). Moreover, the pool of discouraged unemployed, formally counted as economically inactive, is expanding due to the realistically scarce job opportunities. Others abandoned the labour force (employment or unemployment) by taking early retirement, by focusing on household duties or because they emigrated in search of better opportunities. A significant increase in the death rate of the working-age population also occurred in the fastest reformers, such as Kazakhstan and the Kyrgyz Republic.

Despite record growth, China's unemployment has risen. Until recently, official unemployment grew very slowly and remained low. But the official unemployment rates underestimate considerably the real level of unemployment. This is explained by the government's restrictive

Table 3.4 Registered unemployment rates (unless otherwise stated)

Country	*1980*	*1983*	*1986*	*1989*	*1990*	*1991*	*1992*	*1993*	*1994*	*1995*	*1996*	*1997*
Kazakhstan						0.05	0.4	0.6	1.1	2.1	4.2	3.9
Kazakhstan*										10.9	12.7	
Kyrgyz Republic						0.01	0.1	0.2	0.8	3.0	4.5	3.2
Kyrgyz Republic*								1.7	4.1	5.7	7.8	
Uzbekistan							0.1	0.2	0.3	0.3	0.3	0.4
Mongolia				3.8	5.5	6.50	6.3	8.5	8.7	5.4	6.5	
China**	4.9	2.3	2.0	2.6	2.5	2.30	2.3	2.6	2.8	2.9	3.0	

*National statistical offices estimates.
**Urban only.

Sources: ADB (1997) pp. 82–3, 140–41, 168–9, 218–19; CIS-Stat (1998), Kulakeyev and Katarvaeva (1997); Gudkova et al. (1998).

definition of unemployment and by the incomplete coverage of the labour force. A large amount of rural labour surplus goes unaccounted for. Rural migrant labourers seeking jobs outside their home areas have been estimated in the range of 70 to 90 million. Moreover, in recent years, an increasing number of workers were laid off during industrial restructuring, many of whom did not register as unemployed. In early 1998, while registered unemployment numbered 5.3 million nationwide, the number of laid-off workers was 15 million, or nearly three times as many.[2] In Vietnam, urban unemployment in early 1995 was estimated at over 2 million, and the unemployment rate was as high as 25 per cent in some urban areas (ADB 1996: 28). An estimated 28 per cent of the rural labour force was not fully employed in 1996 (EIU 1997b: 30).

Rural unemployment is also an issue of concern in the CARs. Underemployment was often 'kept behind the farm gate' in collective and state farms. During the transition, agriculture enjoyed employment growth in some countries but agricultural output, more often than not, declined over the period, reducing overall productivity despite the process of privatization. This is due to the fact that agriculture was highly mechanized and the decline in output turned into a decline in agricultural inputs such as fertilizers, pesticides, gas and spare parts for machinery. This is in sharp contrast with the experience of China, where labour surplus in agriculture has not been determined by a fall in production but by labour productivity growth.

Unemployment in ATEs shows some common features in relation to gender, age and skill structures. In particular, a gender bias has been generally observed. A survey shows that about 70 per cent of managers in China reported that their surplus workers were mainly women (Lim et al. 1996: 37). Women, as a rule, are overrepresented in unemployment (see Table 3.5).

In the CARs, the prevalence of women, young and low educated people among the registered unemployed is also evident (Table 3.6). This is not necessarily always the case once we take into account the actual number of unemployed. For instance, in Kazakhstan in 1996 unemployed men were more numerous than women, though it does not appear from employment services statistics because men tend to register less. However, as a rule, women are first to be laid off. A World Bank study (1996: 72) confirmed that in most transition economies women account for a disproportionate share of the unemployed. Much of the decline represents women being forced out of the labour force by economic retrenchment, by more burdensome domestic responsibilities, or by discrimination in the labour market.

Table 3.5 Unemployment rates by gender in China (%)

	1987	*1989*	*1990*	*1991*	*1992*	*1993*	*1994*
Men	0.7	1.3	0.9	1.1	–	0.9	0.8
Women	1.0	1.3	1.2	1.1	–	1.2	1.1

Source: ILO (1997).

Table 3.6 Registered unemployment in the CARs

	1993	*1994*	*1995*	*1996*
Kazakhstan				
% women	70.2	64.8	60.1	63.2
% youth (< 30 years)	54.1	52.4	46.5	40.9
% higher education				7.8
Kyrgyz Republic				
% women	69.7	60.9	59.3	57.9
% youth (< 30 years)	31.3	39.2	40.2	37.8
% higher education		16.6	12.3	10.2
Uzbekistan				
% women	61.0	59.0	60.1	
% youth (< 30 years)		64.1	61.9	63.6
% higher education		5.9	6.1	

Source: CIS-Stat (1998).

3.3.2 Causes and consequences of unemployment

An economic recession is conventionally associated with a sharp rise in unemployment. In the ATEs, unemployment has been everywhere on the rise, regardless of economic performance. In reviewing the different speed, scale and characteristics of the rising unemployment, one finds that in addition to output behaviour, factors such as transition strategies, social policies and development levels played unusually important roles. In other words, the process of transition *per se* determines a rise in unemployment, but this rise can take different forms depending on a large set of structural and policy conditions.

In the CARs, the fall in production hit the labour force through a multiplicity of paths. For those who managed to maintain formal employment, real wages were quickly eroded by hyperinflation, they have been paid occasionally and sometimes in kind. For some, working hours have been reduced while others have been put on forced unpaid leave.

Among those who exited employment in the CARs, some were called to fulfill increasing household duties, some became discouraged unemployed, some emigrated or died, some registered as unemployed and others kept looking for work but did not register. Visible unemployment, and especially registered unemployment, remained relatively low. Not surprisingly, measures such as employment and unemployment do not seem to be procyclical. Sometimes they change in the same direction and sometimes in the opposite direction, depending on how the different 'exit paths' behave. Countries such as Kazakhstan and the Kyrgyz Republic saw registered unemployment increase faster in periods of moderate or no fall in output because of employers' attitudes and because of a certain continuous osmosis between the labour force and economic inactivity.

Thus the nature of unemployment is not only determined by a combination of macroeconomic factors such as fall in output in the case of the CARs, increase in productivity and a dominant agricultural sector in the case of China, but also by a combination of microeconomic processes which determine labour flows in times of adjustment. Unemployment, as it is currently measured in transitional Asia, is a fairly poor indicator, leaving out a substantial number of individuals in need of a job.

The fight against transitional unemployment, therefore, depends in general on the overall output performance and on the growing ability of the non-state sector to re-absorb not only the visibly unemployed but all those willing and able to work. Government policies have an important role in guiding labour flows in the right direction by creating the right pattern of incentives. In this respect, China seems to derive its success from a reform strategy which focused on incentives to economic agents rather than on formal ownership of the means of production.

The initial structural conditions have also shaped the current unemployment structure. China benefited from the start as an agricultural sector structured to respond to state incentives. The CARs' agricultural sector, instead, was organized around large kolkhoz and cooperatives managed in an industrial fashion to produce for a vast Soviet market. In this case, privatization and the redistribution of the use of the land among workers could not turn instantly into better productivity but needed a process of restructuring similar to that needed in the industrial sector. Tractors designed to plough large extents of land are difficult to re-deploy for household production and cannot be split into smaller units.

Where pre-transition structural conditions were similar in China and the CARs, such as for the urban state industrial sector, Chinese SOEs faced similar problems to those observed in the CARs during the transition. Restructuring remained a difficult task to accomplish, the government has been reluctant to resort to mass layoffs, and state firms were encouraged to maintain their labour. However, as is the case for the CARs, this policy proved unsustainable and, in recent years and despite favourable macroeconomic conditions, SOEs have been forced to lay off workers in large numbers. This relatively new phenomenon represents a major challenge for the Chinese labour market in the years to come.

Rising unemployment also led to the exit of an increasing number of working-age population from the formal sector of the economy. The growing incapacity of the formal sector to provide minimum means of subsistence in the CARs has pushed many people to enter the informal sector, characterized by low-skilled, low-value-added activities in the agricultural and trade sectors. Even in the formal sector, the category 'self-employment' often hides what is in reality a subsistence activity such as homegrown food commercialized in the local market. The result is a net loss of workers' income, a decline in living standards, and an increase in poverty.

Unemployment results in income losses, thus affecting the living standards of the unemployed. In particular, in countries where the provision of welfare benefits and social services was linked to the place of employment, such as in China or in the CARs, a job loss leads to reduction or loss of access to these benefits and services. The negative consequences of unemployment go far beyond the loss of income. As Sen (1997) pointed out, unemployment also leads to loss of freedom, to social exclusion, skill losses, psychological harm, ill health and mortality, motivational loss, loss of human relations and family life, racial and gender inequality and loss of social values and responsibility. These aspects are likely to be exacerbated in most ATEs.

3.4 Wages and equity

Before transition, wages were commonly under the strict control of the government, in most cases more so than employment. Wage differentials were relatively small, and wage levels were based on individuals' personal endowments, in particular level of education and work experience within any profession. Differences existed between different professions. Workers such as miners, producing physical goods, had generally higher wages than service workers such as medical doctors. This was in line with the socialist view of work and with the necessity to maintain a certain level of production. With the transition, the pattern of wages and incentives was expected to change.

3.4.1 The level and structure of wages

Theoretically, the essential function of wages in a market economy is to allocate labour resources efficiently. It is not the aggregate response of wage levels that matters here, but whether wages can send correct signals to workers in the market. In practice, this process has been hampered in all ATEs by inherited structural rigidities and by new distortions introduced by the process of transition.

Looking at the change in the overall wage level, patterns of wage adjustment were basically of two types. China, which went through the transition process with no macroeconomic crisis, showed steady growth in real wages combined with increasing wage employment. The CARs and Mongolia, which experienced a sharp recession, suffered from a drop in real wages and, in addition, a decrease in wage employment.

As the economy grew, real wages in China increased. Between 1986 and 1992 real wages increased by 17.2 per cent (World Bank 1997: 100). The rate of increase has been different in different sectors, but generally speaking all sectors enjoyed a growth in income or wages. On the contrary, the CARs experienced a tradeoff between wages and employment. Levels of employment were maintained while real wages fell, in line with the decline in output.

The CARs and Mongolia seemed to have opted for keeping labour at work by lowering wages so as to avoid mass layoffs. While this attitude may have been widespread and facilitated by soft budget constraints, at the beginning of the transitional process it was rather the result of a given development. Hyperinflation reduced real wages to very low values in a very short time and enterprises adjusted nominal wages slowly to absorb the output shock. As a result, wage declines have been severe and registered unemployment has remained relatively low. As these economies became more open and subject to market forces, firms started to lay off surplus labour. Real wages slowly readjusted but remained below the pre-transition level and low by any standard.

Irrespective of transitional performances, wage inequalities have been increasing in all ATEs. In China, between 1985 and 1992 joint ventures and foreign-owned firms had on average considerably higher wage levels, and the TVEs had the lowest. The former offered nearly twice as much as the latter. At the same time, average wages in collective TVEs and SOEs rose gradually and steadily, while wages in enterprises with foreign participation showed fluctuations during periods of government tight financial control and adjustment policy such as in 1988 and 1990 (Ying Zhu 1995). In Vietnam, while wage levels in the non-state sectors were far from homogeneous, the highest wage levels were found in private enterprises (Ronnås and Sjöberg 1995).

There are several factors affecting wage levels in different sectors in China. Some of the non-state sectors offer substantially higher wages than the state sector, but other employers such as TVEs and many foreign-funded enterprises do not. A major problem with alternative employment in the non-state sector is the relatively low welfare content. Although wages seemed to be relatively low, the overall pay in China's state sector including benefits was roughly 60 per cent higher than in the non-state sector (World Bank 1996: 73–4). This is an important reason why state sector workers have been reluctant to move to non-state sectors. This factor, however, did not force non-state entities such as TVEs to raise wages in order to attract workers because the major source of their labour came from agriculture, where average income remained still low relative to any other sector. As a consequence, real wage increases occurred throughout the system, pulling workers out of rural farms and into TVEs, out of rural areas and into urban areas and out of slow-growing regions and into fast-growing ones. Therefore, irrespective of distortions present in state employment, wages in China contributed efficiently to the allocation of labour.

The CARs did not benefit from a large relatively low-income sector which could act as a reservoir, and did not manage to create the conditions for a private sector growth which could pull workers out of other sectors. Thus, even when wage restrictions and regulations were lifted, the wage did not perform the function it plays in market economies, except for a restricted number of urban workers employed in service activities. The industrial labour force, squeezed between wage decline and unemployment prospects, either compromised on working conditions or turned to the informal sector as a primary or additional source of income.

Thus in CARs, wage inequality has increased but not as one would expect. In many cases, wage increases have occurred in those sectors which showed the sharpest output decline. For instance, in industry and construction, the sectors hit most by the recession, wages have increased relative to better-performing sectors such as agriculture, trade

Table 3.7 CARs' relative wages (averages, selected sectors)

	1990	*1991*	*1992*	*1993*	*1994*	*1995*	*1996*
CARs (all sectors)	100	100	100	100	100	100	100
Industry	111	115	136	148	150	162	174
Agriculture	97	105	97	80	74	62	61
Construction	127	120	126	154	159	160	162
Transport	111	103	109	124	124	139	133
Communication	92	98	104	113	130	146	150
Trade, catering and wholesale	85	82	79	86	81	76	78
Education	77	73	74	74	71	69	66
Credit, finance, insurance	139	190	198	226	225	202	195

Source: Authors' calculations from CIS-Stat (1998).

and catering. This is so because sectors such as industry and construction are those where wages are not paid and where the provision of social services is still an important factor. The only sector which performed as one would expect is finance, credit and insurance, where wages have increased relative to other sectors. However, even in this sector, the relative gain made between 1990 and 1993 has been eroded since (Table 3.7).

The flows between the formal and informal sectors and between labour force participation and non-participation led to significant hiring and separation rates. This has led some observers to believe that the CARs and other CIS countries have 'buoyant' labour markets, with new opportunities emerging at all times. In reality, the jobs on offer, while on paper they look relatively attractive, often do not materialize in cash at the end of the month and/or real occupations and tend to have a short life, thus influencing the buoyancy of the labour market. Moreover, the practice of not paying salaries, while initially induced by necessity, became a widespread business practice even in profitable sectors. This is possible thanks to non-existent or non-enforceable labour laws and to a large skilled labour supply available on the market. Therefore new forms of labour market distortions determined by the emerging of unregulated markets have replaced the old ones and the wages still send distorted signals to the workers.

3.4.2 The role of inflation

In a market economy, when inflation generally remains low, cost-push factors, in particular wages, are believed to influence inflation. Thus governments pay particular attention during tripartite negotiations to keep nominal wage growth below certain targets. In transition economies that witnessed hyperinflation right after deregulation of prices, the inverse causation was predominant at the initial stage of transition, that is, price liberalization and the following inflation determined real wage fluctuations. Countries facing major economic difficulties saw a sharp decline in real wages. In Mongolia, up to 1991 wages were increasing, but the gains were wiped out in the next two years due to inflation, with wages ending up much lower than their pre-crisis level.

Inflation has been a factor of concern for all ATEs. Prices increased beyond the control of governments, becoming a potential source of social unrest. In all economies inflation has been sparked by price liberalization though it is recognized that inflation was inherited from the monetary overhang in the pre-reform period. The size of the overhanging inflation is difficult to estimate and probably varied a great deal between ATEs, which makes it difficult to compare countries during the post-liberalization period (see Table 3.8).

From a government perspective and in the short run hyperinflation carries some advantages. It works as a government tax by eroding government debts to its citizens, it reduces real wages and it encourages employment retention. But from a household or firm perspective, hyperinflation undermines self-financing capacity, reduces private investments and aggregate demand and creates a new demand for social protection, which in turn puts pressure on the government. While the rationale for price liberalization is correct in its essence, the big-bang approach under conditions of large inflation overhang (and

Table 3.8 Inflation in ATEs

(A)	*1990*	*1991*	*1992*	*1993*	*1994*	*1995*	*1996*
Kazakhstan		79.0	1381	1662	1892	176	39.1
Kyrgyz Republic		85.0	855	772	229	53	30.0
Uzbekistan	3.1	82.2	645	534	1568	305	54.0
(B)	*1978*	*1985*	*1990*	*1991*	*1992*	*1993*	*1994*
China	100	128.1	207.7	213.7	225.2	254.9	310.2
Vietnam		100.0	26 851	49 165	67 750	73 373	80 270

(A) *Source*: EBRD (1997). Average CPI (annual changes).
(B) *Source*: ADB (1997). RPI (changes on base year).

absence of monetary control) may be self-defeating by disrupting production, the fundamental cycle of savings and investments and the potential for medium- and long-term growth. This is what happened in the CARs and Mongolia.

Paradoxically, in terms of labour market outcome, price liberalization in a regime of large inflation overhang acts as an additional form of distortion. Hyperinflation, encourages a shift of financial resources out of financial assets and into physical assets. It encourages a reallocation of labour out of wage labour and into non-wage labour, out of industrial production and into home production, out of the formal sector and into the informal sector. If price liberalization ignites hyperinflation it produces exactly the opposite effect it is designed for. The lesson from China for other ATEs is that it is wise to address the supply–demand imbalances in the goods market before unleashing prices. Perhaps China had more favourable initial structural conditions to be successful in this sense, but a piecemeal approach to price liberalization deserves reconsideration in the light of the CARs' experiences of the early 1990s.

3.4.3 Wage-setting mechanisms

Under the administrative allocation of jobs, wages were based on individual endowments in accordance with wage scales set up by the government. Age, education, profession and working experience were some of the main criteria used to establish the wage scales. During transition the shift towards a more democratic tripartite negotiation mechanism has been slow and often hampered by governments. Thus enterprises in ATEs gained increasing autonomy in wage setting, contributing to wage flexibility and inequality. The basis of wage setting has been shifting towards a pattern in which the performance of enterprises in the market, or enterprise profitability, became a determining factor. In China, and especially since the mid-1990s, when firms such as SOEs performed poorly, wage levels have dropped.

Research efforts to identify the relative importance of a number of factors in wage determination have not been conclusive. Normally, education serves as an important determinant of wages. Better-educated people tend to find employment faster. The current wage levels in different sectors in ATEs do not always show a close correlation between education and wages. In Vietnam, the private sector offers generally higher wages than the state sector, regardless of the generally higher education level of state sector employees (Ronnås and Sjöberg 1995: 24). Empirical studies also found that at least up until

1987 the rate of return to human capital in the urban labour market was much lower in China than in many market economies (Meng and Kidd 1997).

Nevertheless, the role of education and especially marketable skills in wage determination has been growing. Wage differentials within the non-state sector are comparatively wider. Competition from non-state sectors and in particular from foreign enterprises over highly skilled workers had forced the government in Vietnam to adjust official state wages, and SOEs have had to raise the relative pay of educated workers (O'Connor 1996). As a result, wages increasingly reflect the levels of education and training. This is also true in the CARs, where the original bias in favour of non-skilled workers involved in physical production has been reversed. Especially in the service sectors, highly skilled workers now have better chances to find a job and to be better paid.

3.5 Labour market policies

Labour allocation under central planning has been viewed as similar to the allocation of other production factors. But the principles and practices of setting employment and, to a lesser degree, wages evolved over time. For instance, on the eve of transition, in the USSR, 'the labour market became more of a market than other markets' (Jackman and Rutkowski 1994: 121). Restrictions on labour mobility, and on hiring or changing jobs, were maintained but limited, although restrictions on wages were greater. Comparatively, China had perhaps the most rigid labour market, in which labour allocation was far more tightly controlled than in the USSR. Strict government regulations on labour mobility were universally applied, not only restricting urban-bound migration of rural labour, but also labour turnover in urban areas.

In looking at labour market policies in Asia we observe again a major difference between the experiences of China and the CARs. While the CARs followed an orthodox approach to the treatment of unemployment by following a European type of model, China has followed its own path of rather innovative solutions. The main difference between the two approaches is perhaps the fact that China focused on employment rather than unemployment policies – on the demand side of the labour market rather than on the supply side.

China put a greater effort into encouraging the growth of non-state sectors, particularly the new private sector, in order to provide opportunities for those entering the labour market and for those made redundant. These policies include the establishment of a favourable environment for the development of firms of various ownerships. Many administrative obstacles, such as licences, regulations and discriminatory taxes, were reduced or removed. Market entry was made easier for non-state firms. Instead, the CARs, while deregulating prices and wages, maintained rather clumsy rules and norms for the establishment of new businesses in an already poor macroeconomic environment. Thus the fight against unemployment remained in the hands of the receiving end of the problem, such as the employment services.

Employment policies have also aimed at encouraging particular branches or areas that showed some potential for job creation. Sectors such as agriculture and heavy industry were in general oversized and sectors which were underrepresented under central planning, such as industrial activities in agriculture, light industry and especially services, have been encouraged. The development of TVEs in China is a good example of a successful strategy, while the CARs have lagged behind in formulating an industrial policy consistent with new market needs. Some of the CARs have had a much stronger *laissez-faire* attitude in the belief that individuals would find themselves alternative opportunities while others preferred to maintain the *status quo*, avoiding significant restructuring.

Policies aimed at encouraging labour mobility and reducing labour market rigidities are crucial to the establishment of efficient labour markets. Increasing labour market flexibility in ATEs has mainly meant the removal of barriers to labour mobility. Most of these countries had legal or administrative restrictions on the mobility of the labour force before transition. Pre-reform China is an extreme example, where not only were rural residents virtually unable to leave the countryside or engage in non-farm activities, but it was also extremely difficult for urban employees to change jobs. Lifting or relaxing these restrictions has boosted labour mobility. Some of the CARs such as Kazakhstan and the Kyrgyz Republic have also been active on this front by rendering mobility easier, while others such as Uzbekistan and Turkmenistan have been more conservative in this respect. In all CARs, however, internal labour mobility remained constrained by the scarce opportunities emerging and by the relatively homogeneous poor opportunities offered by different regions within countries.

Employment services (ESs) became the main instrument to record unemployment and assist the registered unemployed. Job brokering and the provision of unemployment benefits to a selected number of registered unemployed have been the main activities entrusted to ESs. The CARs have been quite quick to establish such services during the early phase of transition and initially both the capacity to put people back into work and the coverage of unemployment benefits were satisfactory. With the acceleration of unemployment growth and the decreasing capacity of enterprises to finance the employment funds, ESs found it increasingly difficult to cope with the numbers of unemployed. Re-employment rates decreased, together with unemployment benefits coverage. In some cases, such as in the Kyrgyz Republic, a substantial share of enterprises' contributions to the employment fund were made in kind, and the products were distributed to the unemployed in lieu of cash. In Kazakhstan the average level of benefits was 30 per cent and 20 per cent below the average wage and below the subsistence level, respectively (CIS-Stat 1998). The poor level of assistance provided by ESs in recent years led to disillusionment among job-seekers which induced many to try alternative job-seeking paths and to bypass ESs.

Other ESs activities, such as retraining and public works, have generally gained ground. In the CARs, retraining tends to have a fairly successful re-employment rate but it covers generally less than 5 per cent of the job-seekers, with a clear bias towards the better educated. Public works have also been a popular activity, though it remains a measure of last resort rather than an instrument to facilitate labour market changes. In this case, too, the coverage is small though it tends to be biased towards the less skilled.

3.6 Conclusion: transition, development and employment

In looking at labour market changes in ATEs we observed two distinct patterns exemplified by the experiences of China and the CARs. Factors explaining the difference between the two patterns remain an important area of research, but this chapter has identified two major elements which distinguish the two types. One is the substantial structural initial conditions. In China, SOEs provided a relatively small share of employment at the outset of reforms, while in the CARs they provided almost the totality. The other is represented by the different choices made by China in terms of speed and content of transitional reforms. China emphasized the creation of an appropriate pattern of incentives through a piecemeal approach to government policies designed for this specific purpose and tailored to different economic sectors and geographical areas. The CARs expected a big-bang approach to price liberalization and privatization to deliver the same result, with no further intervention in any economic sectors or geographical areas and in the absence of a clear industrial policy. Thus China focused on employment creation while the CARs opted for unemployment assistance – two rather different views on the role of governments in relation to labour in transition.

Adaptable labour markets play an essential role in determining the success of adjustment and reform and their impact on living standards. Reforms to promote labour mobility and income transfers, and policies to equip workers for change are all necessary to increase adaptability. Support to the unemployed in terms of active or passive measures is instrumental in easing the pain of unemployment. However, active and passive measures as well as supply and demand measures are unlikely to be substitutes in transitional economies, where most people remain unemployed because of low labour demand rather than ineffective supply.

Many have pointed to the limits of labour market policies. For transition economies where labour markets are yet to function 'normally', government policies are necessary to assist the labour force in adapting to the emerging labour markets, by establishing legislation, institutions and regulations. For the long run, the governments of ATEs need to pay greater attention to many employment-related issues, including the following:

- While growth is the most important source of job creation, the type of technology used is equally relevant. Thus, when importing technologies, the developing Asian countries should take their impact on employment into consideration. While it is justifiable to upgrade the technology level, conscious efforts should also be made to encourage labour-intensive methods of production in economic processes.
- Government should incorporate the objective of equity much more forcefully in the overall development strategy. This would require overriding free-market forces, for example, by guaranteeing minimum wages and ensuring distribution of essential goods and services. This may not appear optimal for short-term growth, but is essential for long-term and sustained social and economic development.
- Renewed attention needs to be paid to the agricultural sector. Agriculture employs a great portion of the labour force in ATEs. Increasing agricultural productivity is imperative to ensure the industrial transformation of the economy.
- Governments must confront the issue of the non-state sectors, especially the informal sector. So far these sectors have provided a 'safety net' for retrenched workers and their families in transition

economies. But their weaknesses should not be underestimated. Problems such as the lack of occupational health and safety standards, the utilization of child labour and the abuse of labour in general are common to most ATEs. There is a danger that these sectors become a 'sink' for the growing numbers of unemployed in urban areas.

Notes

1. In Kazakhstan, the share of total employment occupied in agriculture increased because employment in agriculture declined less than employment in other sectors, not because employment in this sector increased.
2. Reported in 'Dian Ran Shiyezhe de Xiwang' (Light the hope of the unemployed) (1998), in *Shi Dai Chao* (The Trend of the Times), No. 2.

References

Allison, Christine and Dena Ringold (1996), 'Labour Markets in Transition in Central and Eastern Europe 1989–1995', *World Bank Technical Paper*, No. 352, Social Challenges of Transition Series, Washington, DC: World Bank.

ADB (Asian Development Bank) (1997), *Key Indicators of Developing Asian and Pacific Countries 1997*, Manila: Oxford University Press.

ADB (1996), *Annual Report 1995*, Manila.

CIS-Stat (1998), *Labour Markets in the CIS countries*, Interstate Statistical Committee of the Commonwealth of the Independent States, Moscow.

CSAK (Committee for Statistical Analysis of the Republic of Kazakhstan) (1997), *Statistical Bulletin*, No. 1, Almaty.

'Dian Ran Shiyezhe de Xiwang' (Light the hope of the unemployed) (1998), in *Shi Dai Chao* (The Trend of the Times), No. 2.

EBRD (European Bank for Reconstruction and Development) (1997), *Transition Report*.

EIU (Economist Intelligence Unit) (1997a), *Country Profile: Vietnam 1996–97*, London.

EIU (1997b), *Country Report, 2nd quarter 1997*, London.

Gudkova, N., E. Kasibekov, L. Kusnezova, A. Riskulova and N. Sadovenko (1998), 'The State of the Labour Market in the Republic of Kyrgyzstan in 1991–1996', in *Social Policy Strategy: Labour Market, Employment and Social Assistance* (in Russian), Ministry of Labour and Social Protection, Bishkek.

ILO (International Labour Office) (1997), *Yearbook of Labour Statistics 1997*, Geneva: ILO.

Jackman, R. and M. Rutkowski (1994), 'Labour Markets: Wages and Employment', in N. Barr (ed.), *Labour Markets and Social Policy in Central and Eastern Europe: The Transition and Beyond*, New York: Oxford University Press.

Jamal, Vali (1996), 'Transition, the Asian Way: Growth, Employment, Equity', unpublished paper, ILO East Asia Multidisciplinary Advisory Team.

Kulakeyev, J. and A. Katarvaeva (1997), 'Labour Resources in the Republic of Kazakhstan', *Business Weekly*, 12 September 1997 (in Russian), Almaty.

Lim, Lin Lean, Gyorgy Sziraczki and Zhang Xiaojian (1996), 'Economic Performance, Labour Surplus and Enterprise Responses. Results from the China Enterprise Survey', *Labour Market Papers*, 13, Employment Department, ILO, Geneva.

Meng Xin and Michael P. Kidd (1997), 'Labour Market Reform and the Changing Structure of Wage Determination in China's State Sector during the 1980s', *Journal of Comparative Economics*, Vol. 25, pp. 403–21.

O'Connor, David (1996), *Labour Market Aspects of State Enterprise Reform in Viet Nam*, OECD Development Centre, Paris, France.

Ronnås, Per and Örjan Sjöberg (1995), 'Economic Reform, Employment and Labour Market Policy in Viet Nam', *Labour Market Papers*, 9, Employment Department, ILO, Geneva.

Sen, Amartya (1997), 'Inequality, Unemployment and Contemporary Europe', *International Labour Review*, Vol. 136, No. 2, pp. 155–72.

World Bank (1995), 'China: Macroeconomic Stability in a Decentralised Economy', *A World Bank Country Study*, Washington, DC: World Bank.

World Bank (1996), *World Development Report 1996: From Plan to Market*, New York: Oxford University Press.

World Bank (1997), *World Development Report 1997*, New York: Oxford University Press.

Zhu, Ying (1995), 'Major Changes under Way in China's Industrial Relations', *International Labour Review*, Vol. 134, No. 1, pp. 37–49.

III Country Studies

4
Economic Reforms and Welfare Changes in China

Aiguo Lu

4.1 Introduction

Conventional wisdom has it that the well-being of a population is correlated with positive economic development. However, the empirical evidence indicates that economic and social development are not synonymous and the relation between the two is not straightforward. Studies have suggested that, in addition to per capita income, which is a key indicator of economic development, the degree of income equality and access to welfare provisions have played a significant role in determining the well-being of the population (for example, Milanovic 1993). In general, socialist countries had better human development records as compared with others at similar economic and per capita levels. China is not an exception. Under the central planning system, China made progress in promoting human development to the level that matched the mid-income countries even though its per capita income was among the lowest.

The pre-reform record of favourable social development in China can be characterized as a 'support-led' process (Drèze and Sen 1989). This type of process does not operate through fast economic growth, but 'works through priority being given to providing social services (particularly health care and basic education) that reduce mortality and enhance the quality of life' (Sen 1995: 15).

The support-led security in pre-reform China was sustained by well-established institutions, government policies and the overall framework of central planning. Major components included: employment-based income and social provisions; full employment; an equity-biased wage system in urban areas and labour-earning distribution in the countryside; low-priced and subsidized consumer goods and services; a public welfare system in the state sector and a collective welfare provision in the non-state sector; work-unit-sponsored[1] execution of welfare provision; the rationing system of bulk food and other daily necessities in short supply; government-financed health services for the urban population and cooperative health care in the countryside; free education from primary schools to universities; and social support provided by neighbourhood organizations for those without work unit affiliation.

Hence an extensive support system was in operation, covering virtually all segments of the population. This welfare system, vastly different from that in Western countries (Esping-Andersen 1990; Ahmad and Hussain 1991), was designed to ensure accessibility of the population to the basic provision of goods and services by focusing on the collective consumption and public sharing of available resources. Organizational effort was a key to the successful function of such a system. Equally crucial was the manner in which resources are allocated. Before the reforms, however, although the distribution of income and welfare within economic sectors was in general highly equitable, the gap between urban and rural areas remained significant.

Given the low level of income, the support system proved to have contributed to the good record of human development in pre-reform China. Life expectancy at birth increased significantly, from below 40 years at the beginning of the 1950s to approximately 65 years by the year 1978. At the end of the pre-reform period, China was the 22nd poorest country in the world (World Bank 1980: 110–11), but the 51st from the lowest human development in 1980 (UNDP 1982). In addition, China was among the dozen or so countries to move from low human development in 1960 to medium in 1980, and China's advancement was the most substantial of the group (UNDP 1994: 105).[2] A UNDP report concluded that

> over a long period of time, China has invested liberally in human development. So, despite its low per capita income, it falls in the medium HDI category. China also has the largest positive gap (+49) between its HDI rank and its GNP per capita rank, showing that it has made judicious use of its national income. (UNDP 1994: 100)[3]

Rapid economic growth during reforms provides favourable conditions for the improvement of the good social development record inherited from the previous period. But market transition has also entailed the transformation of the existing economic and social institutions which were largely responsible for the support-led welfare progress. It is against such social and economic context that welfare changes have taken place.

The word 'welfare' in this chapter refers to living standards in a broad sense. As Sen and others have long argued, analysis of living standards cannot be reduced to the simple possession of commodities (Sen 1992).

4.2 Changes in welfare conditions

4.2.1 Economic opulence

In the two decades since 1978, China's economy in general maintained a strong growth momentum. Measured using 1987 US dollars, GDP per capita in 1994 has more than tripled since 1980 (UNDP 1997: 159).

More cash income has been translated into greater consumption of commodities by the average person and family. First, ownership of durable goods expanded rapidly in both urban and rural areas, although an obvious gap exists in terms of the quantity and quality. Second, food consumption has significantly improved, indicated by the change in the structure of people's diet from starchy staples to more costly products. For a low-income country like China, the considerable increase in the consumption of meat/poultry is indeed 'a key measure of progress' (Brown 1995: 44). Noticing that meat consumption had a fivefold increase during 1977–94, Brown (ibid. 46–7) stated that never before have so many people moved up the food chain so fast.

Third, the increase in per capita income not only resulted in more money spent but also in more money saved, as indicated by the increasing volume of bank deposits. By 1994, the total savings deposit balance was more than 100 times larger than in 1978, representing an annual growth rate of 33.5 per cent (*CSY* 1995: 257). Since the increase in savings is many times larger and faster than the increase in prices, the growth in total and average savings even adjusted for prices still remains substantial, and the purchasing power of the average savings in the mid-1990s is many times greater than what it was in the late 1970s.

Fourth, the per capita living space doubled in the mid-1990s, reaching nearly 8 m^2 in the cities and expanding from 8 to 20 m^2 in the countryside. The quality of houses improved as well.

Fifth, one of the greatest achievements during the reforms was the large-scale and dramatic reduction in poverty. The population living in poverty was reduced from 260 million in 1978 to 65 million by the mid-1990s. No matter how one measures and assesses it, the tremendous progress in the reduction of absolute poverty is beyond doubt.

Evidence indicates that the impact of the reforms on the general level of economic opulence is mostly positive. On average, Chinese people today have higher incomes, which allow them to eat and dress better, live in less crowded houses, and enjoy greater access to a variety of consumer goods and services than ever before.

4.2.2 Capabilities

Changes in life expectancy during the period of reforms have in general been positive. Although relevant statistics from different sources vary, most authoritative sources agree that life expectancy continued to increase, from 66 to 68 for males and 68 to 71 for females during 1980 and 1995 (World Bank 1997a: 86). China moved to the upper-middle rank of the world in terms of longevity.

Information on infant and child mortality appear to be inadequate and inconclusive. Banister compiled some data which indicate a substantial rise in the infant mortality rate up to the mid-1980s, from 37.2 per 1000 in 1978 to 50.1 in 1984 (Banister 1987: 116). The Chinese 1990 population census placed the infant mortality figure at 35 per 1000, showing an improvement over the record of nearly 50 per 1000 in 1975.

The under-five mortality rate, according to estimates based on Chinese population census data, seemed to have levelled off in the mid-1980s at about 44 per 1000 after four decades of steady decline. But data from the Ministry of Health suggested that the under-five mortality declined from 61 per 1000 in 1991 to 51 in 1995 (World Bank 1997b: 2).

It is difficult to assess the accuracy of these data but it cannot be ruled out that the situation deteriorated in certain locations and in the early 1980s nationwide. A World Bank study concluded that due to the slight increase in the under-five mortality rate in the early 1980s and its weak improvement even thereafter, by the late 1980s China had actually fallen behind countries at similar income levels (World Bank 1996: 127).

The increase in child malnutrition in the midst of a general improvement in diets has also caused some concern. The occurrence of child malnutrition has been estimated at 21.3 per 1000 in 1987, 25 in 1990 and 24 in 1993 (World Bank: see World Tables 1996).

Educational attainment has improved since the reforms. Table 4.1 summarizes the education levels as reported in the population censuses of 1982 and 1990.[4]

Table 4.1 Population aged 15 years and over by educational level, China, 1982 and 1990 (%)

	1982		*1990*	
	Women	*Men*	*Women*	*Men*
Illiteracy	49	21	32	13
Primary education	25	36	34	35
Junior middle-level education	18	30	24	36
Senior middle-level education			7	11
Technical secondary level	8	12	2	2
College			1	2
University		1		1
Total	100	100	100	100
Number (million)	325	341	399	419

Sources: 1982 and 1990 Population Censuses, cited in Department of Social Science and Technology Statistics (1995), p. 54.

As the result of the increasing school enrolment, the censuses of 1982 and 1990 indicate a decline in illiteracy rates. The trend has continued since 1990 (World Bank 1997c: 48). In 1995, 12 per cent of the total population, or 145 million people, were illiterate or functionally illiterate. Illiteracy, however, remains highly gender-biased in that nearly 3 out of every 4 illiterate people continue to be women (Department of Social Science and Technology Statistics 1995: 54).

4.2.3 Human ecology

China's industrialization in the pre-reform period and, in particular, its rapid economic growth during the reforms have had a marked effect on the ecology. Without a doubt, economic growth had positive results, and the increasing availability of safe water is one example. From 1978 to 1992, urban households with tap water grew from 81 per cent to 93 per cent and those with access to gas increased from 14 per cent to 52 per cent (*CSY* 1993: 627). Progress has also been made in urban sewage systems, garbage disposal, increased green areas, and so on. These developments helped protect the urban living environment from degradation, a common occurrence during rapid urbanization.

But the general condition of the natural environment nevertheless seems to have deteriorated. Industrial pollution is no longer an urban problem. The impact of environmental problems on the health of the rural population can at least partly be confirmed by the much higher morbidity rate from respiratory disease, the number one cause of death for both rural men and women.[5] A World Bank report concluded that the environment has in general suffered during the rapid economic growth in the last 18 years (World Bank 1997d).

The government authorities have become increasingly aware of the problems, and legislation on environmental protection has been accelerated particularly since the early 1990s. The current level of investments in environmental protection stands at 0.7 per cent of GNP, which compares favourably with developing-country standards. As the economy continues to expand at a high rate, pressure on environment protection may become more severe.

Human security is an indispensable part of overall human welfare. In this regard, crime has become the greatest threat to personal security. Since the reforms began, crime has risen and increased sharply in 1988–89. In spite of government efforts, the tendency of growing criminal activities has not been stopped.

Two tendencies have been especially conspicuous in the rising crime wave: first, organized crime is surfacing; and, second, there has been a revival of such criminal and degrading activities as drug abuse and trafficking, prostitution, abduction and selling of women and children, smuggling people across borders and illegal possession of weapons. In terms of geographical location, rising crime appears to be a more serious problem in coastal and border areas, where economic and social transformation has proceeded most vigorously.

Side by side with rising crimes, corruption has reached a level that contributes to the unfair redistribution of wealth, thus causing popular social discontent. The most common form of corruption has been the exchange of power for material gain. Admittedly, it is difficult anywhere in the world to bring dishonest dealings, particularly at a high level, into the open and even more problematic to have them tried in court, largely because of the nature of the act. Corruption is the misuse of public trust in the interest of private gain and its prerequisite is political position or public role. In the process of marketization, the temptation and opportunities of illicit wealth are enormous for low-paid government officials in control of scarce resources.

From 1988 to 1992, nearly a quarter of a million cases of so-called criminal corruption were indicted and these involved 4600 government officials at above the county level. Since the second half of 1993, the central government has made greater efforts to purge bribery, leading to an unprecedentedly large number of indictments. An annual report by the Supreme People's Court revealed that over 20 000 people were jailed in 1994 for corruption. Cases against grafters totalled 30 000, up almost 70 per cent from 1993 (Wen 1995: 136–51; Transition Economic Division of the World Bank 1995: 3).

4.3 The haves and the have-nots

Talking about the standard of living, Amartya Sen asks, 'Can the living standard of a person be high if the life he or she leads is full of deprivation?' (1987: 8). This question concerns a crucial aspect of human welfare which is associated less with the general level of a nation's wealth than with the distribution pattern of wealth. Since one cannot be deprived of something that is not available to others, the *possibility* of deprivation is actually increased – not reduced – in the face of economic growth which ensures additional goods and services. To assess the situation of well-being, one must look at the issue of relative deprivation.

4.3.1 The rich and the poor

A market economy produces both winners and losers, and this is what has happened in China. At the same time, the tempo and characteristics of the transition process are determined by the initial conditions, state policies, the economic structure and, in particular, the emerging pattern of property relations.

The first newly rich emerged in the early 1980s, labelled *wanyuanhu*, meaning households with incomes exceeding 10 000 yuan. At the time, *wanyuanhu* was almost entirely a rural phenomenon, resulting from rural reforms which allowed households to resume responsibility for production. Assuming an average rural family size of five and given per capita rural income at about 200–400 yuan, the average rural household income would have amounted to approximately 1000 to 2000 yuan per year. This suggests that the *wanyuanhu* had annual incomes five to ten times the rural average.

When the focus of the reform programmes began to shift to the cities, a new breed of urban rich began to emerge, and the accumulated wealth quickly surpassed the high income levels of the *wanyuanhu*. The number of Chinese who have accumulated vast amounts of wealth is likely to be small and the information on high-income groups is mostly anecdotal. One source contended that the rich families accounted for about 2 per cent of the total households, and in 1993, 40 per cent of the total savings deposit in the bank was owned by less than 3 per cent of the population.[6]

By the early 1990s the newly rich were said to have begun to form a distinctive layer of society. Members of the so-called 'high-income group' range from profiteers in the stock market, private entrepreneurs and stars in show business, to taxi drivers and re-employed retirees (Ge 1995: 104), and appears to be composed of very diverse professions. As observation and some popular anecdotal reports indicate, a fraction in the high-income group, mostly composed of well-connected businessmen and entrepreneurs, has become ultra-rich.

The poorest at the other end of the social spectrum are beginning to form another layer of society, that is, those who live in absolute poverty. Although reforms significantly reduced absolute numbers of the poor, the persistence of poverty remains an extraordinary problem. While some have managed to shed poverty, newly impoverished people continue to join the ranks of the destitute. According to sources from the Civil Affairs Ministry, 2 to 3 million households since the early 1990s were rescued each year from absolute poverty, but the poor population has remained stable, because similar numbers of households have fallen into this group.

One factor that has accelerated income inequality has been the increasing proportion of non-wage earnings in urban income and the increasing share of non-labour-related earnings such as profits, rent and dividends from stocks and bonds. Overall, income polarization has been accelerated during the reforms. China's future development faces an increasing challenge as to what degree of social stratification can be justified for the sake of economic growth and in the name of reforms.

4.3.2 Urban–rural divide

The income gap between the rural and urban areas has been a problem in both the pre- and the post-reform periods. Life under the central planning system had witnessed an increasing rural–urban income gap[7] which continued to widen after 1978 (Ge and Yue 1993: 278; Ge 1995: 103). In 1995, the ratio between the disposable income of urban and rural residents was 2.49 : 1, up from 2.36 : 1 in 1978. Taking into consideration the fringe benefits of urban residents, the urban–rural income gap would be much larger, estimated at over four times (Zhu 1996: 151).

The urban–rural income gap continued to exacerbate despite the extraordinary growth of rural industries. One explanation lies in the fact that rural industries are far from evenly spread, and far less developed in economically backward regions which, unfortunately, remain large.

What has become clear is that if the central planning system is to be criticized for failing to eliminate the rural-–urban divide, market forces have not been able to do the job any better. Because rural residents constitute the majority of the population, an overall improvement in the welfare of the entire nation depends largely on an improvement in the living standards of the rural population.

4.3.3 Regional disparity

Economic growth has been far more rapid in the east-coast areas than in central and western regions. This uneven development resulted in an income difference among regions, which has become more pronounced, particularly since the beginning of the 1990s. The ratio of average monthly disposable income among the east, central and west areas increased from 1 : 0.66 : 0.71 in 1993 to 1 : 0.64 : 0.67 in 1994.

Regional differences in rural income remained large as well. During 1980–94, rural income in Zhejiang province grew at twice the rate of that of some other provinces such as Guizhou, Gansu and Xinjiang. In the mid-1990s, the richest provinces enjoyed nearly three times the rural per capita income of the poorest territories. Not surprisingly, the poor have been disproportionately concentrated in west and central regions. In 1990, 90 per cent or 27 of the nation's 30 poorest counties, which had a per capita rural income below 200 yuan, were located in the west region (*Green Book* 1993: 118).

The increasing regional disparity presents a problem for China's sustained and equitable development in the future. It poses a serious obstacle to the betterment of the well-being of the people living in the poor regions. Those living in the areas of the interior have poorer access not only to goods and services but also to education, healthcare, and employment opportunities. The 1990 census revealed that the rate of illiteracy and semi-literacy in China was about 16 per cent of the total population, most of which was concentrated in the interior. The interior provinces such as Yunnan, Guizhuo and Xinjiang also have higher maternal and infant mortality rates (World Bank 1996; Howes 1992).

4.3.4 Migrant labourers

A new phenomenon emerging from the process of reforms is the large-scale movement of peasants who seek jobs outside their native villages and who have become known as the 'floating population'. This floating population has been increasing in number and by the mid-1990s reached the colossal size of approximately 80 million.

As in other countries, the single most forceful motivation behind the mass migration is the expectation of wage-earning jobs and a better life. Given the substantial income gap between cities and the countryside as well as among regions, and given the serious underemployment situation in agriculture, it is no surprise that rural labourers are willing to move elsewhere for employment. Institutional changes such as the collapse of the rural commune system and the receding role of central planning in the economy enabled rural people to move more freely.

The precarious living conditions and general vulnerability make the migrant population most susceptible to being victimized and/or turning to crime themselves. Figures verify that urban lawlessness by migrants is disproportionally high and, in almost every major city, they are responsible for a much larger share of crimes than their proportion of the population (Hu 1995: 133). Young women migrants are a particularly vulnerable group and some fall victim to organized crime, abduction or prostitution.

These problems are not caused by the inclination of the rural migrants for crime or other demeaning behaviour. The grim social circumstances under which they work and live prepare the ground for these problems. Because the migrants in general are unable to obtain permanent urban residence, they are not covered by the urban social welfare system which provides the town-dwellers with housing, healthcare and other subsidies. This situation creates an administrative vacuum where crime and anti-social behaviour thrive.

While migrants face problems common to all because of their shared status of 'outsiders', they by no means form a homogeneous body. Social differentiation is very much in evidence. Some have made vast fortunes and have joined the newly rich. Others simply eke out a daily living by toiling in any conceivable job in the sweatshops, or in some highly unsafe and labour-intensive foreign or joint ventures. Still others fall into devastating poverty.

4.3.5 The status of women

There is no simple answer to the question of the changing status of women during reforms. Many studies show that the effects have been largely negative, while others argue that in terms of economic opportunity and social mobility, women have substantially benefited compared to the central planning period, if not to men.[8]

One of the most important aspects of reform measures affecting the welfare of women is labour participation. In the wave of enterprise downsizing, women were usually the first to go. In 1993, according to a survey (Tan 1995: 335–6), women accounted for the majority of the total *xiagang* or 'temporarily laid-off' workers. In addition to those who have already lost their jobs, many more millions of female workers have been considered surplus labour in the public sector, who may lose their jobs when the government moves further in reforming the state enterprises.

The job situation for women in agriculture is different. The proportion of women in the floating population is in general much lower than that of men. In Shanghai and Beijing in 1994, the male to female ratio was 2 : 1. One consequence is that more women are left behind in the countryside and take up farm work. On average, income from non-farm economic activities is five to ten times higher than that generated by farming. Thus the 'feminization' tendency in agriculture has negatively affected the average level of earning power of female rural labour.

On the other hand, there are also women who take advantage of market opportunity and are able to increase their income substantially more than would have been possible previously. In addition, being responsible for farming may increase women's decision-making power in agricultural production as well as within the families.

Nevertheless, women continue to lag behind men in a number of areas of social development. The dropout rate for girls from education is higher than that for boys, and the higher proportion of females in the total illiterate population remains unchanged. In 1994, 128 million women in China could not read, of whom 110 million, or over 85 per cent were rural women (Tan 1995: 334).

The social and political status of women, if measured by political representation, does not seem to show obvious improvement during the reform period. The ratio of women attending sessions of the National People's Congress, the Chinese Parliament, increased substantially during the 1960s and 1970s. But since 1978 there has been no further progress. No women are represented in the top decision-making bodies of the government, the Party, or the army.

There can be no denial that women have also benefited when reforms have raised general living standards. However, the negative effects have perhaps been especially detrimental to women. Social practices and traditions which plagued women in China in the past and which had been eliminated under the central planning system have re-emerged. Women have been abducted and sold as wives and prostitutes, with a market value. Female infanticide can be found in some areas. It seems that rapid economic growth during the reforms has not automatically led to an overall better position for women in the society.

4.3.6 The social marginals

Post-revolutionary China was known for its success in eliminating social marginals. In the three decades before the reforms, the national institutional frameworks had worked effectively to prevent socially marginal groups from recurring, largely by keeping the rural population tied to the land, and by introducing work units to organize the life of the urban population. Marginal social groups have re-emerged during the reforms. As in pre-revolutionary China, the emerging social marginals today include child labourers, street children, prostitutes, drug users, and so on, who are at the bottom of the class hierarchy of society. They live under a social stigma, not only because they are poor (and some are not) but because their activities waver on the borderline of illegality.

Child labour is a new phenomenon to the cities of China and to the rural non-farming industrial sectors. Official statistics on child labour do not exist. According to unofficial estimates made by the ILO, UNICEF and various NGOs, child labour in China in the early 1990s was about 12 million, or 3.5 per cent of the 340 million youngsters under the age of 16 years.

The Chinese government enacted its first detailed law banning child labour in 1991. Judged by the figures for subsequent years, it seems that the law has not achieved its objectives. The fate of the street children – their actual numbers unknown – may be worse. In 1994, some 200 000 children were estimated to be on the streets of Chinese cities. Government organs routinely round up these children to return them to their home villages, but they keep appearing in increasing numbers. While more common in large urban centres,[9] the problem is spreading to middle-sized cities as well.

In the reform era, prostitution has resurfaced under the disguise of business ventures related to tourism, services, entertainment, or other activities. When the government launches its 'hit-hard' campaigns or clean-up programmes, prostitution temporarily disappears, only to come back more forcefully than ever. Moreover, women, including under-aged girls, forced or solicited into prostitution in neighbouring countries such as Thailand are also reported to have increased in considerable numbers.

The growing social stratification in general and the emergence of a marginal population in particular point to the formation of a social underclass. Solutions to this problem cannot be found in economic growth *per se*, but in the nature of development, that is, in socio-economic conditions under which growth has been produced. At the minimum, the negative aspects of social development clearly point to a policy failure.

4.4 Social policies and institutions

Unlike the Former Soviet Union and Eastern Europe, China did not have nationwide welfare coverage before the reforms. The social security functioned in a 'double-split system', the first being an institutional divide of welfare provision between rural and urban population, and the second being an institutional split between those in the public sector and those outside this sector (White and Shang 1996a). The work units in urban areas and rural collectives in the countryside were the agencies responsible for the provision of welfare. Following the institutional changes in the reforms, the system has largely collapsed in the countryside and been decentralized in the cities. Regional and sectoral diversity in welfare provision became more significant, as experiments in welfare reforms have been conducted in a highly decentralized manner.

4.4.1 Employment and wages

Reforms have led to the emergence of a labour market which, at its heart, meant the breaking of the 'iron rice bowls' of employment.

This was relatively easily achieved in the countryside following the collapse of the commune system, the sole employer of the rural labour force under central planning. Cultivation on household-contracted land became a major source of employment in the countryside. The mushrooming of rural industries has gained increasing importance in providing jobs; this sector was said to have employed about 130 million people in the mid-1990s, larger than the entire labour force in the state sector. However, although industrial employment may bring better income than farming, very few rural households have given up their contracted land. It is common practice to divide family labour so that some members work in non-farm jobs such as in rural enterprises to earn cash, while others cultivate the contracted plots. This division of labour provides a form of security: if earnings in non-farm employment fail, rural families can still rely on cultivation as a source of income.

Largely because of the security provided by the contracted land system, the government has not been especially concerned with regulations on employment, wages and fringe benefits in rural industries. By the mid-1990s, issues concerning wages, benefits, unemployment or job contracts were still largely a matter of negotiation between the rural enterprises and their employees.

In the state sector, state policies since the reforms have been striving for a mechanism which would create flexible labour allocation. An initial step to reforming the state employment system was to implement a contract system. Lifetime employment is no longer offered, and the government intends eventually to extend the contract system to the entire state sector. Another step was to allow non-profitable enterprises to lay off workers and to cut wages. But up until the early 1990s, despite the fact that an estimated 40 per cent of state enterprises were unprofitable, these continued to operate, and workers continued to keep their jobs. This enabled the country to avoid large-scale unemployment. However, following the acceleration of state sector reforms after the mid-1990s, an increasing number of workers have been and are expected to be laid off as the result of industrial bankruptcy or restructuring.

In 1983–92, the official unemployment rate was between 1.8 per cent and 2.5 per cent and only in one year (1989) did it reach 2.6 per cent. Since then, unemployment has been on the rise, climbing from 2.5 per cent in 1992 to 2.6 per cent in 1993, 2.8 per cent in 1994, 2.9 per cent in 1995, and an estimated 4 per cent in 1996–97. The actual number of the jobless is undoubtedly far larger. In some cities unemployment actually reached 15 per cent, or as high as one-fifth of the labour force.

As employment security comes increasingly under attack, and as the number of workers in the rural and other non-state industrial sectors is growing, the establishment of an alternative social security system has become imperative. The difficulty of maintaining the minimum living standards of workers in unprofitable state enterprises was reported to have become an acute social problem which, for example, led to cases of strikes and other forms of demonstration becoming 53 per cent higher in the second quarter of 1996 than in the previous quarter, and 19 per cent higher than in the corresponding period of the previous year. In terms of the number of people involved, the percentages increased by 51 per cent and 23 per cent respectively (Qiao 1997: 252–3).

4.4.2 Housing

The housing system in China was essentially made up of two segments – urban and rural. Under the commune system as well as after its collapse, housing in the countryside has been privately owned by rural families. Housing, after land, was the second most important asset, and in the late 1980s accounted for approximately one-third of rural net worth (McKinley 1993; McKinley with Wang 1992). Even today, because rural households do not have legal ownership title to the land, houses continue to be the major asset. As other forms of property such as fixed productive assets and financial assets have increased, the importance of houses in the total wealth of rural households has declined.

Most houses in urban areas under central planning were publicly owned, managed and distributed by the work units. Because of high subsidies, rents in the cities were largely nominal, constituting about 1 per cent of total urban household expenditure.[10] Investment in housing construction thus was a pure loss. For most urban residents, on the other hand, affordability was not the issue; shortage was.

The key element of housing reform is to change its welfare nature, and eventually to establish a housing market. A number of experiments have taken place since 1978, encouraging urban residents to cooperate with the state and work units in housing reforms.[11] The major measures have been to increase rents, to encourage residents to purchase their current publicly owned apartments, and to create a commercial housing market.

The reform has proceeded slowly. Until the mid-1990s, the old distribution system remained fundamentally unchanged. In places where public housing has been put up for sale, not all current occupants are willing or able to buy. Rents have been increased. But, as income has also increased, rent as a proportion of urban household expenditures has not changed much. Rent in 1994 consumed 1 per cent of the per capita annual living expenditures, the same as in 1985 and 1978 (calculated from *CSY* 1995: 262). Newly built commercial complexes and apartments are becoming available, but prices are astronomically high for the ordinary wage-earner.

4.4.3 Healthcare

In the central planning era, accessibility to healthcare was not equal for all, and the services and benefits enjoyed by various social groups were different. Nevertheless, both the urban and rural population had access to affordable medical services. Urban residents were largely covered by the public healthcare system, while the rural population was brought into the rural cooperative healthcare system, whose coverage in 1979 was 85 per cent in the countryside (Hussain and Stern

1990: 17). Although in the countryside the coverage was not uniform and the quality of service was not particularly advanced, the availability of basic medical services made a considerable difference in the improvement of life expectancy and the general health situation in China.

As the economic reforms progressed, the previous healthcare system underwent important changes, with the countryside experiencing the most radical adjustment. Because cooperative medical care was based on the communes, it crumbled after the commune system was dismantled. For an overwhelming majority of the rural population, cash payments to procure medical services have become the only option.

The compensating factor for the collapse of the rural cooperative healthcare system has been the increase in rural incomes, which allows better-off rural residents to pay for medical services. But a large number of the rural poor who cannot pay are likely to suffer ill health, and their poor health conditions keep many of them in poverty.

In urban areas, the public healthcare system has been modified and efforts have been made to create a medical safety net. Concrete measures included increasing individual responsibility for medical expenses. At present, individuals covered by the public healthcare system usually pay a percentage of their medical expenses, or a set sum for each hospital visit. For enterprises running into financial difficulties, public healthcare for the employees often remains in name only.

The urban-favoured healthcare system continues to dominate. In the early 1990s, less than 15 per cent of China's population, or 163 million individuals, continued to be covered by public healthcare programmes, which utilized 44 per cent of the total health resources of the country (Bo and Dong 1993: 196). Unequal distribution of health resources exists also among various regions, affecting the health situation differently in various parts of the country. In particular, healthcare is weaker in the impoverished areas, where it is often more urgently needed to offset such poverty-related health problems as malnutrition. The lack of healthcare has manifested itself in a decline or loss of labour availability, higher morbidity and higher mortality.

4.4.4 The social security system

Because the old social security system has become increasingly inadequate during the transition, the government has tried to establish schemes to pool diverse resources with the aim of establishing a comprehensive social security system.[12] The social security reforms so far have followed the general pattern of reform, that is, new schemes are promoted and tested while the old system continues to function, albeit with modifications. The government offers general guidance, and practical measures are taken mainly by local authorities at provincial or lower levels.

Urban social security reforms have focused on retirement pensions and unemployment benefits. Pension reforms aim at freeing enterprises from sole responsibility, by setting up funds administratively independent of the individual work units. Enterprises and individual employees are required to contribute to the pension funds. It was reported that most of urban state and collective enterprises have participated in the *shehu tongchou*, or socially/publicly managed pension funds. The massive size of China creates problems in establishing a single unified national pension fund.

Enterprises were required in 1995 to remit 1 per cent of their total wages to unemployment compensation funds. Workers who had been on the job for more than one year before being laid off were entitled to compensation, which in many cases was set at 50 per cent of the average wage of the locality for a duration of two months. At the present time, not all regions in China have established unemployment funds and, where they are available, funds are limited and easily depleted because of the short duration of contributions, untimely payments by enterprises, and/or sharp increases in the number of unemployed.

Provision for old-age security has been especially lacking in the rural areas where an overwhelmingly majority of old people are left without individual income once they stop gainful work, therefore becoming totally dependent on their families for support. Since the late 1980s, various rural old-age security funds have been set up on an experimental basis. One common scheme calls for farmers to contribute an amount specified by the individual to a pension fund from the age of 20 years which would accrue towards a monthly pension at 60 years. The amount of monthly pension would depend on the contributions made during active work years.

It is not easy to gain a clear-cut picture of the extent of national social security coverage and related expenditures because of problems of data classification and highly diverse practices in various localities. Tables 4.2 and 4.3 provide a summary of the situation in 1993.

Table 4.2 Coverage of social security, China, 1993

	Million people	(%)
Population under coverage	192.4	100.0
as % of total population	16.20	
as % of total workforce	30.40	
By urban and rural areas		
Urban population under coverage	180.1	93.6
Workers and staff	148.5	77.2
Retirees	27.8	14.4
College students	2.5	1.3
People receiving allowance and relief	1.3	0.7
Coverage of urban population (%)	92.10	
Rural population under coverage	12.3	6.4
Population under regular allowance, relief and five guarantees*	9.4	4.9
TVE workers (10% of total employees)	2.9	1.5
Coverage of rural population (%)	2.70	
By category		
Workers covered by social security	148.5	77.2
Retirees	31.3	16.3
of which those in homes for elderly, five-guarantee and rural pensioners	3.5	1.8
Population under allowance and regular relief	4.4	2.3
Receiving relief for poverty and laid off	1.1	0.5
Population in welfare institutions	0.7	0.4
Disabled in welfare enterprises	0.9	0.5
Workers of TVE covered by social security	2.9	1.5
College students	2.5	1.3
By ownership		
State enterprises	139	72.3
Collective enterprises	47.5	24.7
Others	5.9	3.0

* Five guarantees: food, clothing, housing, healthcare and burial expenses

Source: Zhu (1996). Calculated by the author, based on 1993 statistics.

Table 4.3 Expenditures on social welfare and security in China, 1993

		Billion yuan	*% of GDP*
i	Social security and welfare of workers and retirees	167	5.3
ii	Relief, allowance and other welfare	8	0.3
	Total expenditure (i and ii)	175	5.6
iii	Welfare expenditure from TVEs and rural public funds	16.7	0.5
	Total expenditure (i, ii and iii)	190	6.1
iv	Housing subsidy	35.6	1.1
v	Price subsidy (grain, cotton, meat, vegetables, etc.)	25.4	0.8
vi	Welfare in kind by enterprises and institutions	52.5	1.7
vii	Social purchasing used for individual consumption	13.6	0.4
	Total expenditure (i–vii)	317	10.1

Source: Zhu (1996). Calculated by the author, based on 1993 statistics and other data.

4.5 The political economy of welfare change: alternatives to social betterment

Welfare changes in China during the reforms can be summarized as follows:

1. The welfare of the population as a whole, measured by indicators of opulence, poverty alleviation, capabilities, and so on, has improved.
2. The welfare improvements represent a continuation of the general development trend of the previous three decades, not its reversal.
3. Going beyond the aggregate and average figures, however, welfare improvements have been far from equally shared, and the gap between the well-off and the rest of the nation has increased.
4. Increasing regional differentiation and social stratification are causing differences in welfare advances between the urban and rural areas, among different regions, and among different social groups.
5. In conjunction with the emergence of a small cluster of the newly rich, a social underclass has emerged in the midst of economic growth. This is a new and distinctive phenomenon in post-1949 China.

Overall, China's general record of social development in the reform period continues to be favourable. However, compared with the achievements of the first 30 years of the People's Republic under far less favourable economic conditions, and, in particular, in view of the far greater wealth available now, welfare improvement in the reform era leaves much to be desired.

The analysis of the reform processes suggests that China has shifted from 'support-led' to 'growth-mediated' welfare improvement. The reforms, especially before the mid-1990s, have allowed a broader sector of the population to benefit from economic growth. As a result, the negative impact of the erosion of the previous support systems has been offset to a large degree by rising incomes. The broadly shared growth pattern has been an extremely important factor in keeping the size of the disadvantaged social groups fairly small. But the tendency towards social stratification has become increasingly alarming. This tendency and other social problems accumulated during the reforms call for solutions that economic growth alone has not been able to provide.

Numerous experimental welfare schemes have been tested for nearly a decade. The experiments so far seem to have incorporated elements of social security systems operating in more advanced market economies. The question remains as to what type of social security system or supporting mechanism will emerge in China. This question is closely related to the future socioeconomic system China is striving for.

It has been argued that China at its current development level is a developing country, and consequently government spending on welfare should be limited. Responsibility for social security should fall mainly on individuals. If China is aiming for a 'normal' market economy, this argument makes sense and the country cannot afford, for example, the type of social security provided by welfare states. But affordability is a relative term. Under central planning with a lower economic level, the majority of the population, including the rural sector, were brought under well-defined welfare coverage. China's own experiences confirm the significance of institutions in providing broadly based welfare and social security, a fact that seems to have been overlooked in the reform visions.

In the process of transition to a market economy, voices calling for the reduction of the role of government have been loud. But, leaving welfare issues for the market to regulate can lead, and indeed has led, government authorities to shirk their responsibilities. Given China's huge rural population and great regional diversity, it is very doubtful that long-term and equitable welfare development can be sustained under government inaction.

It is not the purpose of this chapter to argue in favour of more or less government spending on welfare, or to propose particular models of social security systems. Indeed, family ties remain strong in China as in many other Asian countries. Strong family ties, households' access to farm land, and informal social frameworks in the countryside can continue to complement social security. But family responsibilities are not unlimited. It has been observed that the informal social security support mechanism in one way or another is crucial to survival, but the well-being of the people, that is, the release from 'perpetual poverty', depends on a far broader social and economic context.

In a broader sense, the welfare of the population does not hinge solely on social security systems. It is therefore necessary to go beyond welfare arrangements in addressing the issue of social betterment and to examine possible new alternatives to the problems arising from economic transformation.

The consequences of reform suggest that issues central to social development such as political participation, educational attainment, health, class and gender equality, better environment, and the overall improvement of the quality of life for the entire population cannot be addressed successfully by economic growth alone. Indeed, it took centuries for the capitalist market economies to come to terms with the notion of social development. China should not make the same mistake. Social development should be re-emphasized in order to achieve balanced economic growth and human welfare. In pursuing a human-focused development strategy, the experience of the pre-reform 'support-led' welfare improvement in China and the successful experiences of social support systems in other countries will have valuable lessons to offer.

Notes

1. The work unit, *danwei* in Chinese, corresponds in the formal sense to the Western term 'employer', which identifies the place where people are employed and receive payment for their work, whether government agencies, enterprises or rural collectives.
2. HDI in 1960 may have been somewhat lower than in the late 1950s as a result of the 1959–61 famine.
3. The UNDP report also pointed to the existence of large regional disparities.
4. Since 1949 China has carried out four national population censuses, respectively in 1953, 1964, 1982 and 1990.
5. In the urban areas, it is the third highest cause.
6. 'Zhongguo de furen ceng' (The Rich in China), in *Shichang bao* (The Market), 12 February 1998.

7. The rural–urban income difference in the early 1950s was most likely lower than in 1957. It was said that the ratio of rural and urban consumption level was 1 : 2.4 in 1952, which increased to 1 : 2.9 in 1980 (cf. Li 1993: 112).
8. For assessments of the impact of economic reforms on women, see Croll (1985 and 1994); Davin (1991); Gao (1994a and 1994b); Summerfield (1994); and Lu (1995), among others.
9. For example, more than 3000 child vagrants were picked up in Shanghai in 1992.
10. The national average monthly rent per m^2 in 1978 was 0.13 yuan (Expert Group 1995: 218).
11. Cf. World Bank (1992) and Yang and Wang (1992) for evaluations and processes of urban housing reforms in China.
12. For a comprehensive introduction to the Chinese social security system, see Hussain (1995), Ahmad and Hussain (1991), and White and Shang (1996b).

References

Ahmad, E. and A. Hussain (1991), 'Social Security in China: A Historical Perspective', in E. Ahmad, J. Drèze, J. Hills and A. Sen (eds), *Social Security in Developing Countries*, Oxford: Oxford University Press.

Banister, Judith (1987), *China's Changing Population*, Stanford, CA: Stanford University Press.

Bo Xianfeng and Dong Jianzhen (1993), 'Zhongguo yiliao weisheng gaige de xianzhuang fenxi yu fazhan yuce' (The Current Situation of China's Reform of Health Service and the Future Development), in *Social Blue Book 1992–1993*: pp. 191–211.

Brown, Lester R. (1995), *Who Will Feed China? Wake-up Call for A Small Planet*, New York: W. W. Norton.

China Statistical Yearbook (*CSY*), various issues.

Croll, Elizabeth (1985), *Women and Rural Development in China*, Geneva: International Labour Office.

Croll, Elizabeth (1994), *From Heaven to Earth: Images and Experiences of Development in China*, London: Routledge.

Davin, Delia (1991), 'Chinese Models of Development and Their Implications for Women', in Heleh Afshar (ed.), *Women, Development and Survival in the Third World*, London: Longman.

Department of Social Science and Technology Statistics (ed.) (1995), *Women and Men in China*, Beijing: State Statistical Bureau.

Drèze, Jean and Amartya Sen (1989), *Hunger and Public Action*, Oxford: Clarendon Press.

Esping-Andersen, Gosta (1990), *The Three Worlds of Welfare Capitalism*, Oxford: Polity Press.

Expert Group (1995), *Zhongguo de daolu. Zhongguo gaige yu fazhang baogao (1978–1994)* (The Path of China. Report of China's Reforms and Development 1978–1994), Beijing: Zhongguo caijing chubanshe.

Gao Xiaoxian (1994a), 'Dangdai zhongguo nuncun laodongli zhuanyi ji nongye nuxinghua qushi' (Current Labour Mobility and the Tendency of Faminisation of Agriculture in China), *Shehuixue yanjiu*, 2: 83–90.

Gao Xiaoxian (1994b), 'Zhongguo xiandaihua yu noncun funu diwei bianqian' (Modernization and the Change of Women's Status in China), in Li Xiaojiang, Zhu Hong and Dong Xiuyu (eds), *Xingbie yu Zhongguo* (Gender and China), Beijing: Sanlian.

Ge Yanfeng (1995), '1994 nian shouru chanju baogao' (Report of Income Differences in 1994), in *Social Blue Book 1994–1995*, pp. 101–15.

Ge Yanfeng and Yue Songdong (1993), '1992–93 yian shouru feipei zhuangkuang de feixi yu yuce' (An Analysis and Forecast of Income Distribution, 1992–93), in *Social Blue Book 1992–1993*, pp. 277–88.

Green Book (1993), *1992 nian zhongguo nongcun jingji fazhan niandu baogao* (Annual Report of Economic Development of Rural China 1992). Beijing: Zhongguo shehuikexue chubanshe.

Howes, Stephen (1992), 'Purchasing Power, Infant Mortality and Literacy in China and India: An Inter-Provincial Analysis', Suntory-Toyota International Centre for Economics and Related Disciplines (STICERD) *CP/19*, London: London School of Economics.

Hu Weilue (1995), '1994 Nian mingong liudong zhuangkuang' (The Situation of Migrant Workers in 1994), in *Social Blue Book 1994–1995*, pp. 116–35.

Hussain, Athar (1995), 'Reform of the Chinese Social Security System', in R. Krieg and M. Schädler (eds), *Social Security in the People's Republic of China*, Hamburg: Verbund Stiftung Deutsches Ubersee-Institut.

Hussain, Athar and Nicholas Stern (1990), 'On the Recent Increase in Death Rates in China', Suntory-Toyota International Centre for Economics and Related Disciplines (STICERD) *CP/8*, London: London School of Economics.

Li Qiang (1993), *Dangdai zhongguo shehui fenceng yu liudong* (Social Stratification and Mobility in Modern China), Beijing: Zhongguo jingji chubanshe.

Lu Aiguo (1995), 'Farming System and Woman Labour Participation: The Case of Rural China in Economic Transition', in Makita Toich (ed.), *Culture in Development and Globalization*, Tokyo: The Toyota Foundation.

McKinley, Terry (1993), 'The Distribution of Wealth in Rural China', in K. Griffin and Zhao Renwei (eds), *The Distribution of Income in China*, London: Macmillan.

McKinley, Terry with Li Na Wang (1992), 'Housing and Wealth in Rural China', *China Economic Review*, Vol. 3, No. 2, pp. 195–211.

Milanovic, Branko (1993), *Cash Social Transfers, Direct Taxes, and Income Distribution in Late Socialism*, Policy Research Working Paper No. 1176, Washington, DC: World Bank.

Qiao Jian (1997), '1996–1997 nian zhongguo zhigong zhuanghuang de fenxi yu yuce' (Conditions and Prospect of Chinese workers in 1996–1997), in *Social Blue Book 1996–1997*, pp. 250–63.

Sen, Amartya (1987), *The Standard of Living*, Cambridge: Cambridge University Press.

Sen, Amartya (1992), *Inequality Reexamined*, New York: Russell Sage Foundation.

Sen, Amartya (1995), 'Mortality as an Indicator of Economic Success and Failure', Innocenti Lectures, Florence, Italy: UNICEF.

Summerfield, G. (1994), 'Effects of the Changing Employment Situation on Urban Chinese Women', *Review of Social Economy*, Spring.

Tan Shen (1995), '1994–95 nian: zhongguo fumu zhuangkuang' (1994–95: The Situation of Women in China), in *Social Blue Book 1994–1995*, pp. 332–42.

Transition Economic Division (1995), *Transition*, Vol. 6, Nos 5–6, World Bank.
UNDP (1982), *Human Development Report 1982*, New York: Oxford University Press.
UNDP (1994), *Human Development Report 1994*, New York: Oxford University Press.
UNDP (1997), *Human Development Report 1997*, New York: Oxford University Press.
Wen Shengtang (1995), '1994 nian de fan fubai douzheng xingshi' (Situation of Anti-Corruption in 1994), in *Social Blue Book 1994–1995*, pp. 136–51.
White, Gordon and Shang Xiaoyuan (1996a), 'Reform of the System of Social Relief and Social Services in China', in White and Shang (eds), *Reforms in Chinese Social Assistance and Community Services in Comparative Perspective*, Brighton, UK: Institute of Development Studies, University of Sussex, pp. 1–21.
White, Gordon and Shang Xiaoyuan (eds) (1996b), *Issues and Answers: Reforming the Chinese Social Security System*, Brighton, UK: Institute of Development Studies, University of Sussex.
World Bank (1980), *World Development Report 1980*, New York: Oxford University Press.
World Bank (1992), *China. Implementation Options for Urban Housing Reform*, Washington, DC: World Bank.
World Bank (1995), *Social Indicators of Development*, Baltimore, MD: Johns Hopkins University Press.
World Bank (1996), *World Development Report 1996. From Plan to Market*, New York: Oxford University Press.
World Bank (1997a), *1997 World Development Indicators*, Washington, DC: World Bank.
World Bank (1997b), *Financing Health Care: Issues and Options for China*, Washington, DC: World Bank.
World Bank (1997c), *China 2020: Development Challenges in the New Century*, Washington, DC: World Bank.
World Bank (1997d), *Clear Water, Blue Skies: China's Environment in the New Century*, Washington, DC: World Bank.
Yang Lu and Wang Yukun (1992), *Zhufang gaige: lilun de fansi yu xianshi de xuanze* (Housing Reforms: Theoretical Reflection and Practical Options), Tianjin: Tianjin renmin chubanshe.
Zhu Qingfang (1996), '1995–1996 nian renmin shenghuo zhaungkuang' (The Living Conditions in 1995–1996), in *Social Blue Book 1995–1996*, pp. 143–56.

5
Poverty Alleviation During the Transition in China

Zhu Ling

The imperatives of social stability and economic development have forced transition governments to undertake measures in poverty reduction and eradication during the transition to the market in the formerly centrally planned economies. In this respect, China is among those that have achieved great progress. This chapter offers an overview of poverty alleviation in China. It reviews government strategies and policies, examines current problems in poverty reduction programmes, and discusses policy options for the improvement of poverty alleviation and elimination schemes.

5.1 The nature of poverty

Within both the rural and the urban poor, a vulnerable group has always been the subject of targeted relief since the 1950s. These include the disabled, orphans, the childless old-aged and the families of martyrs. People affected by natural disasters have also been made the target of social relief, but usually for short-term periods. Currently, the Ministry of Civil Affairs and its local bureau have the responsibility for social relief functions. In addition, since the People's Commune era, rural villages have taken care of the traditional target groups. There were about 31.5 million rural relief recipients in 1995 and each of them received 18 yuan on average for the year, while about 4.3 million urban recipients received 19 yuan per person per month in the same year (SSB 1996). Although the relief funds are not large for each individual person, the relief system as a whole plays a significant role in maintaining the social stability of China.

The poor, who are the new target groups of the poverty alleviation programmes in the current economic reforms, consist of those who are able to work but live in poverty. This type of poverty exists not only because China is a relatively poor developing country, but also as a consequence of China's transition process. Poverty in China has the following characteristics.

First, China has the largest population in the world and, to a great extent, poverty in China is closely related to the serious problem of a labour surplus. This situation is similar to that in other developing countries. At the end of 1996, the estimated surplus rural labour was 130 million, while the registered urban unemployment and the surplus workers of the state enterprises totalled 27.53 million.

Second, unlike in many other developing countries, private land ownership does not exist in China as the result of the land reform and the collective land tenure system initiated and completed since 1949. Although there has been increasing inequality in distribution of non-agricultural production assets in the transition to a market economy, the existence of the rural poor is still mainly due to underemployment.

Third, unlike in many other transition economies such as Russia and the Eastern European countries in which the rural people are the minority of the population, poverty in China is mainly rural in terms of location and economic sectors. In terms of incidence of rural poverty, the poorest eight provinces and autonomous regions (Xizang (Tibet), Ningxia, Xinjiang, Gansu, Yunnan, Qinghai, Guizhou and Shaanxi) lie at the northwest and southwest of China, and in each of them the extent and severity of poverty are above the national average. In 1995, after ten years of implementing large-scale poverty alleviation programmes, the head-count indices of the poor in these regions increased by more than 10 per cent, the poverty gaps by 2.5 per cent, and the squared poverty gaps by at least 1.5 per cent (Xian Zude and Sheng Laiyun 1996).

Regional poverty has been essentially the result of adverse living conditions, such as the lack of resources and an underdeveloped infrastructure. A common feature of these regions is that rapid population growth has been exerting an increasing burden on the environment. Food security therefore represents an enormous challenge (State Council 1994a, 1994b). Considerable portions of these areas are inhabited by ethnic minorities. The implementation of family planning and environmental programmes is more difficult in these areas than in other parts of China because of the backwardness of the farming system and certain cultural traditions in the localities.

Moreover, the provision of social services in the poor regions lags behind the national average. The quality of the education service is poor, given the low qualification of teachers and shabby classrooms that hardly have any teaching equipment. In 1992, in 121 out of 2148 counties, the primary enrolment rate was below 90 per cent, lower than the national average (Khan 1996).

The provision of health services in rural areas is far from sufficient to meet the people's needs, while the situation in the poverty-stricken areas is even worse (see Table 5.1). For a long time, the lack of a health-care insurance system has been a factor which discouraged patients from low-income groups from seeking medical treatment. Moreover, sanitation and health education are often ignored in rural development projects and poverty alleviation programmes. The poor sanitation in most villages and the lack of hygiene among the villagers themselves are also among the important causes of the high incidence of illness in the countryside, and illness among women and children in particular. In fact, illness is responsible for keeping 50 per cent of the poor in absolute poverty and is an important factor behind the emergence of the new poor in non-poor areas (Yin Dakui 1994).

Fourth, similar to other countries in economic transition, the acceleration of the process of market reform in China has been accompanied by the appearance of a class of poor people who do not belong to traditionally poor groups. These 'new' poor in the rural sector consist of market losers and other vulnerable groups. A sizeable share of the rural poverty which has been identified statistically appears to be transient. In fact, this transient poverty would not exist if the distribution of household consumption were less concentrated (Ravallion et al. 1996). However, because of the lack of an effective social security system for rural people and because rural credit markets are still highly imperfect, a significant proportion of farming households are unable to maintain the level and quality of consumption in the face of income shocks. Thus in recent years many transient poor have become chronically poor, unable to recover from income shocks.

Fifth, the profile of the rural poor in China is similar to that in other developing countries. The poor in China are often illiterate, in bad health, lacking in skills, and devoid of enterprising ability (Table 5.2). This profile is both a result of poverty and a reason why the poor tend to become poorer.

Sixth, unlike many industrial countries, China has a very small proportion of single-parent families, especially in rural areas. Although a number of female workers have lost jobs during the structural adjustment and enterprise reforms, many of them have been re-employed in the service sector or other growing industries. Moreover, it is difficult

Table 5.1 Selected indicators on basic healthcare in China, 1994

Items	*Urban areas (%)*	*Rural areas (%)*	*Poor areas* (%)*	*National average (%)*
Residents enjoy tap water	94.4	21.8	15	43.2
People with free medical care	53.5	2.7	1.1	15.5
Maternal mortality	50/100 000	85/100 000	200/100 000	100/100 000
Infant death rate	**	**	80/1000	40/1000
Young couple receiving a health check before marriage	49.2	14.1	1.8	23.2
Childbirth at home	10.7	76.7	92.7	59.6
Women receiving gynaecological check and treatment	44.5	12.9	2.6	**

*'Poor areas' are those counties designated as poor by the state and the provinces.
** No data are available.

Source: Yin Dakui (1994).

to distinguish the incomes of a rural household from the earnings of individual family labour, unless there is a clear labour division within the household or a gender-specific engagement in various economic activities. It might be for these reasons that the changes of socioeconomic status of women during transition appear to have been statistically ambiguous. The results of the two sample surveys, conducted by the Institute of Economics of the Chinese Academy of Social Sciences in 1988 and 1995 suggest that, first, the differences in the incidence and severity of poverty between males and females appear not to be substantial either in 1988 or in 1995. Second, there are no large changes in relative status of female poverty in the 1990s (Li and Gustafsson 1996).

Certainly, this does not mean that the existing gender inequality in China has been substantially reduced. In education, for example, the situation has worsened for women. Every year, there are about 1 million children in the poor areas who drop out of school, and three-quarters of them are girls. This implies that gender discrimination exists in families' decisions regarding investment in human resources. This phenomenon can be used to explain educational inequalities between men and women (see Table 5.3).

Table 5.2 Profile of average poor household in rural China, 1995*

Indicators	*Mean of poor households*	*Mean of non-poor households*
Irrigated farming land (mu**)	1.91	4.35
Non-irrigated land (mu)	5.75	3.14
Production assets (yuan)	1824	2780
Financial assets (yuan)	2594	4941
Number of family members (persons)	4.60	4.32
Number working in agriculture (persons)	2.45	2.16
Number engaging in non-agricultural activities (persons)	0.4	0.72
With one or more sick or disabled worker (%)	7.7	5.8
Without sick or disabled worker (%)	92.3	94.2
Average years of education of worker (years)	7.61	8.15

*The sample consisted of 7998 households in 19 provinces selected from the SSB rural survey sample using a stratified sample approach.
**mu = 1/15 ha.

Source: Calculated by Li Shi (1997) on the basis of a rural household income survey conducted in 1995 by the Institute of Economics, Chinese Academy of Social Sciences.

Table 5.3 Comparison of educational backgrounds of sample urban couples with rural counterparts in China (%)*

	Illiteracy	*Semi-illiteracy*	*Primary school*	*Middle school*	*High school*	*University*	*Total*
Urban women	0.72	1.35	8.27	33.22	42.43	14.01	100.0
Their spouses	0.30	0.28	4.75	29.26	37.56	27.85	100.0
Rural women	23.76	12.72	27.84	26.74	7.98	0.96	100.0
Their spouses	3.99	4.80	32.59	42.22	15.97	0.43	100.0

*Figures are calculated based on the survey data collected from 4509 urban couples and 4524 rural couples in Shanghai, Shaanxi, Shandong, Guangdong, Ningxia and Jilin provinces in 1991.

Source: Institute of Population Studies, Chinese Academy of Social Sciences (1995).

Seventh, unlike the rural poor, most of urban poor population have emerged during the transition who do not have any productive assets. In 1996, 84 per cent of the urban poor experienced either job changes or unemployment in the course of structural adjustment. About 40 per cent of such poor people were from state or collective firms (Xinhua News Agency 1997). This phenomenon is similar to the situation in other transition economies (NHDR of Russian Federation 1995; NHDR of Ukraine 1996; NHDR of Uzbekistan 1996). The economic and psychological pressure on the urban poor appears to be heavier than on the rural poor. Although urban poverty is smaller in size and the income threshold is about two times higher than rural poverty, urban poverty has a stronger impact on social stability.

Eighth, urban poverty has been concentrated in the regions where high rural poverty incidence exists. The statistics reveal that 85 per cent of the urban poor live in economically backward areas in the central and western regions of the country. The per capita income of the urban poor in these regions dropped 12 per cent to 1321 yuan in 1996, which is equivalent to 30 per cent of the per capita income for the average urban resident (Xinhua News Agency 1997).

Ninth, the urban poor have similar characteristics as the rural poor: high dependency ratio in households, fewer family assets and poor educational background (see Table 5.4).

The nature of poverty in China has changed during the course of development and transition. Now poverty has come to include a variety of sources: regional chronic poverty in both rural and urban sectors; transient poverty resulting from natural disasters and personal failures in market competition, poverty caused by unemployment

Table 5.4 Profile of average poor household in urban China, 1995*

Indicators	*Mean of poor households*	*Mean of non-poor households*
Number of family members (persons)	3.73	3.11
Number of workers (persons)	1.84	2.22
Financial assets (yuan)	2636	12 011
Average educational level of workers (years)	8.47	10.18

*The sample consisted of 6937 households in 19 provinces that were selected from the SSB urban survey sample using a stratified sample approach.

Source: Calculated by Li Shi (1997) on the basis of an urban household income survey conducted in 1995 by the Institute of Economics, Chinese Academy of Social Sciences.

which is, in turn, related to structural adjustment and enterprise reforms, poverty associated with inflation; and poverty stemming from personal misfortune such as illness and injury, and so on. Thus the challenge of poverty calls for the formulation of a variety of poverty reduction strategies and policies (Riskin 1996).

5.2 Government responses

The Chinese government started anti-poverty programmes with a focus on regional rural poverty in the 1980s, and has extended these efforts to the reduction of urban unemployment-related poverty in the 1990s.

The programmes initially concentrated on dealing with economic problems, but have gradually been extended into the social development sphere. These policy modifications have been brought about, on the one hand, by the changing nature of the poverty that the government has to respond to, and, on the other, by the influence of the new concepts introduced from international interaction. Several recent World Summits on such as the protection of the environment, human rights issues, gender equality, food security and the guidelines of social development have created new commitments. At the same time, unsatisfactory results have also accompanied the implementation and performance of poverty alleviation programmes and have negatively affected overall progress. Thus poverty alleviation strategies have been rethought, and assistance programmes for the poor have been modified. The following sections discuss these strategies by examining the implementation of the most significant policies and programmes.

5.2.1 Rural poverty alleviation programmes

During the 30 years before the reforms, when incomes were low, the coverage of rural social services was rendered universally through government intervention. This has been seen as an example of support-led social development (Drèze and Sen 1989). The long-term commitment to the alleviation and elimination of regional poverty in the rural sector since the mid-1980s can be considered an extension of this tradition of public support.

5.2.1.1 Institutions

The State Council set up the Leading Group of Economic Development in Poor Areas in 1986 as an organizational response of the central government to the poverty issue. The group consists of ministers or their representatives from all government ministries. It formulates strategies and policies, organizes, supervises and coordinates poverty alleviation programmes. The group has a secretariat (OSCEDPA 1989a and 1989b).

5.2.1.2 Resources committed

First, anti-poverty initiatives are being undertaken with the help of intensive public investments. At the time when the '8–7 Programme' (the '8–7 Programme' had the goal of eliminating the existing absolute poverty of 8 million rural poor within the seven-year-period of 1994–2000) was announced in 1994, the level of the funding provided by the central government to alleviate rural poverty had already reached about 10.8 billion yuan each year (Chen 1994). From 1996 on, the amount increased by 4.5 billion yuan per year (Jiang Zemin 1996). This implies that the resources committed by the central government reached around 15.3 billion yuan annually. The resources are composed of three types of funds (see Figure 5.1).

Second, social mobilization has been carried out on a broad scale, so that poverty issues have become increasingly public concerns. Along with the implementation of the development assistance schemes designed by the central government for all poor areas, each line ministry has also allocated additional resources for specific programmes in a few chronically poor counties. The Ministry of Agriculture, for instance, carries out a food security programme (*Wenbao Gongcheng* in Chinese) in the high mountains and deep valleys through the extension of technologies of growing hybrid maize.

Figure 5.1 Composition of resources committed by the central government to poverty alleviation programmes in rural China

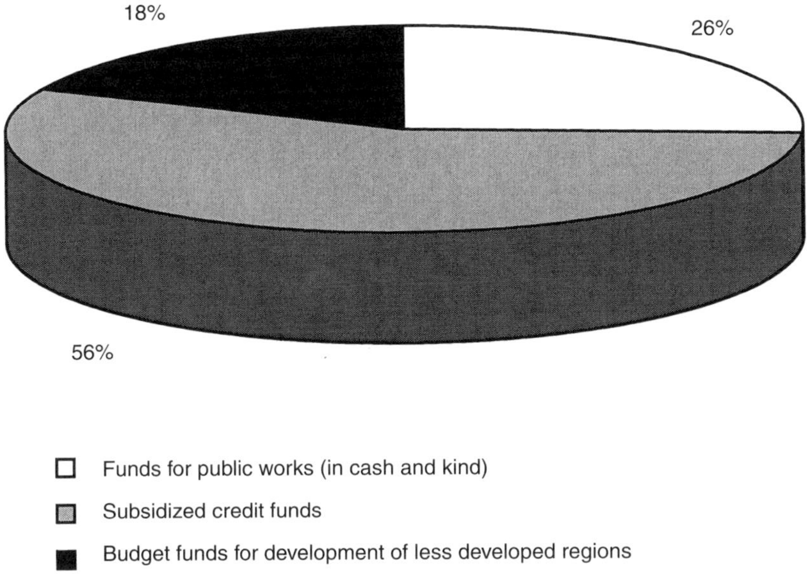

Third, throughout China, individuals make donations every year in support of social development programmes in poor areas, such as programmes for the establishment of village schools and programmes to supply scholarships for the children of poor families, micro-lending programmes for assisting mothers of poor families to develop their mini-business, and so on.

Finally, while the poverty alleviation programmes rely overwhelmingly on domestic resources, especially on the spending of the central government, various international organizations and the development agencies of industrialized countries are playing an active role in the anti-poverty campaign in China through the provision of resources and new ideas and concepts to assist poor areas.

5.2.1.3 *Major programmes for poverty reduction*

The budgetary funds for assisting less developed areas were stipulated by the '8–7 Programme' toward investment in social sectors, but before the publication of the Programme these had quite often been used as matching funds by the local governments to obtain investment projects from different ministries and to apply for credits from financial institutions.

Besides the conventional preferential policies to the poor people and the poor areas, such as fiscal transfers to the local governments and income transfers to individuals, the reduction and exemption of taxation and so on, public works schemes and credit programmes have been the two strategic measures that the Chinese government has undertaken since the mid-1980s (Figure 5.1). The former is designed to improve the infrastructure in poor areas, while the latter aims to stimulate local investments by offering loans at specially subsidized interest.

The public works programme. In contrast to the past practice of providing only relief to the poor, the poverty reduction policy introduced through the current reforms has placed special emphasis on the idea that the existing potential should be tapped. This is accomplished through public works, or *Yigong-daizhen* (which means 'to offer jobs instead of relief').

The *Yigong-daizhen* programme started at the end of 1984. It has differed from formal capital construction projects of the state in the following ways:

1. Central government investments had taken the form of 'in-kind' financing for projects. Since 1996, the investment has mainly been made with funds as the economy became increasingly monetized.
2. Regulations stipulate that the in-kind goods allocated by the central government must be distributed as wages. Local governments are supposed to raise supplementary funds of an equal or greater amount in order to pay for project materials and to cover other expenses. In practice, however, most provinces and counties have not been able to supply matching funds. Therefore, funds from other channels (such as funds from the ministries) have been provided instead, and some of the goods to be transferred have been replaced by cash.
3. Local governments have mobilized rural residents to furnish part of their labour free of charge or at reduced wages. *Yigong-daizhen* projects have made use mainly of simple labour-intensive technologies. Normally, the works have been carried out during slack seasons, thereby providing some additional income to local participants. Between 1985 and 1990, the projects focused on road building and the construction of facilities for the supply of drinking water. Since

Table 5.5 Major achievements of the *Yigong-daizhen* projects in China, 1985–95

Public roads	214 000 km
Public roads connecting	1500 townships
	10 000 administrative villages
Bridges (number of)	20 000
Drinking water supply facilities for	40 900 000 people
	33 000 000 animals

Source: Data supplied by the State Planning Commission and Office of the Leading Group of the State Council for Economic Development in Poor Areas.

1991, the projects scope has extended to farmland and water conservation, new afforestation, the renovation of rural post offices, purchase and supply cooperatives, health care stations for women and children, and old schoolhouses. The results of a study on the *Yigong-daizhen* programme suggest that the programme has helped improve regional infrastructure and social services (see Table 5.5) and directly provided short-term job opportunities and additional incomes for the poor (Zhu and Jiang 1996).

A distinguishing feature of the *Yigong-daizhen* programme has been the nature of the targeting mechanism employed. Some researchers have recommended a sort of self-targeting approach, whereby the wages offered through the public works are fixed so low as to ensure that those seeking to work for the projects really are the poor (Ravallion 1990; Braun et al. 1991). However, this kind of targeting mechanism has not been adopted. Rather, the government chooses the beneficiaries of the projects through the selection of the project sites and the channels of investment. Moreover, the targeting mechanism of the *Yigong-daizhen* projects differs from that of public works projects in other developing countries in several ways, as follows:

1. The *Yigong-daizhen* programme does not directly target the poorest segments of the population. The primary purpose of the projects is to improve infrastructure and social services in poor regions and to create the proper conditions for regional economic growth. These priorities mean that extremely poor villages and the poorest people do not necessarily benefit the most.
2. Within the poor regions, the projects are focused on village communities, that is, administrative villages, and not on rural households

or individuals. During the implementation of the projects, the village communities are responsible for the mobilization of the labour force.

Credit programmes for poverty alleviation. Since the shortages of funds are always extreme in poor areas, investment in the production sector in these areas also depends on the assistance of the central government. Before 1984, the central government appropriated funds mainly through the state finance system in order to support investment in production in poor areas. Starting in 1984, a new approach, the delivery of additional funding through credit institutions, was adopted.

The first priority of the specially subsidized credit programmes (*Zhuanxiang Tiexi Daikuan* in Chinese) has been to achieve food security for the poor (LSCEDPA 1986). Thus, about 1 billion yuan were given as credits to support a project organized by the Ministry of Agriculture for the extension of a special hybrid maize growing technique (He 1994). This project boosted maize yields by at least 100 kg per mu (1500 kg per hectare) and effectively eased food shortages among 15 million inhabitants in mountain areas (Yang 1993).

The central government has set two standards to gauge the success of the credit programmes. One is the food security objective, and the other is the level of loan repayments.

The food security of a poor county is considered achieved if over 90 per cent of the poor households in the county do not experience food shortage problems during a year in which harvests are normal. Households receiving permanent relief or relief because they are eligible for the 'five guarantees' (food, clothing, housing, healthcare, and burial expenses for the elderly or education for the young) are not counted as having a food shortage problem (Guo 1995). In 1990, per capita food grain availability of 300 kg was considered the food security line, and in terms of this line 58.3 per cent of the 331 poor counties receiving state assistance had achieved food security in 1992 (OSCEDPA 1993).

In terms of loan repayments, the situation is not as good as was initially expected by the central government. At the beginning of 1990, a portion of the credits distributed during the 1980s were overdue. Since 1991, the recovery rate for the special subsidized loans issued by the Agriculture Bank has been below 57 per cent. The loan recovery rate for other credit programmes, in particular the credits for county-owned enterprises, has been worse. Moreover, some of the repayments are being made using new loans.

The fact that the poor have lost direct access to the subsidized credits, although the programmes were set up to provide 'credits to assist the poor' (*Fu Pin Dai Kuan* in Chinese), ought to be given more attention. The loss in access has been an inevitable outcome of the way the credits are distributed and the loans used. Although the financial reforms should generate a market orientation, the credit programmes aimed specifically at poor areas are still being carried out according to the principles of a planned economy. The credits are being distributed 'top down' via the administrative hierarchy through a regional targeting approach.

Since 1995, the credits for poverty alleviation and for comprehensive agricultural development projects created by the State Council have been the responsibility of the Agriculture Development Bank, which was set up in November 1994. However, the method of fund allocation remains the same.

Interest rates on poverty alleviation credits are at least 20 per cent lower than normal official rates. The credit periods are usually one to three years, but can run up to five years. The repayments are due in full at the end of the period. The poverty alleviation credits apparently not only provide borrowers with short-term capital, but also represent an interest subsidy. For this reason, the demand for the credits always far outstrips supply.

The specially subsidized credits were originally intended to be distributed mainly to poor households. In 1986–87, household credits represented 60 per cent of all the specially subsidized loans (GHABC 1987). Since local decision-makers frequently argue that it is more efficient to offer the credits to economic entities which can then solve food shortage problems and raise the incomes of poor households, this approach is normally readily approved by the central government. Poor farm households have no opportunity to state their views, for they no longer possess any direct access to the credit programmes. Poor households have not usually been direct project beneficiaries (Wu 1994). Rather, the beneficiaries have included the entities which have organized the projects and those non-poor and 'average poor' households which have participated directly in the projects.

Moreover, the focus of the use of the credits has shifted from the agricultural sector to the non-agricultural sector. In 1986–87, loans to the agricultural sector represented about 55 per cent of all specially subsidized credits (Agriculture Bank of China 1988). By 1993, this share had declined to less than 40 per cent (OSCEDPA 1994). The strategy of accelerating non-agricultural development should certainly not be criticized if a poor county has no agricultural resource potential or has already achieved food security for the poor. However, a thoroughgoing policy and economic analysis of the changes in the priorities for the use of the credits ought to be undertaken.

Non-agricultural rural development is very costly in China. Most of the people who have established non-private enterprises are not experienced entrepreneurs, but government officials. They have very little of their own capital and start their businesses mainly using bank loans. If the enterprises are successful, they become an achievement of the local government leadership and an additional source of local tax revenue. If they turn out to be failures, the biggest losers are the banks and the bank depositors. Most local governments in poor areas run budget deficits and depend on subsidies from the central government. To improve their financial situation and guarantee the support of government employees, local governments in poor counties have a stronger incentive to establish non-agricultural enterprises than do the local governments in better-off counties.

While the central government stresses that the specially subsidized credits should be used to finance agriculture projects so as to alleviate food shortages among the poor, it does not exclude assistance for local processing enterprises. Moreover, the central government also supports poor counties that have already achieved food security to develop industries which can improve the economy of an entire region and generate local financial resources (LSCEDPA 1989). This approach is probably dictated by the fact that healthy local financing systems foster social stability and also tend to lighten the financial burdens of the central government.

The existing socioeconomic framework sets the poor in a position in which they cannot actively make use of the formal financial market. In the implementation process of the credit programmes, both the non-poor and the poor benefit from them through a trickle-down approach. Otherwise, when the programmes are completed, the farmers who couldn't learn how to make investment decisions independently by using credit services would still be left in poverty and need relief intervention in the market economy.

Normally the very poor depend on informal financial services, because the formal sector requires the mortgage of deposit receipts or guarantees. The poor seldom have the required mortgage, nor are their friends, who are usually also poor, capable to be guarantors for them. Therefore the poor who most need credit service are often excluded from it. It is now necessary to improve the institutional arrangements of the present rural credit systems (Zhu et al. 1997).

5.2.2 Programmes for reducing urban unemployment

Up to now, the term 'anti-poverty programmes' in China has referred to actions in the rural sector, while the phrase 're-employment programmes' commonly refers to actions against urban poverty. The difference in terms reflects the fact that the two kinds of programmes are different in nature and are targeted to different groups. Unemployed workers are deemed the most important target group for social policies in the urban sector.

5.2.2.1 Institutions and resources

Unlike the organizational set-up in the rural poverty reduction programme, there is no specific leading group established at the national level to deal with urban poverty issues. Instead, the Ministry of Labour has assumed the responsibility of providing assistance to unemployed and retired workers, the Ministry of Civil Affairs takes care of those groups targeted for traditional relief, and the Ministry of Personnel is in charge of helping those low-income groups associated with public works. In fact, municipalities have played a leading role in reaching the poor with resources and job placements. There are no data available on total amount of resources committed to the urban anti-poverty programmes all over China, but a recent piece of information shows that 4.2 billion yuan were needed in relief funds in 1997 to help keep the 11.76 million urban poor above the poverty line (Xinhua News Agency 1997).

5.2.2.2 Relief intervention

As the newly emerging urban poor overwhelmingly consists of unemployed workers, the first response of the Chinese government was relief intervention and the acceleration of social security reforms with a focus on replacing enterprise-based safety nets by a state-based pension system, an unemployment security system and a healthcare system which are consistent with the operation of a market economy. While the social security reforms are still going on, relief intervention has played a major part in assisting the urban poor. However, because the funds have been extremely limited, donations made by enterprises, labour unions, women's federations and individuals initially provided the major source for the relief actions. Relief by donation could only meet the most urgent needs of the poor for a limited time (see Table 5.6), but could not protect them from falling below the subsistence level in the long term. The system of formulating a poverty line to maintain the minimum living standard of the poor can be

Table 5.6 Statistics on unemployment relief and re-employment programmes for the workers of state-owned enterprises in China, 1986–95

Items	1986–95	1994	1995
Number of unemployed workers receiving relief (million people/times)	6	1.96	2.61
Number of re-employed workers (million people)	3	0.99	1.38

Source: Ministry of Labour (1997).

considered an institutionalized relief intervention. By 1997, 165 cities had established such systems. The resources are provided through two channels: local finance and enterprises (*Workers' Daily* 1997).

The relief programmes for the urban unemployed consist partly of the institutionalized relief interventions to the new urban poor and partly of the rudimentary unemployment security system. Nevertheless, they face many difficulties in operation. First, both enterprises and local fiscal authorities often fail to deliver their share of the funds in time, without a national social security law. Second, in several cities the funds are not effectively managed to prevent misuse and leakages, which have become a serious problem.

Third, because of existing regional differences, a considerable number of the municipalities with poor fiscal positions are not able to set up the relief programmes. Shanghai, the largest city with a growing financial sector and several newly developed high-tech industries, could cover all the unemployed workers in the city, with its unemployment security programmes supported by the sufficient resources committed by enterprises and the municipality. This is impossible for those local governments of the cities in the northeast of China, where traditional heavy industries are located and where both enterprises and governments run deficits to do the same job. Therefore it will be difficult to reach the goal that the Chinese government set for the year 2000: to establish a system for ensuring a minimum living standard for the urban population in more than 600 cities.

5.2.2.3 Re-employment programmes

The institutionalized re-employment programmes started in 1993–94, when a large number of workers in state-owned enterprises were released from their positions. This is why the re-employed in the two years 1994 and 1995 accounted for almost 80 per cent of those who benefited from the programmes during the period of 1986–95 (Table 5.6). The re-employment policies can be summarized as follows:

1. To assist the unemployed in finding new jobs by providing labour placement services. Up to May 1997 the services numbered 8700 over the country (Figure 5.2). There were 70 million urban people who found jobs during the period 1983–96 and most of them obtained the assistance of the labour placement services (Cao Min 1997).
2. To assist the unemployed with training courses for acquisition of new skills or improved qualifications. The training programmes are organized either by labour departments, labour unions and women's federations or by the administrative authorities from the sectors which are actually the former bureau of the industries but are now so-called 'corporations' or 'companies'. The courses are also financed by the contributions of enterprises and local budgets.
3. To encourage unemployed workers to run their own businesses by providing loans and facilities with low rent, facilitating their application for business licences, and so on.

Figure 5.2 Number of employment intermediate institutions in China up to 1997

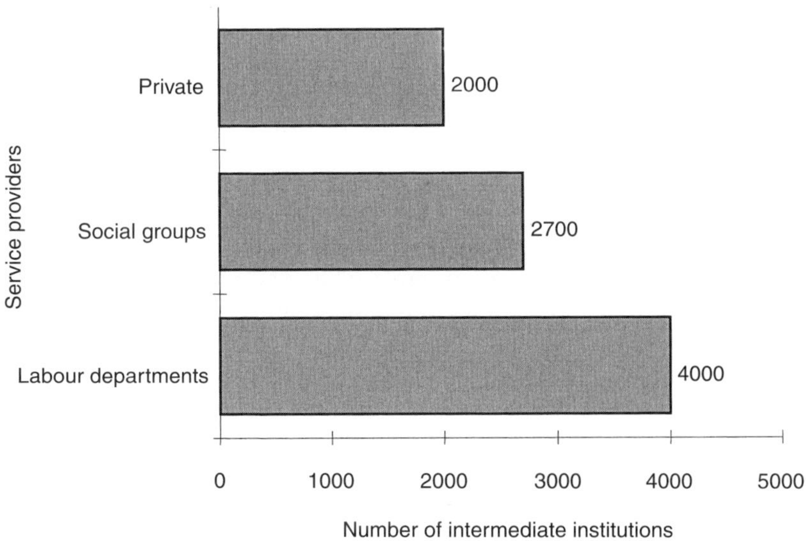

4. To encourage enterprises to recruit the unemployed. For example, for each recruited unemployed worker, enterprises are entitled to obtain a one-time subsidy of 1000 yuan from the Bureau of Labour in Tianjin Municipality (*Workers' Daily* 1997).

What is less well publicized is the issue of driving out rural migrant workers from the cities in order to vacate job positions for the urban unemployed. This idea has already been practised to some extent by most municipalities, which restrict employment opportunities of the rural migrants through a distributed quota to enterprises and impose various fees on both enterprises and migrants for the purpose of raising the costs for enterprises of employing rural migrants as well as of raising the migration costs of the rural labour. These policies could cause an increase in rural poverty incidence, since the rural–urban migration has a significant positive impact on improvement of rural households' income (Li Shi 1997).

Moreover, enterprises in the transition period actually have more autonomy to make their employment decisions than under the centrally planned economy. Most rural migrants are involved in the unskilled labour market. Generally, the enterprises make their employment decisions following market principles: for the job applicants with the same qualifications they prefer to employ the rural migrants at relatively lower wages rather than absorbing urban unemployed workers released from the state and collective enterprises, because the latter usually claim at least their former wage levels, which were artificially higher than they would have been in the labour market.

In fact, state and collective enterprises had already responded to the increasingly expensive urban labour in comparison with the low-priced capital that they were privileged to obtain, by adopting capital-intensive technologies since the beginning of the 1990s (Zhou Qiren 1997). Therefore it can be predicted that the policies to require enterprises to replace rural migrants with urban people might reduce unemployment-related urban poverty in the short term, but will definitely result in a rise in unemployment and poverty of both urban and rural areas in the long run, because of the rational reactions of enterprises.

Beyond the rural versus urban treatment, there is also political discrimination against town and village enterprises and non-state enterprises, which is increasingly unsustainable. Existing state enterprises increasingly cannot support redundant staff and they are even willing to shed more labour, while due to the very tight fiscal conditions the state is not in a position to build enough enterprises to absorb the surplus labour. This implies that a large share of the additions to the labour force and the unemployed have to find their jobs in non-state enterprises or have to create employment opportunities for themselves by starting their own businesses. All these possibilities mean that they have to accept inferior political status, unless they don't care about it.

This is no doubt a reason why a considerable part of the unemployed workers would rather live on relief or the partial payment of wages from their original enterprises and wait to be transferred by labour departments to other state enterprises than be self-employed. These considerations suggest that only when the government succeeds in actually implementing its stated intention to treat firms with different ownership status equally will it be possible for China to tackle its unemployment problems by stimulating investments derived from a variety of channels continuously to create increasing employment opportunities.

The analyses also indicate that urban poverty reduction programmes should not only include standard approaches in other developing countries, but should also be coordinated with the reform of state-owned enterprises, social security reforms and financial reforms. Only by adjusting the existing socioeconomic framework in accordance with the principles of a market economy, which will require eliminating the bias against the rural areas and freeing non-state enterprises and non-key sectors from state administration, can poverty alleviation programmes conducted in cities be more effective.

5.3 Strategies and policy options

In contrast with other transition countries which experienced a drastic decline in the economy and a rapid growth of poverty following the 'shock therapy', China maintained economic growth during its transition. With regard to poverty, it achieved a substantial reduction in rural poverty during the period from the late 1970s until the mid-1980s. From then on, though the poverty in the poor areas identified and intensively supported by the state has been continuously reduced, growing transitional poverty has added to the number of chronically poor in both rural and urban sectors. Such a situation is more complicated than that of the other transition countries.

The initial anti-poverty strategies and policies, which were designed merely with a focus on combating regional rural poverty, have become so extensive as to tackle manifold poverty problems. The goal of eliminating absolute poverty in China by the year of 2000, formulated through '8–7 Programme' with a regional targeting approach, was put forward based on an implied assumption that poverty would not appear in non-poor rural areas, nor would it occur in the urban sector, and neither would the transient poor turn into the chronically poor nor the relatively poor fall into absolute poverty. These assumptions have been overtaken by subsequent developments. It is necessary to revise the existing strategies and policies with a broader view in terms of integrating the poverty reduction programmes into the general development process and the entire transition course, coordinating rural poverty reduction programmes with urban ones, and modifying the operational mechanism of the programmes with further institutional innovations and socioeconomic reforms.

The following points should be taken into consideration in the identification of policy options.

First, since the majority of the poor live on agriculture, it is logical that policies in favour of agriculture should help ease poverty. The adverse direction in the rural poverty trend since the mid-1980s was partly attributed to the shift towards export-led development strategy (Khan 1996).

This interpretation captures the partial truth but not the entire picture: China has been experiencing not only a transition from a planned economy to a market economy, but also a transition from an agricultural society to an industrialized society under a serious labour surplus condition. With the unfavourable land–labour ratio, successful agriculture-led development could not last forever. Unless agricultural productivity could be continuously improved through technological progress and the enormous surplus labour absorbed in non-agricultural sectors, agriculture-led development becomes unsustainable.

Special attention should certainly be given to the phenomenon that the terms of trade to agriculture have fluctuated acutely since the mid-1980s, which is one of the decisive factors pushing the rural poverty incidence up and down (Khan 1996; Xian Zude and Sheng Laiyun 1996).

Extension services, education and training, information services and credit services, and so on all need to be improved with institution building in favour of farmers to enable them to protect themselves from market risks and retain a sustainable agricultural development.

Second, employment-oriented economic growth would help to alleviate unemployment and underemployment, thus reducing both urban and rural poverty. While this has been adopted as a principle for formulating investment policies since the end of the 1970s, the agricultural output-elasticity of employment for industrial and service sectors has apparently declined in 1984–94 compared with that in 1978–84. Between the two sectors, the decline of the elasticity in the industrial sector is sharper, from 0.62 down to 0.27 (Khan 1996).

In fact, the above-stated factors could be considered a cause-and-effect chain: under unemployment pressure, the state attempts to absorb surplus labour by a fast growth in capital investment. It is well known that investment decisions are mostly made by government officials, who take no personal responsibility for decision failures, instead of experienced entrepreneurs at both central and local level. Though China has had a high rate of domestic savings, an enormous amount of failed or inefficient investments have resulted in extremely short-term projects everywhere, such that foreign direct investments are badly needed as a supplement. Foreign direct investments are made with international competitiveness, not necessarily labour absorption, in mind.

A tendency to adopt capital-intensive technologies has gradually appeared in the well-run enterprises in the coastal provinces, where both domestic and foreign investments are concentrated. In these circumstances, it is essential to abolish the financially preferential policies for investors based on classification by ownership rather than efficiency and employment indicators. Employment-oriented investments ought to be given priority by the state for obtaining credit services. In particular, farmers, small enterprises and the self-employed businesses started by the unemployed should be supported with the special credit programmes similar to those successfully carried out in many other transition countries or regions, for instance in the former east Germany (Zhu Ling 1995).

Third, employment-oriented economic growth is one of the strategies that could substantially reduce poverty, while a more equal distribution of income is another. Statistical analyses using a decomposition of the effects from growth (indicated by GDP) and income distribution (indicated by the Gini coefficient) on changes in rural poverty suggest that the growth led to a drop of poverty incidence by 27.3 per cent while the rise of the Gini coefficient brought about an increase in poverty incidence of 10.4 per cent in the period 1980–95. Income distribution has become increasingly and significantly unequal since 1990 and the positive effects of the growth in poverty reduction are being entirely offset by the adverse effects of the income inequality in 1995

(Xian Zude and Sheng Laiyun 1996). It was in 1995 that the Gini coefficient for all of China reached 0.43, while the rural value was 0.34 and the urban value 0.28. These figures imply that income inequality became far worse than in 1988, when the three indicators were 0.38, 0.30 and 0.24 respectively (Zhang Ping 1997).

What the government has not yet substantially tackled is the price control policy on the energy and raw material industries, which are mostly located in the west of China. These products are still priced lower than they should be under market conditions, while the prices of the manufactured products largely made by the industries in the east are market-determined; these terms of trade exacerbate existing regional gaps. For this reason, sectoral price reforms should be undertaken as a means to reduce regional differences (Li Yining 1996).

Fourth, besides the modifications in overall development strategies, poverty alleviation programmes specifically targeting poor groups are still badly needed. The ongoing programmes for the urban areas are just at the beginning phase and lack coordination at the national level. Poverty issues in the rural non-poor areas have also not been covered by the national schemes. Therefore it is suggested that the existing leading group of the State Council for poverty reduction should extend its leadership to the whole of China.

Fifth, with regard to the rural poverty reduction programmes, these now cover only about 45 per cent of the rural poor through their regional targeting mechanisms (Xian Zude and Sheng Laiyun 1996). Within the poor areas designated by the state, the programmes are not adequately supported by initiatives targeted more specifically at the poor. This has meant that, first, the poorest people in poor areas are often not directly integrated into the programmes, and second, the poor in non-poor areas cannot benefit from the programmes. In addition, if the impact of the market on poverty is recognized, the individual poor must be identified case by case, based on specific socioeconomic indicators and by professional personnel. This calls for a network of social workers instead of government officials or administrators. Social work systems should be established as a kind of institution building, integrated into ongoing social security reforms.

Sixth, regional development projects should be differentiated from poverty alleviation programmes. Although the absolute poor are still concentrated in poor areas (partly as a result of policies which, under the planned economy, prohibited the free movement of production factors), 'poor people' and 'poor areas' are not equivalent concepts. The confusion between these two concepts has created difficulties in discussions on poverty issues between China and the international community and led to inefficiencies in the selection of the beneficiaries of assistance. This is clear in the case of both public works and credit programmes.

Seventh, the regional development programmes should consist of environmental, economic and social service components if they are to continue to be conducted in the name of poverty alleviation. Currently, in programme implementation, there are many government initiatives, but limited individual initiatives, and much administrative interference, but little market regulation. Experience both at home and abroad shows that the active participation of the public is essential for sustainable socioeconomic development. Now, during the transition, it is especially crucial to allow individuals the opportunity to create assets, generate employment and increase personal incomes. Such an approach would foster the emergence of entrepreneurs in poor areas and help encourage investors in more developed areas also to become active in poor areas.

Eighth, it is a common concern among decision-makers in developing countries and international development agencies that assistance to the poor be timely and leakage be effectively prevented. It is also realized that policy goals are not really achieved if assistance involves only the provision of funds and materials but no institution building. Various institutional experiments in individual targeting techniques have been carried out in other developing countries through credit programmes, health care and nutrition programmes, education and training programmes, and so forth. The lessons of these innovative programmes are invaluable if the anti-poverty initiatives in China are to be improved. These are also very appropriate areas for which China could seek international cooperation.

Ninth, anti-poverty programmes in various sectors should complement each other in order to generate spinoff effects from each programme. For example, health care and sanitation projects could be combined with projects to promote the use of organic fertilizers, and credit programmes could be linked to programmes to favour the application of new technologies to agriculture or the development of cooperatives in supply and marketing.

Finally, in development projects, particularly in credit programmes for the poor, government efforts should be coupled with individual initiatives and the activities of formal institutions should be supplemented by the activities of informal organizations (such as microlending groups among agricultural women as in the approach of the

Grameen Bank of Bangladesh, mutual-aid credit associations of villages, credit cooperatives and so on).

References

Agriculture Bank of China (1988), 'Improving Rural Financial Services to Support Economic Development of Poor Areas', Beijing: Agriculture Bank of China (February).

Braun, J. von, T. Teklu and P. Webb (1991), 'Labour-intensive Public Works for Food Security: Experience in Africa', *Working Papers on Food Subsidies*, No. 6, Washington, DC: International Food Policy Research Institute.

Cao Min (1997), 'Ministry works hard to solve job problem', in *China Daily*, Beijing, 8 May.

Chen Junsheng (1994), 'Fight with Absolute Poverty', *Development and Common Wealth*, Beijing, 17 October.

Drèze, J. and A. Sen (1989), *Hunger and Public Action*, Oxford: Clarendon Press.

GHABC (General Headquarters of the Agriculture Bank of China) (1987), 'The Report with Regard to Improvement of Utilization of Subsidized Credits Specific for Poverty Alleviation', Beijing: General Headquarters of the Agriculture Bank of China (16 October).

Guo Jinping (ed.) (1995), *Zhongguo shehui baozhang zhidu zonglan* (A Comprehensive Book on the Social Security System in China), Beijing: China Democracy and Legal System Publishing House.

He Linxiang (1994), 'To Promote the Realization of the National Anti-poverty Plan for the Years of 1994–2000', *Development and Common Wealth*, No. 5, Beijing.

Institute of Population Studies, Chinese Academy of Social Sciences (1995), *Survey Data of Women's Status in Contemporary China*, Beijing: International Academic Publishers.

Jiang Zemin (1996), Speech at the Conference of the Central Committee of the Chinese Communist Party on Poverty Reduction Programs, Beijing (23 September).

Khan, A. Z. (1996), *The Impact of Recent Macroeconomic and Sectoral Changes on the Poor and Women in China*, a study prepared for the East Asia Multidisciplinary Advisory Team of the International Labour Organization, University of California, Riverside.

Li Shi (1997), *Impact of Rural–Urban Labour Migration on Income Distribution*, Beijing, Research project report.

Li Shi and B. Gustafsson (1996), 'The Structure of Chinese Poverty at End 1980s', *Social Sciences of China*, No. 6, Beijing.

Li Yining (1996), *Theories on Transition and Development*, Beijing: Tongxin Publishing House.

LSCEDPA (Leading Group of the State Council for Economic Development in Poor Areas) (1986), 'The Summary of the 3rd Plenary Meeting' (20 September), Beijing.

LSCEDPA (Leading Group of the State Council for Economic Development in Poor Areas) (1989), 'The Summary of the 7th Plenary Meeting' (1 February), Beijing.

Ministry of Labour (1997) 'Outline of Social Security Reforms', Beijing, April.

NHDR of Russian Federation (1995), pp. 25–32.

NHDR of Ukraine (1996), pp. 23–33.

NHDR of Uzbekistan (1996), pp. 73–86.

OSCEDPA (Office of the Leading Group of the State Council for Economic Development in Poor Areas) (1989a), *Outlines of Economic Development in China's Poor Areas*, Beijing: Agricultural Publishing House.

OSCEDPA (Office of the Leading Group of the State Council for Economic Development in Poor Areas) (1989b), *Document Compiled on Economic Development of Poor Areas*, Beijing: People's Publishing House.

OSCEDPA (Office of the Leading Group of the State Council for Economic Development in Poor Areas) (1993), 'A Profile of Economic Development and Poverty Alleviation', Beijing, 15 September.

OSCEDPA (Office of the Leading Group of the State Council for Economic Development in Poor Areas) (1994), 'An Analysis Report on the 1993 Statistics of Poor Counties', Beijing, 23 September.

Ravallion, M. (1990), 'Reaching the Poor through Rural Public Employment', *World Bank Discussion Papers*, No. 94.

Ravallion, M., Chen Shaohua and J. Jalan (1996), *Dynamics of Poverty in Rural China*, Beijing: World Bank Resident Mission.

Riskin, C. (1996), *China's Economic Future: Challenges To U.S. Policy*, Study Papers submitted to the Joint Economic Committee, Congress of the United States, Washington, DC.

State Council (1994a), *China Agenda for the 21st Century*, Beijing: Ecological Science Publishing House.

State Council (1994b), *National Planning on Poverty Alleviation for the Years of 1994–2000*, Beijing.

SSB (State Statistical Bureau) (1996), *China Statistical Yearbook*, Beijing: China Statistical Publishing House, pp. 277–8, 724–5.

Workers' Daily (1997), 'The Funds for Guaranteeing Minimum Living Standard Would Not Substantially Increase', Beijing, 24 May.

Wu Guodong (1994), 'Research Report on Credit Policies for Poverty Alleviation', paper presented at the International Workshop on the Anti-poverty Strategies of China, 4–7 December, Beijing.

Xian Zude and Sheng Laiyun (1996), *The Measurement and Decomposition of Rural Poverty of China*, Beijing.

Xinhua News Agency (1997), 'Number of Urban Poor on Decline, Data Shows', in *China Daily*, 3 May, Beijing.

Yang Zhong (1993), 'The Policies of the Chinese Government for Rural Poverty Alleviation and Food Security', paper prepared for the International Policy Workshop on Employment for Poverty Alleviation and Food Security, Airlie House, Virginia, 11–14 October.

Yin Dakui (1994), 'Improving Health Care for the People in Poor Areas', *Development and Common Wealth*, No. 5, Beijing.

Zhang Ping (1997), 'Income Distribution during the Transition in China', *UNU/WIDER Working Papers*, No. 138, Helsinki: UNU/WIDER (July).

Zhou Qiren (1997), *Economic Transition, Structural Adjustment and Urban Employment*, (March), Beijing (mimeo).

Zhu Ling (1995), 'A Healthy Policy Bank of Germany', *Financial Research*, No. 9, Beijing.

Zhu Ling, Jiang Zhongyi and Joachim von Braun (1997), *Credit Systems for the Rural Poor in China*, New York: Nova Science Publishers.

6
Economic Reform and Welfare in Vietnam

Karel Jansen[1]

6.1 Introduction

The transition of the Vietnamese economy started around 1980, when some partial reform measures were introduced to overcome the problems faced by the centrally planned economy. More radical steps were taken around 1989, when prices and trade were liberalized. At present the transition is complete in the sense that Vietnam has a market economy.

The transition has been highly successful. Economic agents in all sectors of the economy, as well as foreign investors, have responded to the new opportunities and the new incentives. In the six-year period 1992–97 the average growth rate has been around 9 per cent per year. After 1997, under the impact of the Asian Crisis, growth slowed down but growth of per capita income remained positive. Incomes have risen and poverty has declined. All available economic, social, demographic and nutritional indicators suggest that significant gains have been made during the transition.

Progress has been widespread but not equal. Some sectors, regions and economic agents have done better than others. Growth in the rural areas has been slower than in the cities, in the mountain regions less than in the river deltas, in state enterprises faster than in the private sector. To some extent these differences are inevitable, some sectors, regions and economic agents are more dynamic than others. But government policies have also contributed to the skewed development. The transition has probably left few people worse off, before almost everybody was poor; now many have escaped the direst poverty. But the remaining poor may have fewer chances than before; their access to basic social services like education and health care is hampered by the increased private cost of such services.

The reforms in Vietnam find their origin in disappointing economic performance and external shocks. The outcomes of the first five-year plan after reunification were very disappointing: actual output stayed far behind stated plan targets. Agricultural output per capita stagnated between 1976 and 1980 and industrial output actually declined between 1978 and 1981. At the same time, Vietnam's military involvement with Cambodia reduced the inflows of (Western) aid. This was the background for a first round of reforms initiated around 1980.

Directive 100 of 1981 is the first step in agricultural reform. Faced with emerging food shortages and with farmers' unrest, the directive gave more autonomy to individual farmers. Household farms were allocated plots of land to cultivate under contract with the cooperative. Farmers undertook to produce a certain quantity of a crop to be sold to the state at a fixed price. Production beyond the contracted quantity could be used for own use or for free sale. Cooperatives continued to control the distribution of inputs and the marketing of outputs. The effect of this measure was a steady increase of agricultural output between 1981 and 1986.

The industrial sector is dominated by the state-owned enterprises (SOEs). Up to 1980, the policy priority in this sector, in line with the Soviet model, was heavy industry. Ambitious targets were formulated in the subsequent five-year plans, for instance, electricity, steel, coal and cement production. Around 1980, after substantial failures in meeting these targets, policy priorities shifted to agriculture and to light industries producing consumer goods. At this time there was also a loosening up of central planning control (Vo Dai Luc 1994). Firms were given some leeway to produce, beyond their plan targets, for the free market. These reforms led to an acceleration of industrial growth in the early 1980s.

However, these early and partial reforms did not lead to a pattern of sustained growth. The inefficiency of the SOEs made substantial government subsidies necessary, which contributed to a large fiscal deficit and rapid inflation. Also in the agricultural sector problems remained (Vo-Tong Xuan 1995). These problems were reflected in the stagnation in agricultural output per capita between 1986 and 1988. More seriously, food output per capita did not grow very much between 1982 and 1986 and declined in 1987. In 1987 bad weather added further to the problems.

The system of dual prices (one for the contracted output and one for the above-contract output) was difficult to administer. Contract prices had to be continuously adjusted to keep track with market prices. An attempt in 1985 at price and currency reform failed badly, resulting in large losses of SOEs, a large budget deficit and a very high level of inflation.

The more radical attack on these problems started in 1986. The Sixth Party Congress of 1986, confronted with problems of production and inflation, made the fundamental political decision to go for economic reform, and decrees and laws in subsequent years implemented this decision. Resolution 10 of 1988 gave the details of these reforms for the agricultural sector. The property rights of the households were strengthened through longer-term land-use rights contracts. These gave farmers a free choice of which crop to grow. They set prices of crops and of inputs free, and privatized the distribution of inputs. Later farmers were also released from the obligation to sell contracted amounts of rice to the state. Private trade in output was now allowed. The 1993 Land Law further extended land-use rights, and made such rights transferable, giving farmers more security of tenure.

These reforms have resulted in a private agricultural sector operating in free input and output markets. Cooperatives still exist, but in most places their functions have been reduced to giving advice and, occasionally, to providing credit or jointly purchasing machinery or organizing infrastructural or irrigation facilities.

The 1986 Party Congress decided to move towards a multisectoral economy where, alongside state-owned enterprises, there would be non-state firms. State firms were given more financial autonomy and market coordination took the place of central planning control. These changes in policy direction were embodied in a series of laws and resolutions that were promulgated in the following years. Of particular interest is the Law on Foreign Investment (1987) and Resolution 16 of 1988 on small-scale and private sector activities. This resolution established the rights of these non-state economic units to operate and the conditions for their operation (Ronnås 1992). In 1990 this was followed by the issuing of a Company Law and a Private Business Law.

The reform of the state enterprise sector was, however, not just a matter of shifting priorities and moving to a multisector economy. The efficiency of the sector had to be enhanced. State enterprises were, at the same time, the main source of government revenue and the main user of government subsidies. The substantial public sector financial imbalances were reflected in very high rates of inflation, over 300 per cent per year during 1986–88. The fight against inflation, that was engaged seriously in 1989, thus included elimination of government subsidies to the state enterprises. The enterprises were given greater financial autonomy and responsibility. Their input and output prices were set free and they were free to decide on procurement of inputs, production and output marketing, investments, hiring and firing of personnel and setting of wages. Government subsidies were terminated but state-owned enterprises obtained preferential access to commercial bank loans.

At the same time, a decree was issued requiring all centrally and locally state-owned enterprises to register anew. This re-registration was used to dissolve some loss-making state enterprises and to merge some others. The outcome was a sharp reduction in the number of state-owned enterprises from about 12 000 to 7000 (World Bank 1995a). This rationalization involved substantial layoffs of workers.

The reforms and laws listed above helped to create or formalize the institutions of the market economy. The year 1989 is the watershed year, when the remaining vestiges of central planning were eliminated. In that year all price controls were removed, interest rates were sharply increased and became positive in real terms, the exchange rate was sharply devalued and external trade was liberalized.

The reasons for the radical intervention in 1989 were both external and internal. The internal imbalances were reflected in the high rates of inflation during 1986–88. The external factor was the collapse of communism in the Soviet Union and Eastern Europe which had a severe political, but also economic, impact on Vietnam. Up until 1989 most of the external trade was within the framework of the Council for Mutual Economic Assistance (CMEA) with the Soviet Union and countries in Eastern Europe, but after 1989 trade with these countries sharply declined.[2] On top of this came the decline and, by 1991, the almost complete disappearance of foreign aid from the Soviet bloc. These contractionary impulses were, however, more than compensated by the strong supply response to the reform measures.

6.2 The impact on welfare

6.2.1 Reforms and growth

As argued above, economic reform in Vietnam came in two stages. A first series of reform measures was introduced around 1980. They had a positive impact on agricultural and industrial production, but these positive effects were gradually undermined by growing instability and inflation. The reforms around 1989 were more radical and had a more sustained impact; they have been followed by very high growth rates.

It is also recognized that the benefits of this growth are widespread: the great majority of the population saw its situation improve and is now better off than before.

Production in the newly liberalized private household sector increased immediately and strongly, as is reflected in the high growth rates for the agricultural and the services sectors in 1989 (see Table 6.1). This directly increased the income of a great share of the population. Real exports almost doubled in 1989, with the agricultural reforms resulting in a substantial export surplus (1989 was the first year with rice exports after many years of rice shortages) and with oil exports coming on stream. Growth in the industrial sector, dominated by state-owned enterprises, stagnated in 1989 and 1990 due to the removal of protective prices and government subsidies and to the loss of the CMEA market, but since 1991 industrial growth has been rapid and sustained.

These positive supply responses explain how Vietnam could stabilize and grow at the same time. In subsequent years, increasing flows of foreign investment and the resumption of Western aid further added to the positive developments. These strong responses can only be understood against the background of the preceding repression. They do not reflect the 'normal' response of economic agents to changes in relative prices; they reflect the grabbing of opportunities that did not exist before.

The initial impact of the reforms was on the agricultural sector, where the majority of the population earns its living. Gross output in agriculture increased after the first reforms in 1981, but then fell back in 1987 as inflation eroded real agricultural prices and bad weather hit the sector. The reforms of 1988 and 1989 induced a growth spurt in these years, which, after a fall back in 1990 and 1991, continued in the 1990s (see Table 6.1). The price liberalization helped to turn the terms of trade in favour of agriculture. One of the characteristic policies of central planning in Vietnam had been to keep agricultural prices low so as to generate a high surplus in the state industrial sector (Fforde and de Vylder 1996). The terms of trade were favourable during the period 1987–91. This plus the land reform that gave a greater certainty of tenure gave the farmers a strong incentive to increase production. In the years after 1991 the terms of trade were less favourable.

Agricultural growth resulted from:

1. An increase in the area sown. Total cultivatable area did not increase much, as it is limited by land availability, but the area sown

Table 6.1 Growth in Vietnam, GDP

	1987	*1988*	*1989*	*1990*	*1991*	*1992*	*1993*	*1994*	*1995*	*1996*	*1997*	*1998*	*1999*
Growth, real													
GDP	3.7	5.9	8.0	5.1	6.0	8.6	8.1	8.8	9.5	9.3	8.2	4.0	4.0
agriculture	–0.6	3.9	6.9	1.5	2.0	7.7	3.3	3.3	4.8	4.4	4.3	2.8	4.8
industry	8.8	5.3	–2.6	2.9	8.6	14.4	12.6	13.4	13.6	14.5	12.6	7.0	5.7
services	5.5	9.2	18.3	10.8	7.5	6.0	8.6	9.6	9.8	8.8	7.1	2.0	1.6

Sources: General Statistical Office (GSO) and World Bank (various years)

increased due to irrigation and more intensive cropping from around 8.6 million hectares in 1985/86 to around 10.4 million in 1994/95 and 12.3 million in 1999. Most of this expansion ended up in rice lands (about 2 million hectares) but also in land under industrial crops.
2. An increase in yields per hectare. The yields of most crops increased. There were substantial increases for products like rice, maize, cotton, sugar and coffee. The reforms provided incentives for the more intensive use of inputs and for more intensive cultivation.
3. Diversification. As noted under point 1, most of the new acreage went to rice cultivation, but in relative terms the acreage under other crops increased much more, thus diversifying agricultural output significantly.

The reforms also opened up the opportunity for the establishment of private small-scale labour-intensive firms in construction, industry and services and the growing incomes provided the demand for such enterprises.

Table 6.2 shows the rapid growth of small-scale private industrial firms since the mid-1980s. Most of these establishments are small household enterprises; only a few have a more formal organization. The majority of these firms are active in food processing, textiles and sewing, construction materials and wood products. To some extent these private firms replace industrial cooperatives. The number of such cooperative industrial firms declined from 35 629 in 1985 to 1729 in 1995. Since the mid-1990s the number of private industrial firms has stabilized.

The number of people working in private trade, restaurants and services more than doubled since 1989. The services sector is usually repressed under central planning; hence the reforms opened new opportunities and the growing incomes provided the demand. An emerging tourism market provided further opportunities: the number of arrivals of foreign visitors increased from 280 000 in 1990 to 1.8 million in 1999. The outcome was very rapid growth in the services sector in the early 1990s. Construction is another sector with rapid growth, as reflected in the sharp rise in its contribution to GDP. The private sector claims a growing share of this; private construction made up about one-third of total value added in the mid-1980s, and this share has increased to more than half in recent years.

Table 6.2 brings together data on these three private economic sectors, small-scale industry, services and construction, which are

Table 6.2 Indicators of private sector growth, Vietnam

	1986	*1987*	*1988*	*1989*	*1990*	*1991*	*1992*	*1993*	*1994*	*1995*	*1996*	*1997*	*1998*	*1999*
Number of private industrial establishments ('000s)	207*	–	319	335	378	448	369	456	498	613	624	615	590	–
Number of persons working in private trade, catering and services ('000s)	577	640	718	793	836	899	952	1038	1116	1663	1537	1389	1455	1502
Construction: contribution to GDP (%)	2.7	2.4	2.7	3.6	3.9	4.0	5.6	7.4	7.6	6.9	6.5	6.5	5.8	5.4

* 1985.

Sources: General Statistical Office (GSO) (1996a, 1996b and 2000).

characterized by easy entry and labour intensity. Through the growth of agriculture and of these other private small-scale activities employment and income opportunities were created and a large part of the population saw its income increase.

The 1989 reforms also included trade liberalization and devaluation of the exchange rate. The result was a rapid growth of exports. Since 1989 exports to and imports from the CMEA countries declined rapidly, but the loss of the traditional CMEA market made no difference to overall export performance. The shift in trade, away from CMEA and towards the world market, implied a shift from a stagnating market to the dynamic Asian market. By a stroke of luck, oil exports came on stream just at the time that the CMEA market was collapsing. Agricultural and trade reforms combined to invite a sharp increase in agricultural export supplies. Some industrial exports emerged (particularly textiles and garments) and earnings from tourism increased sharply.

Vietnam's export structure is still strongly biased towards primary commodities. Taking agriculture, fishery and oil and mining products together, more than three-quarters of merchandise exports leave Vietnam in unprocessed form. All export items have recorded high rates of growth in recent years. Foreign exchange earnings from coffee, tea, textiles and garments, shoes and tourism are growing exceptionally fast. All of these represent labour-intensive activities. Their growth is thus likely to create substantial employment. Earnings from foreign visitors are, in recent years, equivalent to 10 per cent of merchandise exports.

In 1987 a Foreign Investment Law was issued and the 1989 reforms made Vietnam attractive to foreign investors, particularly those from nearby Asian countries. The inflow of foreign direct investment (FDI) started slowly but has accelerated sharply. Initially, FDI concentrated on the oil and services sectors, but in more recent years virtually all FDI is aimed at the services and the industry sectors. Implemented foreign investment forms a large share of total capital formation; in some years FDI accounted for more than one-third of total investment. The Asian Crisis affected FDI inflows strongly since a large share of foreign investment came from the region. Although FDI inflows have fallen, they remain an important part of overall investment.

The reforms and the gradual normalization of the relations with the United States have reopened Vietnam's access to Western aid. Consecutive meetings of the donor consortium have pledged large sums of foreign aid. Actual disbursements have come more slowly but are now substantial: in 1995 they amounted to US$640 million and in 1999 to around 1 billion.

6.2.2 Employment

Table 6.3 shows the employment structure. Between 1986 and 1994 employment in the state sector declined by more than 1 million, as the government agencies and state enterprises were rationalized and consolidated. On top of this, the army was slimmed down, putting another half million on the labour market.[3] Since 1994 there has been a slow recovery of state sector employment. Employment in the non-state sector increased by 10 million between 1986 and 1998. The annual growth rate of employment between 1986 and 1998, as recorded in Table 6.3, was only 2.6 per cent per year, less than the growth of the labour force. Even though it is likely that the statistics may fail to record some new employment, the difference between the two growth rates is reflected in increasing open unemployment. Despite the rapid employment growth in the private sector, it is estimated that unemployment is rising and stands at around 7 per cent (GSO 2000).

It is argued that the social cost of the dismissals in the state sector after 1988 were minor because (a) the dismissed workers received adequate compensation; (b) most could be quickly absorbed into the rapidly growing private sector; and (c) in Vietnam, unlike for instance China, the provision of social services is not linked to the place of employment; thus loss of job did not also imply loss of access to social services (World Bank 1995b). Moreover, many of those that were working in the state sector were moonlighting to supplement their incomes. One study estimated that the income from the salary presented only 55.6 per cent of total income of state employees (Le Manh Hung 1996: 221). The loss of the state job thus implies a loss of only part of income.

Most of the new employment opportunities are in sectors that are labour-intensive but also have low labour productivity, so that incomes generated tend to be low. Table 6.4 gives estimates of labour productivity changes. It should be noted that both value-added estimates and employment estimates of some of the sectors are questionable, so that labour productivity, as a quotient of two uncertain estimates, is even more questionable. Still, the data in Table 6.4 may be indicative of broad trends.

There has been a rapid growth of labour productivity, particularly after 1990. This growth concentrated on the industrial sector. The output per worker increased only slightly in the agricultural sector.

Table 6.3 Employment by sector, Vietnam ('000s)

	1980	*1986*	*1990*	*1991*	*1992*	*1993*	*1994*	*1995*	*1996*	*1997*	*1998*
Agriculture	15 140	20 246	22 319	22 841	22 876	22 935	24,131	24 765	24 775	24 814	
Industry	3258	3872	3661	3735	3847	4140	4352	4375	4417	4633	
Services	3241	3850	4309	4398	4812	5649	5181	5625	6600	7547	
TOTAL	21 639	27,968	30 289	30 974	31 819	32 724	33 664	34 765	35 792	36 994	38 200
State sector	3316	4028	3416	3144	2976	2960	2928	3053	3138	3267	3339
Non-state sector	18 323	23 940	26 873	27 830	28 844	29 764	30 736	31 712	32 654	33 727	34 861
				Percentage distribution							
Agriculture	70.0	72.4	73.7	73.7	71.9	70.1	71.7	71.2	69.2	67.0	
Industry	15.1	13.8	12.1	12.1	12.1	12.7	12.9	12.6	12.3	12.5	
Services	14.9	13.8	14.2	14.2	15.1	17.2	15.4	16.8	18.4	20.4	
TOTAL	100.0	100.0	100.0	100.0	100.0	100.0	100.0	100.0	100.0	100.0	100.0
State sector	15.3	14.4	11.3	10.2	9.4	9.1	8.7	8.8	8.8	8.8	8.7
Non-state sector	84.7	85.6	88.7	89.8	90.6	90.9	91.3	91.2	91.2	91.2	91.3

Sources: McCarty et al. (1992); IMF (2000).

Table 6.4 Value added per worker, Vietnam (in VND 1989 prices)

	1986	*1990*	*1995*	*1999*
Agriculture	536	538	633	664
Industry	1518	1810	2696	3912
Services	2196	2528	2239	2881
TOTAL	892	975	1233	1488
State sector	2021	2810	5599	6811
Non-state sector	680	742	823	979

Sources: calculations based on General Statistical Office (GSO) (1996a, 1996b and 2000).

Agricultural growth has taken place through the extension of sown acreage and more intensive cultivation, reflected in increasing yields per acre. The area of cultivatable land has not increased and so the land–labour ratio has declined sharply but, as noted above, more of the land is double cropped and cultivation has intensified, thus increasing the demand for agricultural labour. Still, the increase in demand is outpaced by the growth of the labour force. A growing number of those registered as being employed in agriculture are in fact only partially employed and are engaged in low-return activities. Underemployment rates in the rural areas are estimated as high as 30 per cent. The agricultural sector seems to operate as the employment sink. As the agricultural sector is absorbing excess labour, output and income per capita stagnate despite the rapid growth of total agricultural output. This stagnation is behind the increasing gap between income in agriculture and that in the other sectors of the economy; as productivity and incomes in other sectors have grown rapidly, income inequality has increased.

There has been a very rapid growth of labour productivity in the state sector. There is the combination of, on the one hand, increased output and, on the other, declining levels of employment. The rationalization of the state sector thus had significant positive effects. This is also reflected in the rapid growth of average income of state workers from VND 57 200 per month in 1990 to VND 274 200 in 1993 (or 132 400 at 1990 prices) (MOLISA 1994).

The impression given by the above economic statistics about increasing levels of living is confirmed by other indicators. Table 6.5 includes demographic statistics on which data are available for different points in time. They all show improvements over the period of transition. Life expectancy has increased by five years since 1980. Infant and child mortality, and the total mortality rate, have fallen significantly. The incidence of low birth weight has fallen.

Table 6.5 Trends in demographic and nutritional indicators, Vietnam

Life expectancy at birth[1]		Low birth weight (under 2.5 kg)[5]	
1994	68	1994	6.4
1990	67	1991	10.8
1980	63		
Total fertility rate[2]		Crude birth rate[6]	
1998	2.3	1993–94	25.3
1993	3.1	1985–89	31.0
1989	3.8		
Infant mortality (per 1000 live births)[3]		Crude death rate[7]	
1997	39	1992	7.1
1989–93	44.2	1989	8.4
1984–88	46.0	1976	11.6
1979–83	54.8		
Under-five mortality (per 1000 live births)[4]		Maternal mortality (per 1000 deliveries)[8]	
1989–93	55.4	1990	1.1
1984–88	68.7	1980	2.0
1979–83	82.1		

Sources:
[1]World Bank World Tables and Kerkvliet and Porter (1995), p. 15. The UNDP (1995) gives for 1993 an estimate of 65.2 years (male 62.9 and female 67.3).
[2]World Bank (2000) for 1997. *Vietnam Intercensal Demographic Survey (VICDS)*. World Bank (1995b) gives figures for 1992/93, on the basis of VLSS 3.3.
[3]*VICDS* (1994) and UN and MOLISA (1999).
[4]*VICDS* (1994). The sharp fall between 1984/88 and 1989/93 is due to the fall in mortality between one and five years; infant mortality changes little between these periods. The fall is ascribed to the effective immunization programme.
[5]Pham Huy Dung (1996), based on Ministry of Health data. The World Bank (1995b) gives for 1992/93 a figure of 5.6 per cent.
[6]*VICDS* (1994).
[7]Center for Population and Human Resources Studies (1995).
[8]Pham Huy Dung (1996).

The improvements in the crude birth rate, the total fertility rate and in maternal mortality indicate that women have participated in the process of progress. The economic and social position of women is relatively strong, when compared to that of women in many other countries. Labour force participation is high: about 90 per cent of adult women work outside the home. There is discrimination in the labour market: women in employment earn less than men and this gap has probably increased with the transition. Still, households headed by women, that is, about one-third of all households, are less likely to be poor. And, as will be noted below, women also participate equally in education.

6.2.3 Poverty and income inequality

Although incomes have grown, Vietnam remains a poor country. Its current per capita GDP is estimated at around US$370 (1999). Poverty has fallen in recent years with rapid growth. Between the Vietnam Living Standards Survey of 1992/93 (VLSS 1994) and the survey of 1997/98 (VLSS 2000) the poverty headcount declined from 58.1 to 37.4 per cent.

Poverty and inequality in Vietnam can be approached from three overlapping perspectives: location, occupation and assets. The poor are concentrated in certain geographical areas, in particular occupations and sectors, and they are characterized by their lack of possession of, or lack of access to, assets such as land, capital and credit, human capital and entrepreneurial talent.

In Table 6.6 the seven regions of Vietnam are ranked by the level of their per capita consumption expenditure as recorded in the VLSS of 1992/93. The gap between the regions is substantial. The expenditure in the poorest region (the Northern Central Coast region) is less than half that of the richest region (the Southeastern region around Ho Chi Minh City). Of course, the regions are all rather large, and within regions there are sharp differences as well. Table 6.6 also shows that the ranking of the regions changed only a little between 1992/93 and 1997/98, and that the gap between the richest and the poorest regions widened.

There is a direct relationship between the level of expenditure and the incidence of poverty. The region with the highest level of per capita income and expenditure has the lowest proportion of population below the poverty line. This link confirms that rapid income growth is the best way of reducing poverty: Table 6.6 shows that the regions with rapid growth (Southeast, Red River Delta, Northern Central) showed the sharpest decline in poverty incidence. But it is clear that economic growth, as it is happening in Vietnam now, is not enough. First of all, economic growth tends to be stronger in the regions that are already relatively rich. And second, regions that are already relatively rich and have higher growth also tend to have a higher level of income inequality as reflected in the Gini coefficients. It would thus appear that economic growth in Vietnam may lead to a further concentration of poverty in certain regions and will increase inequality both between and within regions.

The VLSS data can be used to list some characteristics of the poor in Vietnam, apart from their low income:

Table 6.6 Regional income inequalities, Vietnam

Region	*Average expenditure per capita('000 VND)*[1] *1992/93*	*Average expenditure per capita('000 VND)*[2] *1997/98*	*Growth rate expenditure 92/93–97/98*[3]	*Poverty rate (%) 1992/93*[4]	*Poverty rate (%) 1997/98*[4]	*Gini coefficient*[5] *1992/93*	*1997/98*
Southeast	2008	5019	12.4	32.7	7.6	35.7	34.0
Mekong Delta	1506	2536	3.6	47.1	36.9	31.4	29.8
Central Coast	1457	2641	5.4	49.6	35.2	33.6	33.5
Red River Delta	1349	2938	9.5	62.9	28.7	31.0	32.1
Central Highlands	1159	1942	4.8	70.0	52.2	31.1	30.9
Northern Uplands	1007	1920	5.9	78.6	58.6	24.4	27.4
North Central	974	2197	8.1	74.5	48.0	24.4	28.9
Vietnam	1373	2746	7.2	58.1	37.4	33.0	34.8

Sources:
[1] VLSS (1994) in current prices.
[2] VLSS (2000) in current prices.
[3] VLSS (2000), in constant 1998 prices.
[4] VLSS (2000), percentage population below poverty line.
[5] VLSS (2000). World Bank (1995b), p. 27.

- 90 per cent of the poor live in rural areas and are predominantly engaged in agricultural activities; of the households whose head is occupied in agriculture, 59.9 per cent fall below the poverty line (World Bank 1995b). Poor households tend to have smaller land holdings;
- the size of their households tends to be larger as they have more children per family, with women having a higher fertility rate;
- their children suffer more from malnutrition, wasting and stunting;
- the poor have a lower literacy rate and have completed fewer years of schooling;
- they use the health services less frequently;
- poverty is not gender-determined. In fact, households with female heads are less likely to be poor;
- they tend to live in remote areas with less access to piped or safe water, to hygienic sanitation, and to electricity. They are also less well linked to passable roads and to permanent markets;
- in general, they own smaller and non-permanent houses. Only a few have items like radio, furniture, or bicycles. None have more expensive assets like televisions, refrigerators, motorbikes, videos or washing machines;
- they have a very small capacity to save and thus own little wealth. They have hardly any access to borrowing, especially not from formal financial institutions.

With the rapid growth, the incidence of poverty has declined. The growth process implied rapid structural change (shifting the sectoral balance away from agriculture and towards industry and services) and growing disparities among regions, with urban areas, particularly around Hanoi and Ho Chi Minh City, doing much better than rural areas, and rapidly growing disparities within sectors and within regions between those that could fully benefit from new opportunities and those that could not. The outcome of these three factors is a sharp increase in income inequality.

Pre-reform Vietnam was a relatively egalitarian society. The northern part of the country had been shaped by years of collective effort and the integration of the southern economy in the collective mould had reduced the pre-1975 inequalities that had existed there. Although there are no comparable surveys available to assess the income distribution before the reforms, it seems fair to conclude that inequality was low.[4] The commune system in agriculture controlled the income-generating activities of the majority of the population. Basic necessities (such as food and housing) were kept cheap through price controls, and basic social services (health care and education) were provided cheaply or for free. Good teachers and health care workers could be maintained despite low wages, as they had no alternative employment opportunities. Hence a good system of education and health care could be provided at low cost, resulting in exceptionally good social indicators for a country at Vietnam's level of income.[5] Pre-reform Vietnam was a society with low, but relatively equally distributed, incomes and a broad provision of basic social services.[6]

Developments since then have fundamentally changed this picture. All indicators presented in the previous section show improvements. Economic reform in Vietnam has been an unmitigated success; the great majority of the people are better off than they were before. Incomes have increased, although they remain low, but inequality has significantly increased. While most farmers are better off, they have not become part of the 'new rich'. The 'new rich' are to be found in the newly emerging non-farm private sector. Another element of the new rich, not so well captured by the statistics, are those in positions in state enterprises and government where greater autonomy gives them control over the firm's surplus or those that can grab the 'fringe benefits' that come from positions of monopoly and from control over assets or that are associated with the inflows of foreign investment and aid.

6.2.4 Social services

6.2.4.1 Education

Educational attainment is high for a country of Vietnam's level of development. The gross enrolment ratio for primary education is in excess of 100 per cent, indicating substantial over-age enrolment due to late start and repetition. The *Vietnam Intercensal Demographic Survey 1994* (*VICDS* 1994) reported figures for 1994 as shown in Table 6.7.

Table 6.7 Participation rates in primary school by age group, Vietnam

Age group	*Ever attended* primary school (%)	*Finished* primary school (%)
15–19	93.0	75.8
20–24	92.8	80.4
25–29	94.2	81.1

These figures suggest that almost all Vietnamese children go to school, but that a substantial number of them drop out before they finish primary school. The lower proportion of 15–19-year-olds that have finished primary school (compared to older age groups) suggests that some of that age group are still in school, although the official age for the primary school is 6–10 years. The VLSS reported that 84 per cent of the 6–10-year-olds and 69 per cent of the 11–14-year-olds were attending school in 1992/93 (VLSS 1994: 49). In the VLSS 1997/98 the numbers had changed to 93 and 63 per cent respectively (VLSS 2000).

With such high participation in primary schooling it is not surprising that literacy is high. The VLSS 1997/98 estimated the literacy rate for population of ten years of age and older at 89 per cent, 94 per cent for males and 86 for females and a urban literacy rate of 94 per cent against 88 for rural areas (VLSS 2000: 47).

The *VICDS* reported that about 80 per cent of the recent cohorts finished primary school and that about 70 per cent attended any secondary education; this would mean a rather high rate of progression between primary and secondary. On the other hand, only about 18 per cent of the younger age cohorts finished upper secondary school, so that the drop-out rate at this level is very high (*VICDS* 1994).

The levels of educational attainment are lower in rural areas and vary with household wealth and income. Also regional differences occur, with levels being lower in the Northern and Central Highlands and in the Mekong Delta. Related to the regional pattern is the lower level of attainment for ethnic minority groups (Nguyen Thi Canh 1996). Educational attainment does not vary by sex. The figures in Table 6.8 show that the gender gap in education has been closed in recent years (the exception is the ethnic minorities, where the female participation in education is lower).[7]

Table 6.8 Educational achievement by gender, Vietnam

	Finished primary education		*Finished upper secondary education*	
Age group	*Male*	*Female*	*Male*	*Female*
15–19	76.5	75.2	6.7	6.4
20–24	80.5	80.2	16.8	19.2
25–29	83.7	78.6	20.5	16.0
30–34	84.7	77.2	16.9	14.8

Source: *VICDS* (1994).

Enrolment numbers showed a period of decline and stagnation that started around 1988 and affected all levels and types of education (see also Chapter 2 in this volume). Primary enrolments started growing again fairly soon, but the stagnation lasted longer for other levels of education and still continues in technical education. The most likely reason is that the government introduced school fees and other contributions to be paid by parents. Although no school fees were introduced for primary school, direct and indirect cost for parents also increased at this level. The trend of declining enrolments in technical education is worrying for a country in the process of industrialization.

The VLSS (1994: 73) gives as private educational expenditure per student per year in VND for 1992/93:

Primary	73 000
Lower secondary	175 000
Upper secondary	355 000
Post-secondary	688 000

These figures can be compared with the estimates of total annual consumption expenditure per capita, as given in Table 6.7, to show that for a household with children educational expenditure will take up a considerable part of total expenditure. In the years 1986–88 state expenditure on education (as a percentage of GDP) stagnated, but in 1989 it started to increase again and in subsequent years increased sharply. Within educational expenditures there has been a shift: the share devoted to pre-primary and primary education increased from 34 per cent in 1994 to 43 per cent in 1998. This helped to shift the burden of the cost of education. The PER (2000) estimates that in 1998, 61 per cent of the cost of primary education was covered by the public subsidy and 39 per cent was covered by the parents (in 1993 these percentages were 45 and 55 per cent respectively). At lower secondary level the state contributed 42 per cent of total costs (34 per cent in 1993), at upper secondary level 33 per cent (40 per cent in 1993) and at post-secondary level 46 per cent (71 per cent in 1993). There has thus been a clear trend towards the state subsidy taking care of a larger share of the costs at the lower levels of education and a smaller share at the higher levels. This trend is clearly to the benefit of the poor, who participate in the lower levels of education and hardly at all at the higher levels. Of course, even though the state subsidy has increased, there remains a significant cost burden that has to be carried by the parents.

Table 6.9 Net enrolment rates by income quintile, 1997–98, Vietnam

	Poorest	*II*	*III*	*IV*	*Richest*
Primary	84.8	94.5	94.8	96.3	96.8
Lower secondary	35.1	53.7	65.0	70.9	90.8
Upper secondary	5.2	13.2	21.7	36.3	64.2
Post-secondary	0.5	0.8	3.4	7.9	28.1

Source: VLSS (2000), p. 51.

It is not surprising that the increased private cost of education has led to a stagnation in the growth of student numbers. But the stagnation was only temporary, in the early 1990s enrolments started to grow again. The fact that the substantially higher private cost of education did not reduce participation is due to the increase in income that made it possible for parents to shoulder the cost of education, but it also reflects the high value and priority given to education. Education probably now requires a much higher share of household expenditure than in the past. The higher cost of education will make it more difficult for the poor to participate. Table 6.9 gives the enrolment ratios by income quintile. At all levels of education, the poor have a lower participation rate. In fact, the poor hardly participate in education after lower secondary schools. Still, between 1992/93 and 1997/98 there has been a significant increase in participation by the poor. In 1992/93 the net enrolment rates of the lowest income quintile were only 68 per cent for primary level, 19 per cent for lower secondary and 2 per cent for upper secondary.

Despite the higher public and private expenditure on education, the relative salaries of teachers have stayed behind the general increases in income. The average income of state employees working in education increased from VND 64 200 per month in 1991 to 309 600 in 1995 (or 146 660 in 1991 prices) (IMF 1996). This seems to be a considerable improvement, but the 1995 salary is still low and inadequate to maintain a family. Teachers will receive some additional income from school fees, but will still feel the need to engage in out-of-school activities to supplement income. These secondary jobs will reduce the attention and time they can devote to the school. Good students can no longer be attracted to teacher training and good and experienced teachers leave the profession in large numbers to search for better-paying jobs (Fforde and de Vylder 1996). As a result the quality of education suffers considerably.

Educational expenditures are concentrated on post-primary education. The share of educational expenditure in GDP is not high, but comparable to other Asian countries at Vietnam's level of development. Within educational expenditures there has been a shift: the share devoted to pre-primary and primary education increased from 34 per cent in 1994 to 43 per cent in 1998. This distribution gives an in-built anti-poor bias in public educational subsidies. The levels of education on which most state funds are spent are not much attended by the poor (see also World Bank 1995b: 89).

6.2.4.2 Health services

Health centres are found in virtually all communes to provide first-line health services. But their functioning has suffered from the dismantling of the rural cooperatives that used to finance them. Many centres have closed down and the effectiveness of those that remain is reduced as there is no money for replacement of equipment and medical supplies.

As in education, in 1989 user fees were introduced into health services and utilization rates declined. The number of consultations of public health services declined from 2.10 per 1000 persons in 1987 to 0.93 in 1993. Also the number of inpatients declined (World Bank 1995b: 205). Three reasons are given for this decline: first, the increased cost after the introduction of fees; second, the declining quality of service as public subsidies were reduced; and third, the growing availability of private health services.

By 1993 about two-thirds of all outpatient consultations were done by private doctors and virtually all medicine was purchased in private shops. More than 80 per cent of all health expenditures were privately financed.[8] The government has created a health insurance scheme that by 1996 covered about 7 million people, mainly public sector employees, retirees and school children. The government seeks to enlarge the coverage of the scheme, but its present financial basis seems weak (WHO 1996).

Despite the privatization and the increased cost, the level of medical care remains relatively high in Vietnam. According to *VICDS* (1994):

- 79 per cent of urban and 53 per cent of rural women enjoy some form of pre-natal care;
- 90 per cent of urban and 38 of rural births take place in a health facility;

- 87 per cent of urban and 72 per cent of rural children receive some form of immunization;
- 57 per cent of all women ever used (and 44 per cent currently use) modern methods of contraception.

But the increased cost of health services does make it more difficult for the poor to participate. The VLSS 1992/93 reported that 14.5 per cent of persons in the poorest income quintile and 27.2 per cent in the highest quintile consulted medical services for illness in the last month before the survey. Per capita health expenditure varies from VND 43 670 for the lowest income quintile to 197 030 for the richest quintile. The utilization rate of health services (public and private, including hospitals, doctors, paramedics, but excluding self-medication) increases from 0.79 contacts per person per year for the poorest income group to 1.52 per person for the highest income quintile (World Bank 1995b: 205).

Government expenditure on health as a percentage of GDP declined up to 1988 and then recovered. After 1990 the ratio remained stable. The share of total spending going to basic health services has increased from 32 per cent in 1991 to 40 per cent in 1997 (UN and MOLISA 1999). It seems that, since the economic reforms, total expenditure of education and health have substantially increased and that a major share of these expenditure are now borne by the users. They can afford to pay more as their incomes have risen. It is estimated that of total expenditure on health, about 20 per cent is made by the government and 80 per cent consists of private contributions. The high share of private contributions makes it difficult for the poor to participate; the lower income quintiles are underrepresented in the use of all types of health facilities and programmes.

Government expenditure on social security is rather large at about 13 per cent of total government spending, or between 3 and 3.5 per cent of GDP. Virtually all of this is used to pay pensions to retired civil servants and military personnel. The amounts that remain for programmes targeted at the poor are very small (World Bank 1995b). There are local programmes for employment generation and poverty alleviation, but the amounts involved are small, much too small to have a significant impact on the big problem.

6.3 Reforms and welfare: conclusions

Drèze and Sen (1995) argue that 'One way of seeing development is in terms of real freedoms that citizens enjoy to pursue the objectives they

Table 6.10 Results of survey on evaluation of change in living standards since 1990, Vietnam

	Total	*Urban*	*Rural*
Better	51.8	47.3	52.7
Worse	17.5	19.9	17.0
The same	30.7	32.8	30.3

Source: MOLISA (1994), p. 97.

have reason to value, and in this sense the expansion of human capability can be, broadly, seen as the central feature of the process of development' (Drèze and Sen 1995: 10). Growth of income will be instrumental in increasing capabilities and options open to people. Improved health and education may also expand opportunities, apart from being valuable in themselves. And, significantly in the case of Vietnam, removal of excessive government controls will increase the range of choice people have. From this perspective it is undeniable that the economic transition in Vietnam has fostered development. When the VLSS asked in its community questionnaire whether the quality of life of the commune had increased in the iast five years, 114 out of 120 communes answered yes (World Bank 1995b: 9). In a 1993 survey of the General Statistical Office, respondents were asked to evaluate the change in their living standards since 1990. The answers are shown in Table 6.10.

In answer to a similar question in the VLSS 1997/98, 95 per cent of communes answered that living standards had improved over the last five years and only 4 per cent observed declining standards. There was little variation between the regions in the answer to this question. When asked to which factors they attributed the improvement of living standards, 90 per cent of the communes mentioned the changes in agricultural policy, 55 per cent the expansion of non-agricultural production and 42 per cent the ability to get more education. Only 8 per cent of the communes mentioned the ability to use health services (VLSS 2000, 409–10).

The transition brings greater individual economic opportunity and freedom, but also greater risks and the collective structures that existed to cover personal risk have largely disappeared. Apart from the greater uncertainty, there are also concerns about growing individualism and about the increased occurrence of social vices like corruption, which is widespread, and drunkenness, drug abuse and prostitution.

Probably not many people were hurt by the reforms and the subsequent growth. But many of the poor may have been so isolated that the growth spurt has passed them by.

Notes

1. I am grateful to Tran Kim Dung and Butch Montes for comments that helped to improve this chapter.
2. In 1988, 73 per cent of Vietnam's imports came from Eastern Europe and the Soviet Union, and 54 per cent of exports went there. Starting in 1989 both the absolute value of these imports and exports and their share in Vietnam's total trade fell rapidly. By 1994 only 6 per cent of imports and 3 per cent of exports were with the former CMEA countries.
3. There was further pressure on the labour market due to the repatriation of refugees and because the outflow of contract labour to the Former Soviet Union and Eastern Europe came to an end.
4. Dao The Tuan (1995: 143) gives estimates of Gini coefficients based on GSO surveys of 26.3 for 1989 and 29.8 for 1992. The VLSS gives a Gini coefficient of 33.0 for 1993. Such a sharp increase between 1992 and 1993 seems unlikely, and the two surveys may thus not be fully comparable.
5. Vietnam ranks 120 out of 174 countries on the UN's Human Development Index for 1995, considerably higher than it ranks in terms of its per capita income.
6. See Lu Aiguo (1996) for a similar account for pre-reform China.
7. UNDP (1995) suggests that the gender gap is re-emerging, with girls dropping out more in primary and lower secondary education. This does not agree with the statistics of the GSO on pupils dropping out of school in a sample of cities and provinces. According to these data, in the school year 1993/94, the proportion of pupils leaving school were:

	Total	*Male*	*Female*
Primary	1.9	2.0	1.7
Lower secondary	4.1	4.3	3.9
Upper secondary	1.9	2.4	1.3

   At the primary level the main reason for leaving is economic (50 per cent of the cases). Economic reasons explain 35 per cent of cases for lower secondary and 26 per cent for upper secondary. Economic reasons are more dominant in explaining girls leaving school than boys (GSO 1996).

8. In 1993 the state budget on health services amounted to VND 1.4 billion. According to the VLSS, household expenditure on health totalled VND 7.5 billion. Of this amount about 3 billion was spent on fees and drugs related to the use of public health services and the rest was spent on private providers and on self-medication.

References

Center for Population and Human Resources Studies (1995), *Analysis, Evaluation of the Relation between Population, Migration, Human Resources and Employment*, Report Hanoi (January).

Dao The Tuan (1995), 'The Peasant Household Economy and Social Change', in B. J. T. Kerkvliet and D. J. Porter (eds), *Vietnam's Rural Transformation*, Boulder, CO: Westview Press.

Drèze, J. and A. Sen (1995), *India, Economic Development and Social Opportunity*, Oxford: Clarendon Press.

Fforde, A. and S. de Vylder (1996), *From Plan to Market; The Economic Transition in Vietnam*, Boulder, CO: Westview Press.

General Statistical Office (GSO) (1996a), *Statistical Yearbook 1995*, Hanoi, Statistical Publishing House.

General Statistical Office (GSO) (1996b), *Impetus and present situation of Vietnam society and economy after ten years of Doi Moi*, Hanoi: Statistical Publishing House.

General Statistical Office (GSO) (2000), *Statistical Yearbook 1999*, Hanoi: Statistical Publishing House, Hanoi.

International Monetary Fund (IMF) (1996), *Vietnam, Recent Economic Developments*, IMF Staff Country Report (December), Washington, DC: IMF.

International Monetary Fund (IMF) (2000), *Vietnam, Statistical Appendix and Background Notes*, IMF Staff Country Report (August),Washington, DC: IMF.

Kerkvliet, B. J. T. and D. J. Porter (eds) (1995), *Vietnam's Rural Transformation*, Boulder, CO: Westview Press.

Le Manh Hung (ed.) (1996), *Kinh Te Xa Hoi Viet Nam, Truc Trang, Xu The va Giai Phap*, Hanoi: NXB Thong Ke.

Lu Aiguo (1996), 'Welfare Changes in China during the Economic Reforms', *Research for Action* No. 26, Helsinki: UNU/WIDER.

McCarty, A., M. Paunlagui and Vu Quoc Huy (1992), *Vietnam Data Bank 1976–1991*, National Centre for Development Studies, Research School of Pacific Studies, Australian National University, Canberra.

Ministry of Labour, Invalids and Social Affairs (MOLISA) (1994), *Statistical Yearbook 1993*, Hanoi.

Nguyen Thi Canh (1996), 'Report on the Education Sector in Viet Nam', paper for final meeting on Social Sector Issues in Asian Transition Economies, Asian Development Bank, Manila.

Pham Huy Dong (1996), 'Study on Health and Health Systems in Vietnamese Transitional Economies', paper for final meeting on Social Sector Issues in Asian Transition Economies, Asian Development Bank, Manila.

Public Expenditure Review (PER) (2000) *Joint Report of the Government of Vietnam-Donor Working Group on Public Expenditure Review*, Hanoi, June.

Ronnås, P. (1992), *Employment Generation through Private Entrepreneurship in Vietnam*, Geneva: ILO (ARTEP).

United Nations and Ministry of Labour, War Invalids and Social Affairs (MOLISA) (1999), *Basic Social Services in Vietnam, an Analysis of State and ODA Expenditures*, Hanoi (December).

United Nations Development Programme (UNDP) (1995), *Viet Nam through the Lens of Gender*, Hanoi: UNDP.

Vietnam Intercensal Demographic Survey 1994 (VICDS), Birth Spacing and Child Mortality in Viet Nam, Hanoi: Statistical Publishing House.

Vietnam Intercensal Demographic Survey 1994, Contraceptive Knowledge and Practice, Patterns and Differentials, Hanoi: Statistical Publishing House.

Vietnam Intercensal Demographic Survey 1994, Education in Vietnam, Trends and Differentials, Statistical Publishing House, Hanoi.

Vietnam Intercensal Demographic Survey 1994, Infant Feeding Practices in Viet Nam, Statistical Publishing House, Hanoi.

Vietnam Intercensal Demographic Survey 1994, Major Findings (VICDS) (1996), Statistical Publishing House, Hanoi.

Vietnam Intercensal Demographic Survey 1994, Major Findings, Statistical Publishing House, Hanoi.

Vietnam Living Standards Survey 1992/3 (VLSS) (1994), Hanoi: State Planning Committee and General Statistical Office.

Vietnam Living Standards Survey 1997/8 (VLSS) (2000), Hanoi: General Statistical Office, Statistical Publishing House.

Vo Dai Luc (1994), *Vietnam's Industrial Development Policy in the Course of Renovation*, Hanoi: Social Science Publishing House.

Vo-Tong Xuan (1995), 'Rice Production, Agricultural Research, and the Environment', in B. J. T. Kerkvliet and D. J. Porter (eds), *Vietnam's Rural Transformation*, Boulder, CO: Westview Press.

World Bank (1995a), *Viet Nam Financial Sector Review, an Agenda for Financial Sector Development*, Washington, DC: World Bank.

World Bank (1995b), *Viet Nam, Poverty Assessment and Strategy*, Washington, DC: World Bank.

World Bank (2000), *World Development Report 2000/1, Attacking Poverty*, Oxford: Oxford University Press.

World Health Organization (WHO) (1996), *The Development of National Health Insurance in Viet Nam*, Technical Paper No. 23, Geneva: WHO.

7
Poverty and Economic Transition in Kazakhstan

*Mamta Murthi, Menno Pradhan and Kinnon Scott**

7.1 Introduction

Kazakhstan is located at the heart of Asia, bordered on the north and west by Russia, on the east by China, and on the south by Turkmenistan, Uzbekistan and the Kyrgyz Republic. Per capita GDP in 1999 was US$1250. It is a vast country of over 2.7 million square kilometres with a population of around 16.5 million. Population density is among the lowest in the world and has declined further since independence, largely as a result of emigration. Kazakhs are the largest ethnic group (48 per cent) with Russians forming a large minority (34 per cent). The country is divided into 14 provinces (*oblasts*). The national capital until 1998 was Almaty, its largest city, located in the southeast of the country. Its new capital, Astana, lies to the north. The north of the country is its major grain bowl as well as its industrial heartland. The south is mostly agricultural, with some light industry. The major mineral resource of the country, oil, is located in the west.

Poverty, in the sense of low or inadequate income, is not a new phenomenon in Kazakhstan.[1] However, during the Soviet period, the severity of poverty was limited by state action. Low administered prices for a range of key goods and services (food, rent, utilities) kept the cost of living strictly under control. Guaranteed employment, and a relatively generous system of pensions, family allowances, sick pay and maternity benefits insulated households from major income shocks. Subsidies to child care helped maintain a fairly high level of labour force participation among women. Access to education and healthcare was universal. This system of social provision underlies the strong achievements in the field of human development that is characteristic of the countries of the Former Soviet Union (FSU). At independence, most human development indicators were higher in Kazakhstan than in countries with comparable levels of income, an achievement that largely persists despite recent difficulties (see UNDP 1995, 1996).

Since independence, poverty has been aggravated by economic decline. As in other transition economies, economic activity has contracted significantly since independence. Although macroeconomic performance has improved recently, output remains well below 1990 levels. The fall in output has resulted in a substantial decline in real wages and incomes, while hyperinflation during the early years of the transition has virtually destroyed household savings. The weakened fiscal position of the state has limited its ability to mitigate the impact of these changes on household welfare, and has reduced the quality and quantity of public services.

This chapter investigates the effects of the economic transition on poverty and provides an assessment of the effectiveness of the social safety net. It is based on the 1996 Kazakhstan Living Standards Survey (KLSS), the only nationally representative household survey available for the 1990s. Section 7.2 contains an overview of the economic changes since independence from the FSU up until the period of the survey. Section 7.3 contains a profile of the poor based on the KLSS, and sections 7.4 and 7.5 discuss two important aspects of any poverty alleviation strategy for Kazakhstan: growth and social assistance. Section 7.6 concludes.

7.2 Economic transition

The most important factor affecting living standards in Kazakhstan in the period under consideration is the unprecedented fall in output. After declining continuously for five years, GDP expanded modestly in 1996 and 1997, but remained at a little above 60 per cent of pre-independence levels (see Table 7.1). The contraction in output in Kazakhstan was related to the twin challenges of adjusting to the dissolution of the FSU while at the same time managing the transformation of a planned to a market economy. Kazakhstan was part of a Union-wide division of labour in which the Central Asian Republics specialized in production of food and raw materials. The Russian hinterland was (and still remains) the major source of inputs and the main market for output. Transport and other infrastructure was designed with a view to meeting these needs, not those of the local economy.[2] Social spending was high, maintained in part by transfers from Moscow. Central budgetary support to Kazakhstan was estimated to be of the order of

Table 7.1 Selected macroeconomic indicators in Kazakhstan since independence

	1991	*1992*	*1993*	*1994*	*1995*	*1996*	*1997*
Real growth in GDP (%)	–9.8	–2.9	–10.4	–17.8	–8.9	1.1	2.1
Index of real GDP (1990 = 100)	90.2	87.6	78.4	64.5	58.7	59.3	60.5
Index of real consumption (1993 = 100)			100	78.2	76.5	80.3	n.a.
Inflation (end-of-year change in CPI)	90	1 381	1 662	1 880	60	29	11
Fiscal deficit (% GDP)	7.9	7.3	1.3	7.2	2.5	3.1	3.8
Nominal rate of exchange (annual average tenge/US$)			2	36	61	68	76

Source: National Statistical Agency (1997a, 1997b).

12 per cent of GDP in the early 1990s (World Bank 1994). These arrangements were seriously disrupted by the dissolution of the FSU.

Massive inflation, associated with uncontrolled deficit financing and loosely directed credit, was an additional problem in the early years. After the introduction of a new currency (the tenge) and some initial hiccups, the budget deficit was gradually reined in and money supply growth brought under control. In response, inflation dropped to 11.5 per cent in 1997 after peaking at 1880 per cent in 1994.

The reduction in the budget deficit came at a cost. Wage and pension arrears mounted steadily from around 4 per cent of GDP at the end of 1995 to 6 per cent at the end of 1996 despite progress in clearing the bulk of central government wage obligations during the year. More generally, there was a massive build-up of payment arrears in the economy, with arrears and barter arrangements substituting to a large extent for money and credit. Delays in the payment of wages and pensions became a significant source of public dissatisfaction with the economic transition. Despite the resumption of growth in 1996, public opinion remained firmly pessimistic, perhaps because the recovery was relatively modest (see International Foundation for Election Systems 1996).[3]

The rise of open unemployment in Kazakhstan (as measured by the number of registered unemployed) was small compared to the scale of output decline. Registered unemployment rose from 0.3 per cent in 1992 to 3.8 per cent in 1997. Much of the adjustment in the market for labour took place on the price side. According to official estimates, real wages fell by more than 50 per cent during 1991–96.[4] The slow emergence of open unemployment in Kazakhstan may be attributed to three factors: the widespread use by employers of 'administrative' leave and reduced hours (in place of outright dismissal of workers), the growth of informal sector activity (kitchen-gardening, petty commerce), and movements out of the labour force (often through early retirement).

Another feature of the transition in Kazakhstan was the growing incapacity of the government to mobilize resources. Government revenues fell from 39 per cent of GDP in 1992 to 24 per cent in 1996 (see Table 7.2). Combined with the fall in GDP, this resulted in a situation in which public expenditures fell substantially in real terms.

The decline in public expenditure fell disproportionately on public investment, social protection and public services (see World Bank 1996). The social safety net wore thin. Public expenditure on social protection (pensions, unemployment benefits, family allowances, sick

Table 7.2 Fiscal adjustment in Kazakhstan since independence

	1991	*1992*	*1993*	*1994*	*1995*	*1996*	*1997*
Government revenues and grants (% GDP)		38.9	37.2	23.8	23.6	24.0	n.a.
Social protection expenditures (% of GDP)		11.2	8.3	4.6	6.6	6.6	7.9
Index of real per capita expenditure on healthcare (1992 = 100)	168	100	94	59	72	66	80
Index of real per capita expenditure on education (1992 = 100)	177	100	100	51	63	49	62

Sources: World Bank (1996); World Bank staff estimates.

pay, maternity benefits and social assistance) fell from 11.2 per cent of GDP in 1992 to 6.6 per cent in 1996 before rising to 7.9 per cent in 1997 as the government cleared pension arrears of the order of 1.5 per cent of GDP during the year. Expenditure on public services suffered considerably. As a result, public outlays in education and healthcare during 1997 were running at about one-third to one-half of 1991 levels in real per capita terms (see Table 7.2). Although private out-of-pocket spending on education and healthcare undoubtedly expanded, the nature of these expenditures raises questions of access and equity.

7.3 Poverty

The huge changes since independence affected not just the general standard of living in Kazakhstan, but created new groups of people vulnerable to poverty. This section investigates which groups suffered most from the prevailing economic circumstances and examines the main correlates of poverty. While drawing on other material, it relies largely on the nationally representative, multi-purpose Kazakhstan Living Standards Survey, conducted by the National Statistical Agency in July 1996.

In analysing poverty, the chapter focuses on monetary indicators of household welfare – in particular, per capita consumption. Poverty is a multidimensional phenomenon which encompasses non-monetary dimensions such as access to public services. The declining quality of public services and the emergence of differential access are issues of tremendous public concern in Kazakhstan.[5] By focusing on consumption, this chapter does not mean to suggest that non-monetary aspects are unimportant. However, non-monetary aspects of poverty often reinforce monetary inequities. For example, the rich are in a better position than the poor to insulate themselves against the effects of deteriorating public services.

Per capita consumption is calculated as total household consumption divided by the number of household members. Consumption includes both food (including purchases, home-produced food, as well as food received as a gift or as payment in kind for services rendered) and non-food goods (including utilities, transport, clothing, cleaning, leisure, healthcare and education). An imputed value for the services of durables was also included. However, it was not possible to impute rental values for owner-occupied dwellings. Total consumption was adjusted to take account of regional differences in prices.[6] Poverty was defined as having per capita consumption below the government's 'subsistence minimum' line (*prozhitochnyi minimum*). The 'subsistence minimum' is similar in concept to an absolute poverty line. At the time of the survey, it was equal to around US$40 (2861 tenge) per person per month at market rates of exchange, and around US$70 at purchasing power parity.

According to the KLSS, 34.6 per cent of the population of Kazakhstan was living in poverty in July 1996. The poverty gap was 11.4 per cent and P_2 (the poverty severity index) was 5.2 per cent. Thus average consumption of the poor was nearly one-third below the poverty line.[7] In comparison, in the Kyrgyz Republic the average consumption shortfall among the poor was 49.1 per cent in 1993 (see World Bank 1995a). On these measures, poverty in Kazakhstan is not as deep as that observed in the Kyrgyz Republic.

The KLSS suggests that poverty is higher in rural than in urban areas, although the differences are relatively small (see Table 7.3).[8] While poverty rates between urban and rural areas may not be that different, information on demographic and health indicators do suggest a picture of greater rural deprivation. Rural areas in Kazakhstan show higher infant and child mortality relative to urban areas. The incidence of stunting (low height for age), wasting (low weight for height), and anaemia in children is also higher in rural areas (see National Institute of Nutrition et al. 1996). Housing is of poorer quality and access to public services is lower.[9]

While urban poverty is lower than rural poverty, one group of urban dwellers – residents of so-called one-company towns – are generally

Table 7.3 Urban versus rural poverty in Kazakhstan*

	Headcount ratio, H	*Poverty gap, PG*	P_2
Urban	30.0	8.9	3.8
Rural	39.0	13.7	6.6
Total	34.6	11.4	5.2

*The headcount ratio, *H*, is the proportion of individuals below the poverty line. The poverty gap, *PG*, is a measure of the depth of poverty. It measures average consumption shortfall in the population (the non-poor have zero shortfall) as a proportion of the poverty line. P_2 is a measure of the severity of poverty. It is calculated in same way as the *PG* but gives more weight to poorer households. For further details, see Ravallion (1994).

Source: KLSS (1996).

believed to be poorer than most (see, for example, UNDP 1995). Once, one-company towns were dependent on one or a few enterprises, during Soviet times. These have since closed or have shut down for all practical purposes. There are 57 such towns in Kazakhstan, mostly in the north of the country. Local unemployment rates are extremely high, and public services (formerly financed by the enterprises) vastly underfunded.[10] Public utilities face particular problems due to the lack of effective demand. As the subsample of households from one-company towns in the KLSS is too small to be representative, this chapter was not able to examine the poverty rates in these towns separately.

Perhaps more striking are differences in regional poverty rates (see Table 7.4). More than two out of three people live in poverty in the south compared to a national average of around one in three. Poverty is also significantly deeper in the south than elsewhere. These findings reflect the lower resource endowment of the region, limited employment opportunities, and the disproportionate impact of fiscal contraction (see World Bank 1997). In contrast to the south, one out of 11 people live in poverty in the north. Not only is poverty more limited in the north; it is less deep and far less severe than in other parts of the country. Lower poverty in the north may be related to greater opportunities for cross-border trade with Russia in this region.[11]

Poverty in Kazakhstan is positively associated with household size (see Table 7.5). Households in the bottom quintile of the consumption

Table 7.4 Regional dimensions of poverty in Kazakhstan

*Region**	*Headcount ratio, H*	*Poverty gap, PG*	P_2
North	9.2	1.9	0.7
Centre	26.4	9.0	4.4
East	31.3	9.0	3.6
West	37.8	10.8	4.2
South	69.2	26.4	13.0
Total	34.6	11.4	5.2

*North: Kostanai, Kokshetau, Pavlodar, and North Kazakhstan *oblasts*; Centre: Zhezkazgan, Karaganda, Akmola and Torgai *oblasts*; West: Manghystau, Atyrau, Aktyubinsk, West Kazakhstan; East: Semi Palatinsk, East Kazakhstan, Taldykorgan and Almaty *oblasts* and Almaty city; South: Kzyl-Orda, South Kazakhstan and Zhambyl *oblasts*. In April 1997, the merger of oblasts reduced the total number from 19 to 14.

Source: Authors' calculations.

Table 7.5 Household composition and poverty in Kazakhstan

	Consumption quintile					
	Bottom	*Second*	*Third*	*Fourth*	*Top*	*Total*
Average household size	4.5	4.1	3.5	3.4	2.9	3.6
Average no. of children	1.8	1.4	1.1	0.9	0.8	1.1
Average no. of elderly	0.4	0.4	0.3	0.4	0.3	0.3
Dependency ratio*	1.1	1.0	0.9	0.9	0.8	0.9

*Dependency ratio is the sum of all persons below 16 years or above 59 years divided by those of prime age (16–59 years).

Source: KLSS (1996).

distribution during 1996 had an average of 4.5 members while those in the top-most quintile had slightly fewer than 3 members. Most of the difference is driven by higher average number of children in poor households. In the bottom quintile, households had, on average, one additional child compared to households in the top quintile. This comparison takes no account of economies of scale in consumption.[12] However, the finding that large households are at greater risk of poverty stands up to alternative assumptions regarding scale economies (see World Bank 1998).

Focusing on particular family groups who may be vulnerable to poverty due to life-cycle factors, it can be seen that single elderly people or elderly couples face lower than average risks of being in the bottom quintile (see Table 7.6). Moreover, single-parent households are less susceptible to low levels of consumption than is commonly believed, although families with young children are disproportionately represented

Table 7.6 Poverty incidence among selected demographic groups in Kazakhstan (% of households in quintile and in total)

	Consumption quintile					
% of households which are:	*Bottom*	*Second*	*Third*	*Fourth*	*Top*	*Total*
One person, elderly*	3.1	4.7	5.9	5.4	4.8	4.9
Only elderly*	6.0	10.0	9.4	11.8	7.7	9.0
One adult with dependent children	3.8	4.7	5.4	5.0	5.2	4.9
With children <6 years	40.1	28.7	25.5	20.0	15.3	24.8

*An elderly person is anyone 60 years and over.

Source: KLSS (1996).

in the lower quintiles. Allowing for greater economies of scale in consumption, however, overturns these conclusions about elderly and single-parent households (see World Bank 1998). Such households tend to be small and thus appear poorer as we allow for a greater scale economies. We therefore need to be cautious when interpreting findings for these households based on per capita consumption.

Although households with young children are more likely to be poor, the extent of malnourishment among young children appears to be limited. According to the Demographic and Health Survey conducted in 1995, 3 per cent of all children under three years were wasted. Moderate or severe stunting was found in 16 per cent of children in the same age group (National Institute of Nutrition et al. 1996). The prevalence of both wasting and stunting in children in Kazakhstan is not higher than what might be expected in a normally nourished population. Micro-studies focused on poorer regions of the country suggest that even the less well-off populations have avoided serious malnutrition (see Ismail and Hill in Falkingham et al. 1997).[13]

Unemployment is seen to be strongly associated with poverty. As shown in Table 7.7, individuals in the higher quintiles are more likely to be economically active (working or seeking work) than those in lower quintiles. But what truly separates the poorer individuals from the others is the level of unemployment. In 1996, the poorest individuals suffered an unemployment rate of 9.4 per cent while their counterparts in the top quintile of the population had an unemployment rate of only 2.6 per cent.[14]

The importance of employment for living standards is best illustrated by looking at the number of household members being supported by each employed person. In the top quintile, each employed person supported 1.4 other household members, including children and

Table 7.7 Labour force status and poverty in Kazakhstan (ILO definitions)

	Consumption quintile					
	Bottom	*Second*	*Third*	*Fourth*	*Top*	*Total*
Labour force participation rate	51.2	54.8	60.9	66.0	68.6	60.8
Unemployment rate	9.4	8.2	6.0	6.0	2.6	6.0
Dependency on employment*	2.5	2.3	1.7	1.7	1.4	1.9

*Dependency on employment is the number of household members being supported by each employed person.

Source: KLSS (1996).

unemployed or inactive adults. In the bottom quintile, each employed person supported 2.5 persons. Even if the average worker in the poorest households earned the same amount as his or her counterpart in the top quintile, consumption per capita would be significantly lower due to the greater dependency on that income.

While unemployment is strongly associated with poverty, the limited rise in open unemployment has meant that as a proportion of all working-age individuals the number of unemployed is relatively small. In 1996, in the bottom quintile, 46.3 per cent of working-age individuals were employed, 4.8 per cent were unemployed and 48.8 per cent were inactive (neither employed nor actively seeking work). In the bottom two quintiles, the figures for employed, unemployed and inactive were 48.3 per cent, 4.7 per cent and 47.0 per cent respectively. Thus the bulk of the poor were 'working poor', that is, they were at work but were poor either because they had too many dependents to support adequately, worked in low-wage occupations, were subject to involuntary leave without pay or reduced hours, were paid irregularly, or some combination of these factors. Another large proportion of the poor were inactive, including women who stayed at home and those individuals who were too discouraged to look for work.

In accordance with international experience, education and poverty are inversely correlated in Kazakhstan. Individuals in the lowest quintile are seen to have less schooling on average than those in the topmost quintile, though the difference (1.2 years) is relatively small (see Table 7.8). A stronger correlation appears to exist between poverty and level of schooling (basic or additional). Individuals in the top quintile are much more likely to have additional schooling (beyond grade 9). University degrees are positively correlated with consumption, while vocational and technical degrees are *negatively* correlated with consumption. The latter is perhaps a reflection of the collapse in the industrial employment in the post-1991 period, and the greater versatility of university education in the changed circumstances.

The gender of the household head is not seen to be correlated with poverty. The proportion of households headed by women was around 30 per cent in the bottom two quintiles, compared to 40 per cent in the population as a whole. Although female-headed households faced no greater risk of poverty, this is not to suggest that there are no gender inequalities in Kazakhstan. Women's work was traditionally associated with low pay in the FSU, as in other parts of the world. Much of this difference has persisted: in Kazakhstan in 1996, official

Table 7.8 Education and poverty in Kazakhstan

	Consumption quintile		
	Bottom	*Second*	*Top*
Years of schooling	10.6	11.2	11.8
% with more than basic schooling*	55	68	79
Degree if more than basic schooling (%):			
Vocational	21	21	17
Technical, no secondary	9	8	7
Technical with secondary	18	16	15
Technical college	36	29	37
University	16	25	24
Postgraduate	0.4	0.0	0.4

*Basic schooling is grades 1–9.

Source: KLSS (1996).

wages in the female-dominated sectors (education, healthcare) were about half the official average wage. Women appear to face a marginally greater risk of unemployment than men, and possibly higher rates of long-term unemployment. However, inequality in access to education and healthcare are not significant (see UNDP 1995, 1996, 1997; Asian Development Bank 1997).

One group who may very well be poor but about whom relatively little can be said are migrants and refugees. The transition has been accompanied by a sharp increase in migration in Kazakhstan. In addition to substantial emigration, Kazakhstan has received immigrants, including ethnic Kazakhs from other CIS countries and Mongolia, and refugees escaping conflict in other parts of the CIS, and Afghanistan.[15] In thinking about the living standards of the two groups, it is important to distinguish between ethnic Kazakh immigrants, who are entitled to state assistance, and refugees, who are typically not covered by the social welfare system. Within each group there are likely to be those who are better placed to cope with changed circumstances. Further research is needed to establish poverty rates and living conditions among these groups.

The composition of consumption and income suggests different ways in which households have responded to changed economic circumstances. The ability to grow one's own food is a vital coping strategy. This is reflected in the share of own-production in food consumption (see Table 7.9). The poor in Kazakhstan are those who are

Table 7.9 Structure of consumption and poverty in Kazakhstan

	Consumption quintile					
Source of expenditure	*Bottom*	*Second*	*Third*	*Fourth*	*Top*	*Total*
Total food	73.5	74.2	72.7	73.7	77.9	74.3
Food purchased	51.3	47.5	44.9	35.3	24.8	40.7
Food self-produced	19.0	23.8	23.3	30.7	40.5	27.4
Food eaten out	1.0	0.6	1.3	1.8	1.6	1.3
Food as gift	2.2	2.3	3.2	5.9	11.0	4.9
Utilities	8.5	6.9	7.0	5.5	4.2	6.4
Durables	2.5	2.5	2.8	3.2	2.6	2.7
Transport	2.2	2.8	3.0	2.8	2.7	2.7
Cleaning	3.4	3.0	2.7	2.4	1.9	2.7
Clothing	6.5	6.1	6.5	7.0	5.9	6.4
Leisure	2.8	3.2	3.9	4.0	3.7	3.5
Health (chronic)	0.7	1.1	0.9	0.9	0.6	0.8
Education 6–16	0.1	0.2	0.5	6.0	0.7	0.4
Total	100.0	100.0	100.0	100.0	100.0	100.0
Average per capita consumption (tenge)	1 524	2 610	3 684	5 245	9 562	4 545

Note: Owing to data limitations, total health and education expenditures are underestimated.

Source: KLSS (1996).

not able to meet a large proportion of their food consumption needs from self-production and need to rely on purchased food.

Other informal activities, such as holding a second job, offer alternative ways of making ends meet (see Table 7.10). Gifts and transfers between households are also an important source of cash income. The KLSS recorded private transfers between households, including assistance from immediate and extended family, other households, charities, cultural and religious organizations and NGOs. The data suggest that parents are the single most important source of private cash transfers in Kazakhstan, followed by other relatives, reflecting the importance of the extended family network as a source of informal social security. In terms of overall magnitude, private transfers are a smaller share of household income than pensions, *but are significantly larger than the sum of all other public transfers*. In fact, private assistance is nearly five times the size of all government transfers excluding pensions. This probably reflects the erosion in the value of benefits and the impact of arrears.

Table 7.10 Structure of cash incomes in Kazakhstan

	Consumption quintile					
	Bottom	*Second*	*Third*	*Fourth*	*Top*	*Total*
Primary wage	45	49	55	51	50	51
Pensions	16	21	14	13	9	13
Other public transfers*	6	4	4	3	3	3
Secondary/other occupation	6	4	6	4	4	5
Own business	8	3	7	8	8	7
Sale of food	2	1	1	1	3	2
Private cash transfers	14	13	9	14	19	15
Other	4	4	4	4	4	4
TOTAL	100	100	100	100	100	100
Average per capita cash income (tenge)	957	1 535	2 167	3 067	4 116	2 370
Average per capita income (including imputed income from own production)	1 371	2 412	3 229	5 156	9 473	4 743

*Includes all transfer payments excluding pensions.

Source: KLSS (1996)

Before concluding this section, it is worth mentioning one caveat. As the KLSS was conducted over one summer month when own production of food is likely to have been high, it probably overstates consumption and, consequently, underestimates poverty, especially in rural areas. The estimates presented in this section may therefore be thought of as a lower bound on poverty during 1996. It is also possible that the share of own-produced food in total food consumption, and its importance as a coping strategy, is overstated.

Turning briefly to inequality, we see that the Gini coefficient for consumption is 0.35. Consumption in Kazakhstan appears to be more equally distributed than in neighbouring countries. Contemporary estimates from Russia and the Kyrgyz Republic place the Gini coefficient in both countries at around 0.46 (see World Bank 1995a, 1995b).

The analysis presented above suggests that poverty has many dimensions. A poverty alleviation strategy for the country will therefore require a multifaceted approach based on growth, social safety nets and human capital investment. The first two components of a poverty alleviation strategy, growth and safety nets, are covered in the next two sections. Data limitations impede inclusion of an assessment of programmes investing in human capital. This latter aspect is important, and further work is needed.

7.4 Growth

Economic activity in Kazakhstan contracted by around 40 per cent during 1991–96, leading to a sharp fall in wages, and a rise in unemployment and underemployment. Over one-third of the population was living in poverty in 1996. Given the scale of output decline, and the level of poverty, it should be clear that broad-based growth that both raises wages and creates employment will be key to reducing poverty in Kazakhstan. Growth is critical not just for raising incomes but also for providing the resources for a fiscally sustainable safety net to help those who might be temporarily or chronically disadvantaged.

Although Kazakhstan is vulnerable to external shocks (particularly those emanating from Russia), the prospects for a sustained increase in output over the medium term are generally good, both because of a relatively stable policy environment, and because it is well endowed with natural resources.[16] As in other transition economies, the private sector is likely to provide the main impetus for growth. Continued macroeconomic stability and low inflation will be important for growth to occur. Further developments, such as improving the legal and regulatory framework for the private sector, improving the management of public resources and the process of enterprise restructuring, and improvements in the areas of health and education services, will also be critical. As with other oil-exporting countries, Kazakhstan will need to adjust to large inflows of foreign exchange and increased competition from imports. Over the medium term, attention will need to be focused on policies that raise the competitiveness of the non-oil sectors, particularly as these sectors are vital from the viewpoint of employment creation.

While growth is a necessary condition for the reduction of poverty in Kazakhstan, it is not a sufficient condition. First, growth will not necessarily result in net increases in employment, at least in the short run. The further restructuring needed in the non-service industries, notably in agriculture, but also mining, transportation and utilities, will involve significant net reductions in employment, given inherited levels of overstaffing and the limited adjustment of employment to falls in output.[17] Information from the KLSS on employment probabilities suggests that differences between those with university education and those with technical and vocational training have already emerged. Many of the semi-skilled, and those with inappropriate skills, may experience greater unemployment in the near future.

Second, growth is unlikely to be distributionally neutral. Wage and earnings differentials were suppressed under the former system, with skilled manual labour compensated relatively well compared to other professions.[18] With the growth of the private sector and the market economy, earnings differentials are likely to grow. In other words, wage growth cannot be expected to be distributed evenly across the population.

7.5 Social safety nets

Given the limitations of growth, a strong social safety net will be necessary to protect the population from the worst effects of the transition. The social safety net in Kazakhstan incorporates elements of both social assistance and social insurance (see Table 7.11).[19] Social assistance includes: (a) child allowances, of which the major programme is the means-tested child allowance; (b) means-tested housing allowances; and (c) other benefits in cash and kind. Social insurance includes: (a) pensions; (b) unemployment compensation; and (c) allowances related to events such as births and deaths and temporary incapacity to work, including sickness and maternity.[20] In 1996, spending on all social protection programmes in Kazakhstan was 6.6 per cent of GDP. Pensions were the most important programme, with 75 per cent of all spending on social protection going to pensions.[21] The second largest programme was the means-tested child allowance. The housing allowance scheme was small but is likely to have expanded substantially since then.

The social safety net circa 1996 reflects a series of important changes from the pre-independence system. The old social safety net was a comprehensive social security system that combined guaranteed employment with a generous system of pensions, sickness and maternity benefits and subsidies for food, fuel, transport and a range of consumer items. Normal pension ages were low by international standards and significant groups of the population were entitled to early retirement on full pensions. Social assistance relied on universal child allowances and a range of benefits targeted at specially identified vulnerable groups, including single pensioners, war veterans, victims of environmental disaster, nuclear testing and political and social repression.

Table 7.11 Social safety net expenditures in Kazakhstan as a percentage of GDP, 1992–97

	1992	*1993*	*1994*	*1995*	*1996*	*1997*
Total social safety net expenditure	11.2	8.3	4.6	6.6	6.6	7.9
of which:						
1. Pensions	8.2	4.1	3.8	4.3	5.0	7.1
2. Labour market programmes (including unemployment benefits)		0.1	0.1	0.2	0.2	0.2
3. Social insurance fund benefits	0.8	0.8	0.5	0.7	0.6	0.4
of which:						
Sickness	0.4	0.4	0.3	0.4	0.4	0.3
Maternity	0.1	0.1	0.1	0.1	0.1	0.1
4. Social assistance	1.4	0.6	0.6	0.7	0.8	0.3
of which:						
Means-tested child allowances	1.4	0.5	0.4	0.5	0.5	0.2
GDP (million tenge)	1 213 616*	29 413	423 484	1 019 722	1 425 000	1 742 000

*Million ruble.

Source: Ministry of Labour and Social Protection, Kazakhstan.

Due to the demands of the new economic structure, the government took a number of steps to make the social safety net both less generous and more targeted. The employment guarantee was abolished and programmes designed to assist the newly unemployed (training, unemployment benefits and job placement services) were introduced. Utility subsidies were reduced and a housing allowance scheme introduced to cushion the impact. The main child allowance scheme moved from being a universal entitlement to a means-tested programme in 1994. Finally, the age for retirement pension eligibility was increased.

The composition of social safety net expenditure, divided among pensions, other social insurance, and social assistance remained by and large unchanged from 1992 through 1996 (see Table 7.12). Within these three broad groups of programmes, however, there have been

Table 7.12 Composition of social safety net expenditures in Kazakhstan, selected years, 1992–96

	1992	*1993*	*1996*	*1997*
1. Pensions		100	100	
Old age		80	79	n.a
Disability		8	8	n.a.
Loss of breadwinner		7	8	n.a.
Social		2	2	n.a.
2. Labour market programmes	100	100	100	
Unemployment benefit	5	5	56	n.a.
Administrative costs	36	28	18	n.a.
Assistance to migrants	0	43	3	n.a.
Training	11	11	13	n.a.
Public works	0.6	0.5	1.2	n.a.
3. Social insurance fund benefits	100	100	100	100
Sickness	52	50	68	77
Maternity	15	14	18	20
Sanatoria	29	32	10	0
4. Social assistance	100	100	100	100
Means-tested child allowances	97	92	83	82
Other child allowances	3	7	10	5
Local social assistance	0	0.4	6	0
Housing allowances	0	0	0	12

Source: Ministry of Labour and Social Protection, Kazakhstan.

substantial changes in the importance of the different sub-programmes. Unemployment benefits increased in importance over time within labour market programmes (up from 5 per cent in 1992 to 57 per cent in 1997), sickness and maternity programmes increased their share among other social insurance, and the means-tested child allowance programmes declined as a share of social assistance programmes, largely due to the increase in the housing allowance benefit.

The decline in the overall level of resources, combined with the changes in composition of spending, led to declines in the level of some benefits as well as a fall in the number of beneficiaries (see Table 7.13). The real value of pensions fell by over two-thirds between 1993 and 1995, although there was a modest increase thereafter. The number of pensioners declined from 2.82 million in 1993 to 2.67 million in 1997. Maternity benefits fell by one-half in real terms between 1994 and 1995, although the number of beneficiaries remained the same. Unemployment benefits fell to 40 per cent of their previous level in 1994. But, in 1996, they rose sharply and in 1997

Table 7.13 Programme beneficiaries and average benefit levels in Kazakhstan, 1993–96, selected programmes

	1993	*1994*	*1995*	*1996*	*1997*
1. Pensions					
Number of beneficiaries (000s)	2 829	2 814	2 819	2 771	2 670
Index of real average benefits (1993 = 100)	100	41	35	44	43
2. Labour market programmes – unemployment benefits					
Registered unemployed (000s)	40	70	139	282	258
Index of real minimum benefits (1993 = 100)	100	41	40	103	127
3. Social insurance fund benefits – maternity					
Number of beneficiaries (000s)	283	284	n.a.	n.a.	n.a.
Index of average real benefit	100	48	n.a.	n.a.	n.a.
4. Social assistance – means-tested child allowances					
Number of beneficiaries (000s)	2 417	1 674	1 795	1 469	1 232
Index of average real benefit	100	94	186	235	247

Source: Ministry of Labour and Social Protection, Kazakhstan. Indices computed by authors.

stood well above their 1993 level; the number of beneficiaries in this programme also rose continuously. The expenditure per beneficiary also rose for the basic child allowance, due in large part to the substantial decline in the number of beneficiaries.

Cash transfers are an important source of income for many poor households but, in general, coverage is limited and available assistance is not well targeted. Data from the KLSS show that 37 per cent of households in Kazakhstan receive at least one transfer (see Table 7.14).

Table 7.14 Coverage and average value of cash transfers in Kazakhstan, 1996

	Poor		*Non-poor*		
	Proportion of households in receipt of benefit	*Receipt rate**	*Proportion of households in receipt of benefit*	*Receipt rate**	*Average benefit per household (tenge per month)*
Pensions					
Old age	23	68	24	81	2 619
Disability	5	74	3	76	2 586
Loss of breadwinner	1	42	1	76	2 683
Unemployment benefit	2	40	1	40	1 382
SIF – Sick pay	0.2	10	0.8	15	10 353
SIF – Maternity benefit	0.0	0	0.5	8	1 063
Child allowances					
Means-tested	6	36	3	25	2 603
Other	1	n.a.	2	n.a.	776
Other social assistance	4	n.a.	4	n.a.	2 345
All benefits	37		37		

*Receipt rate is proportion of eligible households who received benefits during the month of the survey. Eligibility is self-reported with the exception of mean-tested child allowances.
Subsistence minimum (poverty line) in the survey month was 2 861 tenge per capita.

Source: KLSS (1996).

Table 7.15 Share of public transfers in consumption in Kazakhstan

	Consumption quintile					
	Bottom	*Second*	*Third*	*Fourth*	*Top*	*Total*
Pensions	15.2	19.3	12.8	11.3	5.6	12.2
Mean-tested child allowances	2.2	1.2	1.2	0.3	0.1	0.9
Unemployment benefit	0.7	0.1	0.2	0.1	0.1	0.2
All others	1.2	1.5	0.6	1.1	1.3	1.1

Source: KLSS (1996).

But over 60 per cent of poor households receive no cash benefits at all. Of the different transfers, pensions are the most common, being received by over 28 per cent of households. Other transfers are relatively uncommon, with child allowances being received by only 4 per cent of households, and unemployment benefits by around 1.5 per cent of households. Average benefits are modest compared to the subsistence minimum (poverty line), especially for unemployment benefits.

As a result of falls in benefit levels and limited coverage, cash transfers played a modest role in protecting living standards in Kazakhstan in 1996 (see Table 7.15). Pensions and other transfers accounted for nearly 20 per cent of consumption on average in the bottom quintile, and over 20 per cent of consumption in the second quintile. Public transfers fell to a little over 7 per cent in the top quintile. For the population as a whole, transfer payments accounted for around 15 per cent of total consumption. In terms of relative importance in household consumption (or income), pensions are the most important transfer, while child allowances come second. In the lowest quintile, pensions contributed over six times as much to household resources as child allowances.

There are two additional issues associated with the effectiveness of the social safety net. First, a large proportion of households appear not to receive the transfers they are entitled to (see Table 7.14).[22] Receipt rates were the highest for pensions and the lowest for maternity benefits. In the case of the means-tested child allowances, the major social assistance programme, *only one in three eligible households actually received payments during the month of the survey.* Receipt rates were slightly higher for unemployment benefits, which were received by around two in five eligible households. The proportion of beneficiary households, and the impact of the transfers, would obviously be significantly higher if a greater proportion of eligible households were actually to receive benefits. The main reason cited for not receiving benefits was the shortage of cash on the part of the local authorities. There is a distinct locational pattern to non-receipt of transfers – higher in rural areas and in the south and the east than in other parts of the country. The incidence of non-receipt in Almaty city is, however, small.

A second issue relates to the targeting of transfers. The largest programme in the social safety net programme is the pension programme, which is, by definition, not a targeted programme. As might be expected, pensions are not progressive (see Table 7.16).[23] Benefits flow largely to the middle income groups, with the bottom quintile receiving 11 per cent of total programme expenditure. There is some evidence that sickness and maternity benefits are also largely enjoyed by the non-poor, but this finding should be interpreted with caution given the small proportion of households in the sample that actually receive these benefits.

Table 7.16 Proportion of programme expenditures reaching different quintiles in Kazakhstan

	Consumption quintile				
	Bottom	*Second*	*Third*	*Fourth*	*Top*
All pensions	11	21	20	25	23
Old age pensions	11	21	19	26	23
Disability	13	29	25	11	23
Loss of breadwinner*	0	39	17	31	13
Unemployment benefit*	33	4	33	12	18
SIF – sick pay*	11	1	6	38	44
SIF – maternity benefit*	0	16	33	45	5
All child allowances	21	25	33	13	8
Means-tested child allowances	24	25	31	13	7
Other child allowances	1	26	44	11	17
Other social assistance	6	19	9	19	47

*Owing to the small number of sampled households who receive these transfers, the results should be treated as indicative.

Source: KLSS (1996).

Other benefits are, however, progressive. Child allowances are mildly progressive, with 45 per cent of benefits going to the two lowest population quintiles. The means-tested programme is much more progressive than the categorical child allowance schemes, suggesting that there is scope for improved targeting of other social assistance. Unemployment benefits, although not intentionally targeted, largely flow to the poor. Over one-third of the benefit was received by the bottom quintile. This is not surprising given the observed correlation between unemployment and poverty. Additionally, given the low real value of the benefit, this may also reflect self-targeting by the poor. However, the earlier caveat on small numbers applies here as well.

These findings suggest that there is scope for improved targeting of social assistance. Further reforms in targeting could increase the allocation of resources to the poor. There is a high level of leakage of resources to the non-poor in the means-tested child allowance. Improving the targeting mechanism, using either a full-fledged proxy means test[24] or simply incorporating some additional characteristics of the household along with the income measure, could substantially reduce leakage and increase the impact of the programmes. Other social assistance programmes could follow this model as well.

Rationalizing the social assistance system would further improve the impact of the social safety net. The present multiplicity of programmes increases the administrative costs of the system without substantially increasing the number of beneficiaries.[25] And the overlap of programmes, such as the child allowance, with contradictory targeting schemes undermines their ability to reach the poorest groups in the population.

Beyond the savings that can be had through better targeting, further assistance for the poor would have to come from an expansion in social protection spending. In this context, it is worth considering the introduction of targeted income support for the poor. At the time of writing, there was no targeted benefit for those who are poor but do not qualify for public means-tested assistance through the child allowance or housing allowance schemes.[26] The lack of benefits for people who are generally poor and do not fall into one of the predetermined categories partly explains why coverage among social assistance programmes is so low. This would suggest that the various non-means-tested and local programmes are perhaps best replaced with a targeted poverty benefit. In any such scheme the level of the benefit would need to be carefully considered to preclude adverse incentives. At the very minimum, the benefit should be lower than the level of other social insurance payments. It should also provide an encouragement for people to help themselves. This would suggest that the level of the benefit should be austere, and given the considerable reliance on self-production and informal safety nets in Kazakhstan, about one-third to one-half of the level deemed necessary for minimum subsistence would not be inappropriate. Significantly, the poverty benefit would *not* be aimed at bringing the individual or household up to the subsistence level, but to provide a helping hand in the process. For administrative efficiency, the programme could be administered by the local departments of social protection.

The observed correlation between poverty and unemployment, and the difficulty of targeting transfers, also suggests a role for public works programmes in targeting assistance through self-selection among the poor. Public works programmes operate on a very limited scale in Kazakhstan, accounting for less than 1 per cent of all spending on labour market programmes in 1996. These schemes could, however, be expanded significantly and play an important role in targeting assistance to the poor. Given the possible association of such schemes with the forced labour of former times, it would be important to emphasize community services at the expense of heavy manual labour. This would also favour women, who face a marginally higher risk of unemployment. Community services worthy of consideration for inclusion in public works programmes include cleaning and sanitation activities, home care for the aged, and informal child care.

7.6 Conclusions

This chapter has examined the impact of economic transition on living standards in Kazakhstan and suggested ways in which the social safety net could be made more effective. There are three principal conclusions. First, over one-third of the population of Kazakhstan was living below a 'subsistence minimum' living standard in 1996. Second, given the extent of poverty, this is a problem that cannot be eliminated by public transfer programmes. Indeed, the social safety net has shrunk substantially since independence under the combined impact of falling revenues and the need to maintain fiscal discipline. Strong and sustained growth that raises wages and reduces unemployment will therefore be key to poverty reduction in Kazakhstan. Third, the social safety net will none the less be critical for easing the costs of economic restructuring, and to assist those who may not be able to take advantage of changing economic opportunities. The social safety net should be made more effective through greater regularity in the payment of benefits and improved targeting of benefits to those in greatest need. An expansion of programmes that assist the poor should also be considered.

Notes

*Mamta Murthi and Kinnon Scott are at the World Bank. Menno Pradhan is at the Free University in the Netherlands. The authors would like to thank the National Statistical Agency of Kazakhstan for permission to use data from the 1996 Kazakhstan Living Standards Survey. The findings, interpretations and conclusions expressed in this chapter are entirely their own. They do not necessarily represent the views of the World Bank, its executive directors or the countries they represent.

1. Estimates from the 1989 Family Budget Survey (FBS) suggest that around 15 per cent of the population had incomes below the 'socially acceptable minimum' compared to 33–52 per cent in other Central Asian SSRs. The figures should be treated as indicative, as the FBS sample is not nationally representative. For further discussion, see Atkinson and Micklewright (1992).
2. For example, the lack of pipeline capacity is a key constraint on the export of oil and gas outside the FSU.
3. In December 1996, 82 per cent of adults polled said they were dissatisfied, and 38 per cent very dissatisfied with the overall economic situation. A year earlier, the figures were 77 per cent and 32 per cent respectively.
4. There are numerous problems with official wage and unemployment data. Registered unemployment tends to underestimate real unemployment as it only captures those who seek unemployment benefits and meet all eligibility requirements. See Klugman and Scott in Falkingham et al. (1997), and World Bank (1998).
5. Over 86 per cent of adults polled in November–December 1996 stated they were dissatisfied with the quality of healthcare, while 68 per cent expressed dissatisfaction with the system of education. See International Foundation for Election Systems (1996).
6. Further discussion of data and methodology may be found in World Bank (1998), Appendix 1.
7. Average consumption shortfall among the poor is given by dividing the poverty gap by the headcount ratio.
8. Allowing for economies of scale in consumption makes the difference between rural and urban poverty rates even smaller. See World Bank (1998), Appendix 4.
9. Nearly 59 per cent of urban households have in-house toilets, compared to 5.6 per cent of rural households. Access to piped drinking water (urban 78 per cent, rural 17 per cent) and to central heating (urban 70 per cent, rural 10 per cent) are also significantly different. See National Statistical Agency (1996).

10. Tekali, a mining town of around 27 000 people in Taldykorgan *oblast*, provides a good example. In 1996, official unemployment was 20 per cent and another 40 per cent of the labour force was subject to reduce hours or administrative leave.
11. Equally the economic crisis in Russia during 1998 may have affected this region more adversely.
12. Economies of scale are best explained intuitively by the idea that 'two can often leave as cheaply as one'. By taking per capita consumption as our measure of household welfare, we implicitly assume that there are no economies of scale. Allowing for scale economies typically changes the demographic profile of poverty, with large households appearing less poor. For further discussion, see Lanjouw and Ravallion (1995) and Lanjouw et al. (1998).
13. On the basis of a representative survey of three *rayons* (regions) in Kzyl-Orda *oblast*, which is affected by the Aral Sea crisis, Ismail and Hill (1997) found no evidence of wasting (0.5 per cent) and limited evidence of stunting (15 per cent) in the region.
14. Unemployment is defined here as being without a job and having actively searched for work in the preceding seven-day period.
15. Over 150 000 Kazakhs arrived in Kazakhstan during the first half of the 1990s. The number of refugees is more difficult to estimate. Ethnic Kazakhs have tended to settle in the southern half of the country while the south-eastern *oblasts* have received refugees from the Afghan and Tajik conflicts.
16. Natural resources can be a mixed blessing. The competitiveness of non-oil sectors of the economy has been found to be a problem in almost every country that has experienced a rapid expansion in foreign exchange earnings from petroleum exports. In a study covering growth in 97 developing countries during the period 1970–89, Sachs and Warner (1995) found that countries with high export earnings based on natural resource wealth grew more *slowly* than those without such natural resources.
17. Employment norms that are several times levels found in other countries are still common in Kazakhstan. In Kzyl-Orda, for example, sheep farms typically employ about one person per 200 animals compared to the international average of one person per 600 animals. In water utilities there are 50 staff members per 1 000 connections, compared to 10–20 employees per 1 000 connections in relatively inefficient utilities, and 2–3 employees per 1 000 connections in efficient ones (see World Bank 1997).
18. This pattern of remuneration was common to many command economies (see Barr 1994).
19. In discussing the social safety net, we exclude general production and consumption subsidies.
20. A fourth component is health insurance, which this chapter will not consider in detail.
21. As a result of the payment of pension arrears in 1997, pensions rose from around three-quarters to nearly 90 per cent of total social safety net expenditure, but this was a one-off event.
22. For this analysis, eligibility for the means-tested child allowance was determined by applying the means test to the income per capita of households with children. For other transfers, eligibility is self-reported.

23. A subsidy is considered 'progressive' if the benefits go disproportionately to the poor in absolute terms.
24. Along the lines of the Ficha Cas in Chile or the SISBEN in Colombia.
25. For example, there was one child benefiting from the programme for children with HIV in 1996.
26. For example, to qualify for the means-tested child allowance, household income (largely based on the official wage) must be below a particular threshold. If the official wage is above the threshold, the household becomes ineligible, *whether it has received that wage or not.*

References

Asian Development Bank (1997), *Women and Gender Relations in Kazakhstan.*

Atkinson, Anthony B. and John Micklewright (1992), *Economic Transformation in Eastern Europe and the Distribution of Income,* Cambridge: Cambridge University Press.

Barr, N. (ed.) (1994), *Labor Markets and Social Policy in Central and Eastern Europe,* New York: Oxford University Press/World Bank.

Falkingham, J., J. Klugman, S. Marnie and J. Micklewright (eds) (1997), *Household Welfare in Central Asia,* London: Macmillan.

International Foundation for Election Systems (1996), *Public Opinion in Kazakhstan.*

Ismail, Suraiya and Hereward Hill (1997), 'National Statistics in the Kyzyl-Orda Region of Kazakhstan', in Falkingham, et al. (1997).

Klugman, J. and K. Scott (1997), *Measuring Labor Market Activities in Kazakhstan: The Implications of Using Official Statistics,* in Falkingham et al. (1997).

Lanjouw, P. and M. Ravallion (1995), 'Poverty and Household Size', *Economic Journal* , Vol. 105, No. 433, pp. 1415–34.

Lanjouw, P., B. Milanovic and S. Paternostro (1998), *Poverty in Transition Economies: A Case of Children Pitted Against the Elderly?,* World Bank (mimeo), 15 May.

National Institute of Nutrition, Kazakhstan, Academy of Preventive Medicine, Kazakhstan and Macro International Inc., USA (1996), *Kazakhstan Demographic and Health Survey 1995.*

National Statistical Agency, Kazakhstan (1996), *Living Standards Measurement Survey 1996 Final Report.*

National Statistical Agency, Kazakhstan (1997a), *Kratkiy statisticheskiy yezhegodnik Kazakhstana 1996* (Short Statistical Yearbook of Kazakhstan 1996).

National Statistical Agency, Kazakhstan (1997b), *Kazakhstan: Report on National Accounts.*

Ravallion, M. (1994), *Poverty Comparisons,* Switzerland: Harwood.

Sachs, Jeffrey D. and Andrew M. Warner (1995), NBER Working Paper.

UNDP (1995, 1996, 1997), *Kazakhstan Human Development Report.*

World Bank (1994), *Kazakhstan Economic Report.*

World Bank (1995a), *The Kyrgyz Republic: Poverty Assessment and Strategy,* Report No. 14380-KG.

World Bank (1995b), *Poverty in Russia: An Assessment,* Report No. 14110-RU.

World Bank (1996), *Republic of Kazakhstan Transition of the State,* Report No. 15353-KZ.

World Bank (1997), *Kzyl-Orda: Regional Development Priorities.*

World Bank (1998), *Kazakhstan: Living Standards During the Transition,* Report No. KZ-SR-19398.

8
Gradual Economic Reform and Well-Being in Uzbekistan

Richard Pomfret and Kathryn Anderson

The aim of this chapter is to evaluate the economic and social impact of the transition from central planning to a market-oriented economy in Uzbekistan. The Uzbekistan government has pursued a policy of gradual reform, and, among transition economies, Uzbekistan is typically seen as one of the slowest reformers (Pomfret and Anderson 1997: 1). Uzbekistan provides the only reasonable test of whether gradual reform of a Soviet centrally planned economy could avoid the short-term social and economic disruption associated with big-bang strategies, while remaining on course for long-term economic success; other slow reformers among the former Soviet Republics have been affected by regional tensions or suffered from blatant economic mismanagement.

The first section provides an overview of Uzbekistan's development strategy and of the welfare situation in Uzbekistan before the December 1991 dissolution of the USSR. Section 8.2 discusses the changes in welfare indicators since independence. Sections 8.3 and 8.4 analyse the connections between Uzbekistan's economic and social policies and the welfare changes. Section 8.5 discusses responses that have been made to policy changes or which might be expected, focusing on possible indirect or long-term consequences not picked up in Sections 8.2–8.4. The final section presents some conclusions.

8.1 Introduction

8.1.1 Development strategy and its recent changes

Uzbekistan's development strategy and economic reforms were primarily determined in Moscow until 1992. Uzbekistan was not one of the Soviet Republics which experimented with local reforms during the

Gorbachev era, and even after it became independent in late 1991 the country reacted to Russian initiatives (for example, following the Russian Federation's January 1992 price reform) rather than adopting proactive reforms. The government pursued a gradual reform strategy, seeking to minimize the economic and social impact of the dramatic changes associated with the dissolution of the Soviet Union.

The Uzbekistan government recognized that the pre-independence economic strategy was unsustainable. The cotton monoculture established during the Soviet era led to deterioration in the natural resource base, highlighted by the dramatic shrinking of the Aral Sea and salinization of large tracts of land.[1] Transfers from the central Soviet budget declined in 1991 and, although some subsidization from Russia continued within the ruble zone, the amounts were dwindling. As the situation within the ruble zone became untenable, Uzbekistan issued a provisional national currency in November 1993, followed by a permanent currency in July 1994.

Creation of the national currency was followed by macroeconomic stabilization in late 1994. Uzbekistan has been one of the most successful former Soviet Republics in controlling the budget deficit: Uzbekistan's deficit, equal to 18.8 per cent of GDP, was above the average of those republics in 1992, but below the average in 1995 at 3.4 per cent of GDP (Table 8.1). Uzbekistan, together with other slow reformers, was sheltered from some of these changes and additionally benefited from continued ability to raise revenues from the cotton and minerals sectors. Thus, despite the paucity of external financing, Uzbekistan was still maintaining government expenditures at over two-fifths of GDP in 1994 and 1995. Uzbekistan has used this ongoing public control over resources to maintain social spending and (unlike other slow reformers such as Ukraine) has increased spending on education and health rather than channelling resources into subsidies for enterprises and consumers (the 'social protection' category in Table 8.1).

After the exit from the ruble zone, Uzbekistan adopted a more assertive political and economic nationalism in 1994–95. Attempts to shift agricultural output from cotton to grain were intensified, but the 1995 grain harvest was disappointing.

Uzbekistan has welcomed foreign investors and gradually liberalized its trade regime. The liberal policy towards imports is, however, nullified by strict foreign exchange controls, which also reduce the incentive to export.

Table 8.1 General government spending, 1992–95, former Soviet Republics

(a) Revenue and expenditure in Uzbekistan, and average for former Soviet Republics (as a percentage of GDP)

	1992	*1993*	*1994*	*1995*
General government revenues				
Uzbekistan	32.3	41.5	36.0	35.0
FSU average	33.1	30.3	28.6	23.9
General government expenditure				
Uzbekistan	50.1	52.0	43.6	42.4
FSU average	45.8	44.1	37.9	29.5
General government deficit				
Uzbekistan	18.8	9.4	6.7	3.4
FSU average	13.1	12.2	7.2	4.6

(b) Allocation of general government spending (as percentage of GDP)

	USSR (1989)	*Kazakhstan (1994)*	*Uzbekistan (1994)*
Education and health	7.4	4.7	16.5
Social protection	7.4	5.7	7.4
Support for the economy	14.1	11.4	12.2
Capital and restructuring	7.2	0.2	3.9
Law enforcement	0.9	1.3	–
Defence	8.0	0.8	–
Administration	0.3	0.7	1.0
Interest	0.7	0.3	–
Other	3.5	4.2	7.0
Total	49.5	29.3	48.0

Source: Cheasty and Davis (1996).

The slow pace of reform and concerns over human rights issues contributed to difficult relations between Uzbekistan and the IMF, the World Bank, the European Union and the USA in the post-independence period. The political relations eased in 1996, culminating in President Karimov's meetings with European Union leaders and with President Clinton in June 1996. In the second half of 1996, however, relations with the international financial institutions deteriorated once again. A poor harvest and disappointing export revenues from cotton led the government to start financing expenditures by money creation.

8.1.2 A brief historical account of the welfare situation

Uzbekistan was one of the poorer Soviet Republics and at the time of independence was probably a lower-middle-income country on the World Bank scale. As with all Soviet Republics, Uzbekistan's social indicators were higher than those of most developing countries with similar income levels. In particular there was widespread access to health and education, with almost universal literacy and high life expectancy. Unemployment was non-existent and an effective social security system provided a safety net against extreme poverty.

The Soviet economy was, however, running into ever more severe problems from the 1970s onwards, which made it increasingly difficult to maintain living standards. The environmental problems associated with Soviet planning were especially acute in Uzbekistan, as the cotton monoculture placed exorbitant demands on water resources. Apart from the economic consequences, the over-reliance on irrigation led directly to health problems, with high rates of morbidity and gynaecological ailments being reported especially in the Karakalpak region bordering the Aral Sea.

8.2 Changes of welfare indicators

8.2.1 Economic indicators

Uzbekistan had the smallest decline in GDP over the period 1990–95 of any former Soviet Republic. According to IMF estimates, Uzbekistan's 1995 GDP was 83 per cent of its 1991 GDP (Table 8.2a). Uzbekistan also had relative success in avoiding hyperinflation, never recording a four-digit annual increase in the consumer price index, although by 1995 the Kyrgyz Republic and Kazakstan had made more progress in reducing inflation (Table 8.2b).

Official statistics must be treated with caution. Production figures often appear to be inflated. Estimates of the disappointing 1995 grain harvest were continuously downsized during 1996, revealing the first official reports to have been gross overestimates.

Many of these statistical problems apply to all transition economies, so that comparisons between Uzbekistan and its Central Asian neighbours are more firmly based than attempts to compare Uzbekistan's GDP or inflation rate with established market economies. There are differences in the availability and reliability of data among the Central Asian Republics; the general picture of Uzbekistan's relative success in limiting GDP decline and open inflation is apparent from Table 8.2.

Table 8.2 Output and inflation performance in former Soviet Republics

(a) Real GDP (index: 1991 = 100)

Country	*1991*	*1992*	*1993*	*1994*	*1995*
Uzbekistan	100	89	87	84	83
Estonia	100	78	72	72	74
Belarus	100	90	81	71	63
Turkmenistan	100	95	85	68	61
Russia	100	81	74	65	58
Latvia	100	65	54	56	56
Kyrgyz Republic	100	81	68	55	55
Lithuania	100	62	51	51	53
Kazakhstan	100	86	76	57	52
Ukraine	100	83	71	55	48
Azerbaijan	100	78	60	52	47
Moldova	100	71	70	48	47
Armenia	100	47	40	43	46
Tajikistan	100	71	63	50	44
Georgia	100	55	41	37	35

Source: IMF staff estimates, reported in Horton (1996), pp. 19 and 22.

(b) GDP growth rate (%)

Country	*1971–80 average*	*1981–89 average*	*1990*	*1991*	*1992*	*1993*	*1994*	*1995*
Kazakhstan	4.4	2.0	–4.6	–6.8	–13.0	–15.6	–25.0	–9.0
Kyrgyz Republic	4.4	4.0	6.9	–9.1	–15.8	–16.3	–26.5	–6.0
Tajikistan	4.9	3.3	–2.4	–8.7	–30.0	–27.6	–15.0	-12.0
Turkmenistan	4.0	4.0	0.8	–5.0	–5.4	n.a.	n.a.	–5.0
Uzbekistan	6.2	3.4	2.0	–0.5	–11.1	–2.4	–4.5	–2.0

Source: World Bank (1996), pp. 173–4.

(c) Average annual inflation rates (%)

Country	*1990*	*1991*	*1992*	*1993*	*1994*	*1995*
Kazakhstan	4.2	91.0	1 610.0	1 760.0	1 980.0	180.0
Kyrgyz Republic	3.0	85.0	854.6	1 208.7	280.0	45.0
Tajikistan	4.0	111.6	1 157.0	2 195.0	452.0	635.0
Turkmenistan	4.6	102.5	492.9	3 102.0	2 400.0	1 800.0
Uzbekistan	3.1	82.2	645.0	534.0	746.0	315.0

Source: World Bank (1996), pp. 173–4.

Evidence from the Soviet era suggests a high degree of income equality, although a privileged class with special access to some services and to the perquisites of power clearly existed. Rural–urban and regional differences in income were also apparent, for example, the Karakalpak autonomous republic lagged the rest of Uzbekistan. On average Slav households were more prosperous than households of Central Asian origin. Since independence, inequality of status has been transformed into greater inequality of income and wealth through the alienation of state assets and new opportunities for corruption. Rural–urban and regional inequalities remain, but ethnic differences may have diminished in importance due to Slavic emigration. Poverty among old people is limited by a fairly generous pension system (Section 8.4.2). In sum, transition was associated with an increase in income inequality;[2] poverty also increased but was not visibly widespread (ILO 1996: 151).

8.2.2 Capability-based indicators

8.2.2.1 Health

Life expectancy has risen slightly during the 1990s and infant mortality rates have continued to decline sharply from previous high levels (Table 8.3). Apart from these rough indicators there is little information about trends in health, with only anecdotal evidence on morbidity. Health expenditure fell from 5.9 per cent of GDP in 1991 to 4.7 per cent in 1993, which was still high compared to other CIS countries (for example, 3 per cent in Russia and 2.4 per cent in Kazakhstan). Some changes in health delivery have occurred with the legalizing of private activities, but their extent is hard to assess.[3] Measures of inputs into healthcare are available but difficult to interpret.

Infant mortality fell from 32 per 1000 live births in 1993 to 28 in 1994 and 21 in 1995. The UNDP (1996: 27 and 60) ascribes this to fewer births, longer spacing between births and a lower birth rate among women over 35, which in turn are related to improved maternity services and a dramatic increase in the use of contraception (from 12 per cent of women of child-bearing age in 1990 to 21 per cent in 1991, 33 per cent in 1993 and 38 per cent in 1995).

The Soviet system provided widely accessible healthcare, but was inefficient due to a bias towards intensive use of physical and human capital. Since independence there has been a shift from in-patient to out-patient activities, which has reduced costs and improved efficiency, but the net impact on the quality of healthcare is difficult to assess. Between 1990 and 1994 the number of hospital beds fell by

Table 8.3 Socioeconomic indicators for the Central Asian Republics

Country	*Population (million)* *mid-1994*	*Population growth (%)* *1981–90*	*1991–4*	*Urban pop. (% of total pop.)* *1994*	*Sec. enrol. (% of age group)* *1993*	*GNPPC (US$)* *1994*
Kazakhstan	16.8	1.2	0.1	59.3	90	1 160
Kyrgyz Republic	4.5	1.9	0.4	38.8	n.a.	630
Tajikistan	5.8	2.9	2.0	32.2	n.a.	380
Turkmenistan	4.4	2.5	4.6	44.9	n.a.	n.a.
Uzbekistan	22.4	2.5	2.2	41.2	94	60

Life expectancy at birth (years)

Country	*1971–80*	*1981–90*	*1991–93*	*1994*
Kazakhstan	66.6	68.2	69.0	68.3
Kyrgyz Republic	65.5	65.8	67.9	67.8
Tajikistan	64.8	69.0	68.1	66.6
Turkmenistan	61.9	64.9	65.8	66.3
Uzbekistan	67.3	68.1	69.3	69.8

Infant mortality rate (per 1000 live births)

Country	*1971–80*	*1981–90*	*1991–93*	*1994*
Kazakhstan	32.7	29.2	27.3	27.4
Kyrgyz Republic	46.1	38.5	31.0	29.1
Tajikistan	58.1	47.5	44.5	40.6
Turkmenistan	53.6	52.5	45.5	46.4
Uzbekistan	47.0	42.7	35.0	28.2

Source: World Bank (1996), pp. 172–5.

40 000 (16 per cent) and average length of stay in hospital was reduced by one-third, while daycare facilities were expanded. The UNDP (1996: 59) reports that by the end of 1995 a quarter of all patients who would have been treated in hospitals in 1990 were being treated at day clinics or at home.

Admissions to medical school were cut by half after independence (ILO 1996: 120). The UNDP, however, puts this in the perspective of more efficient delivery of healthcare, observing that although admissions to higher education institutions dropped from 4800 in 1991 to 1500 in 1995, admissions to secondary medical educational establishments increased by 2000 (UNDP 1996: 63). The critical change is towards training doctors for general practice and other healthcare providers at varying skill levels, rather than focusing on training specialists.

In all of this, there is no evidence of whether the change in inputs by substituting for physical and human capital has had a positive or a negative impact on national health.

Despite the official shift in emphasis from cure to prevention, routine child and adult immunization declined after independence. Poliomyelitis vaccine coverage fell from 89 per cent in 1992 to 46 per cent in 1993, when 117 cases were reported of which 94 were children under two. A similar pattern applied to diphtheria, with 37 deaths in 1994. The government responded to these developments with National Immunization Days in October and November 1994, when 98 per cent of children under four were reached, with financial support from external aid donors (ILO 1996: 124).

8.2.2.2 Education

The government has maintained a high priority for education since independence, with over one-quarter of the consolidated government budget being spent on education. The share of public expenditure on education dropped from 11 per cent of GDP in 1991 to just below 9 per cent in 1994, but this remains high by international standards. The distinctive feature of the structure of the education budget is the large share of funds (30–50 per cent) allocated to student subsidies; students and parents make no contribution to the cost of education beyond food and basic school supplies. This feature has helped to ensure that a basic education is open to all, although in future more targeted assistance will be necessary to alleviate fiscal pressures. The literacy rate in Uzbekistan (over 97 per cent) is very high for a country of its income level, reflecting the emphasis on education in the USSR, with ten grades of compulsory schooling.

Primary education continues to be universal, but in the mid-1990s it apparently lasted three years for some pupils and four for others, and some entrants were better prepared than others. Raising the primary school entry age disadvantages children not attending kindergarten, especially as kindergartens have begun to teach basic literacy skills to 6-year-olds. Kindergarten capacity in 1993 was 45 per cent of 4–6-year-olds in urban areas and 21 per cent in rural areas. The shortage was exacerbated in 1994 by the closure of 917 preschool centres, mostly due to the privatization of sponsoring enterprises which then withdrew funding; meanwhile, only 356 new state preschool centres were opened.

Middle schools cover five grades (11–15-year-olds since 1992) and the number of graduates appears to have remained steady at around 96–7 per cent of the age group.[4]

Quality variations are made more likely by the generally recognized teacher shortage. Although 4300 new teachers graduated in 1992 and 4700 in 1993, this is believed to have not kept pace with the rate of dropouts from teaching. Market-oriented reforms opened up new opportunities for people with some skills (for example, foreign-language teachers), and state salaries provided poor a incentive to remain in teaching.[5] Increased emphasis on the use of national languages has been associated with many maths and technical teachers, who were predominantly Slavs, deciding to emigrate from Uzbekistan.

Physical facilities in grade schools had shortcomings in the Soviet era, but the situation is deteriorating, with virtually no funds having been allocated for school repairs and maintenance between independence and the time of the ILO mission in April 1995 (ILO 1996: 100). Less than one-third of schools have a central water supply system, and in rural areas schools have earth floors; some schools even lack facilities for boiling drinking water. Since independence most schools have discontinued provision of free school lunches due to insufficient funds.

Uzbekistan has 55 higher education institutions, in which 272 000 students were enrolled in 1993. This represents a 20 per cent drop from the 1990 enrolment of 341 000. It is unclear whether the declining numbers are mainly due to reduced supply of places or to lower demand, reflecting poor employment expectations and emigration of qualified teenagers.[6]

8.2.2.3 Nutrition

The traditional Uzbek diet has been high in animal fat. During the Soviet era caloric intake levels in Uzbekistan were well below the USSR average, and varied considerably within the Republic; in 1991 average meat consumption was 81 kg in Tashkent and 20–23 kg in the Fergana Valley, while milk consumption varied from 376 kg in Tashkent to 144 kg in Andizhan (Craumer 1995: 31). The same source reports that the poorest households received 60 per cent of their caloric intake from bread alone.

Nutritional deficiencies, specifically lack of micronutrients such as iron and vitamin A, are major causes of anaemia, which is exceptionally prevalent in Uzbekistan, with high incidence among women of childbearing age and among children under five.[7] Anaemia contributes to low birth weight and excessive bleeding during delivery (increasing infant mortality) and aggravates acute respiratory diseases. Since independence, maternity wards have been encouraging breastfeeding, which ameliorates the problems for babies.

Food consumption since independence is difficult to document. Declining incomes have shifted food consumption patterns away from meat towards vegetables and bread. Increased dependence on bread among the poor has raised the potential for bread shortages or price increases to promote social unrest. In January 1995 food rationing was abolished, apparently in connection with the first IMF loan to Uzbekistan, but the following month the government reinstated rationing in order to ensure availability of bread for all. Meat output increased by 9 per cent between 1991 and 1994, that is, about equal to population growth, but meat imports declined. Milk output rose more substantially (by 12 per cent between 1991 and 1994), and there may be underreporting due to the growth of private ownership of livestock. This picture of average food consumption, while more or less stagnant, is better than in most former Soviet Republics.

There is concern about variations in nutritional changes between regions and age groups, with children in poor areas particularly vulnerable. The discontinuation of free school lunches is likely to have contributed to the number of children receiving inadequate nutrition. A summer 1995 household survey of three representative *oblasts* (Fergana, Karakalpakstan and Tashkent), however, showed some stunting among children but no evidence of severe or moderate wasting; stunting tends to indicate chronic malnutrition, while wasting would suggest acute malnutrition in recent years.

8.2.3 Demographic-based indicators

Population in Uzbekistan grew from 20.3 million in 1990 to 22.2 million in 1994. In 1990 and 1994, the population grew at 2.2 per cent per year; at this rate, population will double in about 32 years. However, between 1991 and 1994, there was a fluctuation in growth, from a low of 1.9 per cent in 1991 to a high of 2.4 per cent in 1992. The drop in growth between 1990 and 1991 was partly due to the large emigration of Russians, Germans, and Tatars from Uzbekistan.

The rate of natural increase declined significantly after 1990, from 27.6 per 1000 population to 22.7. The change in natural increase was largely due to changes in fertility; the crude birth rate fell from 33.7 to 29.3.[8]

Even if these reductions in fertility are permanent, the population will continue to grow rapidly for many years, because of high fertility in the past.

Significant rural–urban differences in population growth are evident. In 1990, 8.3 million persons lived in urban areas of Uzbekistan, while 12 million lived in rural areas; urban and rural population growth rates were comparable (2.2 per cent and 2.3 per cent). By 1994, population increased to 8.7 million in urban areas and to 13.5 million in rural areas, with urban growth of only 1 per cent and rural growth of 3 per cent. This change in growth across regions was caused by emigration from urban to rural areas as well as smaller reported drops in fertility in rural areas, where children are an important source of agricultural labour. Outmigration from urban areas was so large that Uzbekistan experienced a decline in the level of urbanization after 1990 (Craumer 1995: 38). A deterioration in agricultural wages has been associated with the relative increase in rural population; agricultural wages were 15 per cent above the Uzbekistan average in 1991, but less than 70 per cent of the average by 1995 (Klugman 1997).

8.2.4 Environment-based indicators

Unemployment was first officially acknowledged in the 1992 Employment Law, after which the figure rose from 13 300 in 1993 to 21 800 in 1994 (UNDP 1996: 96) to 36 200 in March 1995 (ILO 1996: 48) and 41 000 in mid-1996 (SCFS 1996). It is widely believed that the high levels of underemployment in agriculture and in state enterprises typical of the Soviet era still remain, and that many displaced workers are recorded as having entered rural jobs or part-time work, rather than being included among the unemployed. The IMF (1996: 13) reports that 50–60 000 workers were on forced leave in 1995, that is, they had jobs but received no wages during the year, and quotes estimates of disguised unemployment in agriculture at around one million persons. State enterprises are not allowed to dismiss workers for three years after privatization.

By the end of 1994 over 96 per cent of housing units had been turned over to occupants, apparently with little difficulty and at nominal cost to buyers. The IMF (1994: 59) reports that in 1993 the cost per dwelling ranged from 24 per cent to 158 per cent of the average monthly wage. Privatization at nominal prices was inequitable as some people dwelt in superior housing, so the distribution of assets (which had all been paid for by the entire population) was uneven.

The Soviet Union placed a high priority on freeing Central Asian women from traditional restrictions, with the economic consequence of increasing labour participation rates. The USSR's pro-natalist policies also provided significant benefits for women. Maternity leave began after 30 weeks of pregnancy and continued for 126 days at full pay. Women were entitled to three years of unpaid leave without prejudice to their pension entitlements. In a market economy, the protective labour legislation and generous maternity benefits provide a disincentive for enterprises to hire women.

Labour force participation rates for women remain high (71 per cent in 1993, when they accounted for 46 per cent of the workforce), but women receive lower pay and there is evidence of increasing marginalization. Low pay reflects the concentration of women in low-wage activities such as health, education and other services, and light industries such as textiles and food, but there also seem to be barriers to women reaching high levels in industry or government.[9] In 1993, 64 per cent of the registered unemployed were women. More importantly, the World Bank (1994: 20) reports evidence of an increased share of rural labour taking the form of household production, that is, women returning to a traditional role of providing unremunerated labour but not officially registered as unemployed. Some displaced female workers have turned to the informal trading sector, which is among the most entrepreneurial and dynamic parts of the post-independence economy, but by its nature the size of this sector is difficult to monitor.

Organized crime was associated with Uzbekistan, perhaps first amongst all Soviet Republics, even before independence. The extent of organized crime is by its nature difficult to measure, but by all reports it increased after the collapse of central planning and the dissolution of the USSR. Corruption among public officials is also a long-standing feature of Uzbek society, which is widely believed to have increased during the 1990s and to be especially prevalent within law enforcement agencies (Lubin 1995: 8).

Uzbekistan has not, however, experienced the collapse of law and order which has occurred elsewhere in the Former Soviet Union. Official statistics show a decline in the number of crimes from 93 626 in 1992 to 67 026 in 1995, a much lower crime rate than in Kazakhstan, Belarus, Ukraine or Russia (UNDP 1996: 75–6). This corresponds to travellers' tales of relative safety: as long as one keeps on the right side of government officials and criminal organizations, then Uzbekistan is a relatively safe place.

There has been substantial emigration from Uzbekistan during the 1990s, which has been concentrated among non-Uzbeks and among professionals and technicians. Kaser (1997) and Mehrotra estimate net emigration of 1.8 million persons in 1990 and 1.0 million in 1991, that is, 13 per cent of the population in two years (ILO 1996: 20–21). Rashid (1994: 95) reports 1 million Russians having left Uzbekistan by 1993, and few Germans or Tatars remain. Official estimates are smaller, at 274 400 emigrants between 1990 and 1993, but even this represents a significant proportion of the Slavic population.

8.2.5 Assessment of changes

Following the shock of the collapse of the Soviet Union in 1991, Uzbekistan maintained living standards better than other former Soviet Republics. Average material welfare undoubtedly declined, but per capita GDP fell by less than in any other CIS or Eastern European country. National income estimates for transition economies are notoriously unreliable, but the general picture of a limited decline in well-being is supported by other indicators.

The high rate of population growth declined during the 1990s. Unlike the changes in birth and death rates in some Eastern European and CIS transition economies, which are attributed to negative feelings towards the economic future, the changes in Uzbekistan have mainly been in response to a public campaign encouraging smaller families (that is, three to four children instead of as many as possible) and due to lower infant mortality. Health indicators are difficult to interpret, but reduced public spending may have been offset by improved efficiency in healthcare delivery.

The open unemployment to be expected from the changing output mix during transition has been minimal in Uzbekistan. Under-employment is believed by some observers to have increased sharply, but it is difficult to measure both at present and in the previous economic system. The perception among residents is of increased crime, but Uzbekistan has avoided the open lawlessness experienced by other newly independent states such as Kazakhstan or Russia.

The welfare impact of independence and transition has not been evenly spread. Many non-Uzbeks ceased to feel at home in the republic and have emigrated. Long-standing rural–urban income differentials have widened. The élite has turned non-pecuniary benefits into wealth and income, while others have seen their previously guaranteed incomes decline substantially in real terms. Changes in the provision of education and health services are likely to exacerbate these distributional effects. Gender-based differences in economic opportunities also threaten to widen as the active policy of including women in the labour force and ensuring their equal access to education in the Soviet era is replaced by a more passive policy. Nevertheless, extreme poverty has been avoided, and some form of safety net clearly continues to exist for the very poor.

8.3 Macro- and microeconomic impact on welfare changes

This and the following section analyse the links between policies and performance. The distinction between economic and social policies is artificial because the human development perspective has emphasized that increasing human capabilities is central to well-being, but it is useful to recognize the macro- and microeconomic policies which dominated the early debates on transition strategies. Those debates focused on the desirability of shock therapy, involving rapid adoption of market-determined prices supported by anti-inflationary monetary policy, reforming or privatizing state enterprises and opening up the economy to international trade. By the mid-1990s the debate had become more nuanced as it was recognized on all sides that in some policy areas shock therapy was impossible or undesirable, while in other areas gradualism was impossible or undesirable.

8.3.1 Monetary, fiscal, and price liberalization policies

Uzbekistan has espoused a gradualist reform strategy and consistently resisted shock therapy. This is most apparent with respect to fiscal and monetary policy and price reform. Fiscal policy has been cautious, with the government seeking to limit the budgetary deficit rather than commit to a non-inflationary policy. Likewise, monetary policy has not been directed to the single goal of taming inflation. Indeed, monetary policy has been of limited significance, because the government has relied on price controls as its main anti-inflation weapon.

Price liberalization was introduced in January 1992. As a member of the ruble zone with porous intra-CIS borders, Uzbekistan had little alternative but to follow Russia's price reform, but it retained price controls on a number of basic commodities and services. During 1992 and 1993 the potential for commodity arbitrage between Uzbekistan and neighbouring states with freer (and hence higher) prices was a constant source of tension, which led to closure of the borders on several occasions.

Following the introduction of the national currency in July 1994, Uzbekistan pursued cautious but cumulatively significant price liberalization. Following the abolition of profit margin regulations and the shift to full-cost recovery pricing by state enterprises, the IMF (1996: 11) concluded that 'the process of price liberalization was essentially completed' by early 1995. Nevertheless, prices for many public services and some key commodities (for example, bread and flour) were still far below world prices (although oil and gas prices were brought substantially closer to world levels in 1996), and the two most important prices in any market economy, the exchange rate and interest rates, continue to be artificial.

Since late 1994 Uzbekistan has announced several macroeconomic stabilization programmes (IMF 1996: 27–35). Actual policy has been cautious; monetary tightening has occurred, but the drop in inflation in 1995 was less dramatic than in Kazakstan or the Kyrgyz Republic. Financial sector reform has been limited, with entrepreneurial banking discouraged and interest rates controlled. As a counterpart to Popov's (1996) characterization of Russia's transition strategy as 'inconsistent shock therapy', Uzbekistan's macroeconomic policy since 1994 could be characterized as inconsistent gradualism.

8.3.2 Privatization and enterprise reform

The dangers of characterizing Uzbekistan as a slow reformer are most pronounced in the area of privatization and enterprise reform. There has not been any sweeping privatization of state enterprises from above. There have only been limited amounts of privatization from outside in the form of foreign investments. On the other hand, housing was almost completely privatized by 1994 and the incentive structure has been changed in agriculture and in industry.

Before independence, agriculture was divided between state farms (whose workers received a fixed wage) and cooperative farms (which paid workers out of net revenue), with a tiny proportion of personal plots. After independence the state farms were converted into collectives, primarily to relieve the state budget, and by 1994 the only remaining state farms were those engaged in experimental work. The land allocated by collective farms to personal plots increased from 110 000 ha in 1991 to 630 000 ha in 1994, and a limited privatization programme created 10 408 private farms covering 89 650 ha by 1994 (ILO 1996: 75). Potentially more important than the privatization measures is the spread of arrangements within cooperative farms whereby individual farmers contract to produce a certain quota at a specified price and then retain a larger share of revenue from above-quota production. This system, which resembles China's successful household responsibility system, appears to have been adopted in most cooperative farms by 1995.

Key agricultural prices remain partially controlled, especially for cotton and grains. Although agricultural output declined by less than total output in the first half of the 1990s, discriminatory cotton pricing alone transferred income out of agriculture equal to over one-tenth of the value of GDP originating in agriculture (even after taking account of all direct and indirect subsidies), so that rural incomes fell by more than urban incomes (ILO 1996: 71).[10]

Within the industrial sector, enterprises appear to have been captured by incumbent managers. The economic consequences are more difficult to assess, because the change in incentive structure as managers turn from being salaried employees to controlling residual incomes could lead to greater efficiency, although widespread price distortions and absence of efficient financial markets inhibit achievement of allocative efficiency.

The conflicting economic implications of Uzbekistan's enterprise and price reforms are starker in agriculture. The institutional changes have improved the incentive structure, but distorted prices are likely to induce resource misallocation.

8.3.3 Foreign trade and exchange rate policies

Uzbekistan has a relatively open economy but restrictive trade/forex policies. Cotton and gold have both proven to be desirable export commodities in the initial post-independence years, since they face less physical impediments than the oil and gas of Kazakhstan and Turkmenistan, and cotton prices have been buoyant.[11] The government has chosen to focus on its exportables as a tax base and to provide substantial protection to import-competing producers in industry and agriculture. These policies have underpinned the limited change in output mix and relatively small drop in GDP during the transition process. In the mid-1990s trade policy became more liberal but less relevant as the foreign exchange market was tightly controlled.

The foreign trade outcome has been good in so far as large trade deficits have been avoided. In 1996, despite declining cotton revenue, Uzbekistan had a small trade surplus, mainly due to a substantial decline in grain imports (from about 3 million tons per year in the early 1990s to 1.6 million tons in 1996) and to achieving self-sufficiency in electricity, coal, oil and gas. The moves towards self-sufficiency in grain and energy are probably desirable, because pre-1992 policies discriminated against using land for grain and against energy production, so that higher output of these items reallocates resources in the right direction.

8.3.4 Transition strategy assessment

The pattern of limited output decline and less dramatic hyperinflation experienced by Uzbekistan in the 1990s is closely connected to the choice of transition strategy, helped by a favourable resource endowment. Transition in Uzbekistan has been gradual in the sense that the government has retained controls over key prices and hence over resource allocation. This control has been exerted cautiously, so that Uzbekistan is arguably the least changed of all the former Soviet Republics.[12]

The cost of retaining administrative control over resource allocation has been to restrict the emergence of new enterprises and the identification of new activities fitting the country's comparative advantage.

Nevertheless, the beneficial impact of an improved incentive structure is limited by distorted prices; in particular, the two most important prices in any market economy (exchange rates and interest rates) are artificial in Uzbekistan.

Uzbekistan's transition strategy has so far had an adverse impact on the distribution of wealth. Thus, although the economy retains many features reminiscent of the Soviet era, transformation of the non-economic perquisites of the élite into real assets and monetary wealth has undermined the equality which characterized the USSR. Whether the ensuing income inequality is more or less severe than in alternative scenarios, such as a purer market economy, is difficult to assess, but the fact that the *nouveaux riches* became rich as a result of privilege rather than effort has been resented.

8.4 Impact of social policies on welfare changes

Table 8.2 shows that Uzbekistan maintained public expenditure's share of GDP and raised the share of social expenditures (Table 8.1). Given the relatively small decline in GDP, social expenditures must have dropped less in Uzbekistan than anywhere else in the Former Soviet Union. Has this ameliorated the welfare situation?

8.4.1 Taxation

The budget deficit in Uzbekistan fell from 36 per cent of GDP to less than 4 per cent in 1995, with a slight surplus during the first quarter of 1996 (IMF 1996: 20). The reduction in the deficit resulted from the introduction of new measures to maintain revenues, a change in government expenditures, and tight budget management. In 1995, tax revenue was 30 per cent of GDP. The most important sources of revenue were corporate income taxes, individual income taxes, value-added tax (VAT), and excise taxes on cotton and fuels.

To fund the social insurance system (pensions, unemployment benefits, sick pay and maternity benefits), a large payroll tax was imposed on wage income. The payroll tax in 1995 was 41 per cent of the gross wage (Klugman 1997). The effect of a payroll tax was to lower the wage received by workers and to raise the total wage (including the tax) paid. Employment can be adversely affected by payroll taxes, with fewer workers desiring to take jobs at lower wages and firms reducing the number of employees demanded.

8.4.2 Public expenditure

Social policy has moved away from the provision of universal subsidies towards providing a cushion for the economically most vulnerable households – the elderly, the disabled, children, and low-skilled labour. This policy shift probably reduced the spread of poverty in Uzbekistan.

Four major policy initiatives were implemented after 1989: the *mahalla* scheme, child payments, pension reform and unemployment insurance. Beginning in 1994, Uzbekistan implemented the *mahalla* scheme to assist low-income families in need. Government funds were distributed to neighbourhood committees or *mahalla*s. The *mahalla*s decided who should receive money from the fund and distributed the money to these families. The *mahalla*s enjoy significant discretion within broad guidelines set by the government. Allowances were tied to the minimum wage; the average allowance in 1995 was equal to two minimum wages (IMF 1996: 26). While the programme was cheaper to run than a programme of national distribution, it was subject to a great deal of local variation in standards of need and, therefore, which households received aid. One in five households and 30 per cent of the bottom quintile of the income distribution received money from this fund in 1995 (Klugman 1997). The *mahalla* programme cushioned, to a certain extent, the economic disruption experienced by low-wage households. It tended to equalize income within the lowest quintiles by placing a floor on poverty, but it did not reduce the level of income inequality in general (Klugman 1997).

In addition to material assistance to low-income families, the government targeted needy children through two programmes. The first programme served families with children under the age of 16. Payments varied with the number of children in the family and were linked to the minimum wage; families with one child received 20 per cent of one minimum wage, while families with five children received one full minimum wage per month. The second programme targeted mothers with children under the age of two. Eligible women could receive about 1.5 minimum wages per month; however, few women participated.

Spending on pensions fell from 12 per cent to less than 6 per cent of GDP between 1993 and 1995. Under the pension system, men with 25 years of work experience are eligible to retire at age 60, while women with at least 20 years of experience can retire at age 55. Men and women who work in 'dangerous' occupations may retire ten years earlier than other workers and receive a full pension. The maximum pension benefit is 75 per cent of earnings and the minimum benefit is indexed. The decline in benefits occurred through large reductions in the replacement rate or the rate at which earned income is replaced by a pension. The decline in the replacement rate coupled with indexation of the minimum benefit implies a redistribution of pension benefits from higher-income retirees to low-income retirees. This again cushions one of the most vulnerable groups – low-wage elderly workers – from severe poverty during periods of economic disruption. Retirees can supplement their pension income with additional market work to further prevent poverty; about 13 per cent of retirees work and receive a pension (ILO 1996: 156).

The low retirement age and generous pension benefits relative to wage income create incentives for low-wage workers beyond their peak earnings capacity to retire even though they may still be productive workers.

Finally, unemployment benefits are paid by the Employment Fund and financed through a 2.5 per cent payroll tax. Benefits to unemployed workers are low, and only 30 000 workers in 1995 applied for benefits (IMF 1996: 26).

Overall, the social expenditure system in Uzbekistan was designed to reduce the hardship experienced during transition among low-income households and to force higher-income households to contribute to this redistribution of income. Among the elderly, minimum benefits increased, while higher-income retirees received lower benefits. For families with children, cash assistance for each child was provided so that the health and development of children would not be negatively affected by slow growth. For low-income families, general assistance was available and determined from a community standard. Finally, for the unemployed, an insurance programme was developed to support workers in their search for other employment. All these programmes will help reduce the social disruption often experienced when income inequality increases within a relatively short period of time.

8.4.3 Structural policies

Two labour market policies can have significant effects on employment – the minimum wage and the 'wage brake' system. The minimum wage is an important component of wage policy in Uzbekistan. In most transition economies, the minimum wage has eroded in real terms so that it has relatively insignificant effects on employment. However, in Uzbekistan the real minimum wage is set so that 75 per cent of the consumer's market basket can be purchased, and the wage is partially indexed. In 1993 and 1994, the minimum wage was one-third of the average wage. The real minimum wage did fall significantly between 1995 and 1996, so that the 1996 minimum wage was one-sixth of the average, probably due to the stabilization effort and lagged indexation (Klugman 1997).

Benefits paid under the social safety net are linked to the minimum wage. However, if the real value of the minimum wage falls relative to the average real wage, then the real value of benefits paid through transfer programmes falls as well. The lowest-income households are negatively affected relative to other households, and the cushioning effect of transfers on poverty may be reduced.

To control wage inflation, the 'wage brake' system was implemented in July 1994. This system of wage controls in state and private companies in the production sector of the economy capped increases in the firms' wage bill to no more than 70 per cent of the increase in production. In 1995, additional wage incentives were imposed in state enterprises; wage increases over a certain level were taxed at high rates (IMF 1996: 14). These two policies prevented firms from fully adjusting wages and the production process itself to changes in the economy. If, for example, skilled labour needed by firms was in short supply, firms would be constrained in their ability to raise wages to the level needed to fill their labour needs.

8.5 Responses to shock or gradual changes

The Uzbekistan government has been among the most successful of CIS countries in creating a national consciousness and reviving traditional institutions. This is most apparent in the *mahalla* system of decentralized social assistance. There has also been a revival of traditional kinship relations as social security measures, which has reduced individual poverty but may have had a negative impact on the role of women.

Uzbekistan spent over a century under tsarist and Soviet rule, but particular political and social institutions proved resilient. The hierarchical political and administrative system was based on traditional as well as imposed norms. Since independence, the authoritarian leadership has managed to retain power (as in most other Soviet successor states), but also to limit entrepreneurial corruption at lower levels of government (unlike other CIS countries, such as Kazakhstan). Policy implementation, while uneven across regions of Uzbekistan, appears to be better than in any other of the larger CIS countries.

The continuing strength of the extended family in Uzbekistan, as elsewhere in Central Asia, has also provided an important safety net for many people adversely affected by the shocks of the 1990s. The extended family provides a low-cost system of employment information and network of contacts, as well as offering unpaid work and satisfaction of basic needs to family members who would otherwise be unemployed. The phenomenon of underemployment is especially pronounced in the rural and the informal service sectors. This response to rapid economic change is more positive than state-supplied unemployment benefits, which encourage welfare dependency and discourage initiative.

The negative aspects of these responses are as yet potential rather than actual. Hierarchical social and political structures may inhibit future economic development, if access to higher education and to other opportunities becomes limited to an élite. Decentralization of social services could accentuate regional and rural–urban disparities, if organizations in poorer communities have to rely on local sources of revenue without substantial equalization payments from the centre. The role of the extended family in offering economic protection could result in a reinstatement of traditional values for the allocation of work and resources within the family, with particularly negative consequences for younger women.

8.6 Conclusions

The Uzbekistan government's goal, reiterated in several speeches by President Karimov, is to create a socially oriented market economy through 'stage-by-stage transition'. So far Uzbekistan has passed through two stages. In the initial stage, priorities were the establishment of the legal framework for a market economy, institutional reforms such as changing the sectoral specialization of government ministries and removing monopolies, and changing attitudes towards property through housing and small-scale privatization. Large expenditures for social protection were intended to maintain popular support for economic reform. The second stage, following the introduction of the national currency in July 1994, included macroeconomic stabilization and financial reform as preconditions for a strategy of attracting foreign investment and undertaking more general systemic reform.

The common characterization of Uzbekistan as a slow reformer among transition economies is correct, but it is false to categorize it as a non-reformer. Even in the initial phase, privatization of housing was thorough and rapid, and small-scale privatization and (possibly substantial) agricultural reforms were implemented. The commitment to macroeconomic stability and to financial reform has strengthened since the early 1990s, but in both areas Uzbekistan lags behind the rapidly reforming transition economies.

The economic performance of Uzbekistan since independence has been good compared to most other transition economies. The cumulative decline in output has been smaller than in all other former Soviet or East European transition economies, and hyperinflation less than in most of these comparable economies. More debatable is the relationship between gradual reform and relatively little economic decline; the lack of radical change clearly contributes to the absence of drastic output drops associated with major changes in the output mix, but the question is whether that is at the expense of faster medium- and long-term growth once the initial reallocation has occurred.

The most interesting aspect of Uzbekistan's transition strategy has been the explicit concern with the welfare impact on those members of society least able to deal with the shift to a market-oriented economy. By its nature, relying on economic incentives to redirect people's efforts and rewarding those who make the correct decisions, the market mechanism widens income differentials which had been suppressed under the communist regime. Uzbekistan has sought to counteract these tendencies by its expenditure policies and by intervention in the labour market. Unlike some other slow-reforming transition economies, Uzbekistan has not concentrated on providing subsidies to enterprises and to consumers, but has relied more on direct payments to families. Some of these payments have been ineffective (for example, unemployment assistance) and others contain long-term dangers (for example, the generous pension arrangements), but together they have softened the burden of transition on vulnerable groups. The most innovative aspect of the social expenditures has been the revival of *mahallas* as a vehicle for decentralized administration of social security. Another positive aspect of the government's expenditure priorities has been the attempt to maintain the share of spending on health and education, which has fallen by less than in other CIS countries, and which is the best long-term assistance to the less well-off. The structural labour market policies have been less appropriate, since both minimum wages and the graduated wage taxes discourage employment, although the falling real value of the minimum wage in 1995 and 1996 diminishes its economic impact.

Overall, Uzbekistan succeeded in ameliorating the impact of the shocks of the early 1990s better than other former Soviet Republics. This may have been assisted by its gradual reform strategy, but more important was the explicit concern for economic welfare and specific social policies. The long-term economic future of the country remains uncertain. Many of the prerequisites for a flourishing market economy are less firmly established than in Eastern Europe or the more reformist CIS countries, but the gradual reform strategy has not yet put any major obstacles in the way of eventual success as a market economy.

8.7 Annex – Turkmenistan: non-reform in a resource-rich economy

Turkmenistan is often linked with Uzbekistan as another example of gradual reform by the autocratic government of a natural-resource-rich Soviet successor state.[13] The contrasts are, however, more striking than the similarities. Turkmenistan has a far less diversified economy than Uzbekistan, and output is heavily concentrated in natural gas and cotton (66 per cent and 8 per cent of GDP in 1994). Since independence the regime in Turkmenistan has been highly personalized and populist, buying support by sharing the natural resource rents rather than undertaking reforms. This strategy proved unsustainable, and the first significant reforms were announced at the end of 1995. Implementation has been patchy and as yet difficult to assess.

Turkmenistan's natural gas reserves are among the world's largest, and were viewed as a huge advantage at independence. Moving to world prices yielded a huge immediate improvement in the terms of trade, estimated at around 50 per cent by Tarr (1994). President Niyazov sought to cement popular support by making water, gas and electricity free (up to generous limits), charging nominal rents on public housing, and subsidizing retail prices of sugar, rice, tea, butter and flour. The extensive social protection also included guaranteed employment, family allowances, pensions and other benefits. The overall impact of the many provisions is non-transparent, but the social protection helped to cushion vulnerable groups from the immediate negative consequences of the dissolution of the USSR and other economic shocks.

Reform of the economy towards a more market-oriented system was minimal during the first four years following the dissolution of the USSR. Some prices were freed, but many key prices remained controlled. The government sets an average wage, and payments above this level are subject to a punitive excess wage tax (set at 50 per cent on all wages over 20 000 manat following the January 1996 wage reform). Interest rates and exchange rates are tightly regulated.

Privatization has progressed slowly and been constrained by the government's unwillingness to cede control. By 1996, 1652 out of 3980 small enterprises targeted for privatization had changed ownership structure and four medium-sized and one large state enterprise had been privatized by auction, but the government has retained a majority shareholding in many of these enterprises. Urban housing privatization has been suspended. The June 1995 agrarian reform replaced state farms and cooperatives by peasant associations, whose members must fulfil state orders but can retain additional output. Although this arrangement bears superficial resemblance to China's household responsibility system and Uzbekistan's agrarian reform, in Turkmenistan all produce in key sectors (including cotton, grains and livestock) must be sold at official procurement prices rather than market-determined prices, so that the Turkmenistan situation is less favourable to producers.

The IMF staff team diplomatically described the situation in early 1996 as one of 'limited progress' in reform and where 'a heavily subsidized public enterprise sector continued to dominate the economy'. A monetary policy of accommodating the needs of state enterprises, the social protection system and prestige construction projects fuelled high inflation levels. Output performance was negatively affected by the no-reform strategy, which gave no incentive for the development of non-traditional sectors.

Given the structure of the economy, the key to performance since independence has been natural gas exports. Output of natural gas fell from 88 billion m^3 in 1990 to 36 billion m^3 in 1994, with a further drop in 1995. Initially, export earnings increased with the shift to world prices, but then declined from US$1.86 billion in 1993 to US$1.43 billion in 1994. More important than the decline in earnings was the growth of arrears due to non-payment, especially by Ukraine and Georgia.[14] National expenditure during 1993–95 was maintained by foreign borrowing. The external debt increased from zero at independence and US$168 million in 1993 to US$469 million by the end of 1995; although this was only 21 per cent of GDP (and despite the notional external assets), Turkmenistan ran into debt-servicing problems due to high interest rates and the short-term nature of its debt, and was forced to reschedule (notably US$58 million owed to the European Union at the end of 1995).

Table 8.2 illustrates the output and inflation pattern. Output was initially maintained by gas export earnings and minimal reform, but plumeted in 1993 and 1994. Inflation was repressed in 1992 and early 1993 by extensive price controls, but accelerated in 1993 and was still very high in 1995, when most former Soviet Republics had regained macroeconomic control, at least to the extent of ending hyperinflation.

Turkmenistan's policies since independence have differed fundamentally from Uzbekistan's. Rather than undertaking gradual reform, Turkmenistan's president has attempted to maintain popular support by giving away some of the natural resource rents, while consolidating absolute political power and avoiding any economic reform which reduces the government's control. Analysis of the welfare impact of government policy in Turkmenistan is exacerbated by statistics which are even more unsatisfactory than Uzbekistan's.

By the usual economic aggregates, Turkmenistan's economic performance has been significantly worse than Uzbekistan's (Table 8.2). The poorer members of the population may have been sheltered by the social security system, but this worked only in the short term and by the end of 1995 the strategy was unsustainable. In 1996 official policy started to look more similar to Uzbekistan's gradual reform strategy, but implementation was more reluctant and the consequences are as yet unclear.

Notes

1. Cotton accounts for 30 per cent of GDP and over 40 per cent of employment (IMF 1996: 1).
2. UNDP (1996: 77) reports an increase in the Gini coefficient from 0.285 at independence to 0.341 in 1996.
3. Klugman and Schieber (1996) report Uzbekistan's public health expenditures to have been 4.0 per cent of GDP in 1996; comparable figures are 2.0 per cent for Kazakhstan, 3.2 per cent for the Kyrgyz Republic, 6.4 per cent for Tajikistan and 1.2 per cent for Turkmenistan. Private hospitals exist and doctors have left the state sector to open private practices, but the degree of privatization appears to be limited. A more common phenomenon appears to be that of state sector facilities charging for supposedly free services. The mid-1993 survey reported by Lubin (1995) found that surgery in a good clinic cost an average of 50 000 rubles, which was over one-tenth of the average annual salary in Uzbekistan.
4. Tibi (in ILO 1996: 99) reports that admissions into standard comprehensive schools declined from 78 per cent of basic education graduates in 1990 to 73 per cent in 1993, while admissions into vocational schools increased from 14 to 17 per cent.
5. In April 1995 the monthly salary of 300–400 sums (about US$10) was enough to cover living expenses for ten days (ILO 1996: 111). Teachers also receive subsidies from the state (that is, free housing and a 50 per cent discount on electricity, gas, water and transport). In Uzbekistan's state school system more is spent on supporting pupils' living expenses than on teachers.
6. It might also reflect increased cost. Although public sector education is technically free, admission to institutions with good reputations can be expensive, and this applies especially at the university level. Lubin (1995: 8) reports a mid-1993 admission charge for prestigious institutions of higher learning of close to 1 million rubles (that is, double the average annual salary).
7. Hetland and Haycock (in ILO 1996: 123n) report rates over 80 per cent among toddlers in Karakalpakstan. *The Economist* (15 October 1994: 31) quotes one doctor as saying that every pregnant woman he examined in a Nukus (Karakalpakstan) maternity unit was anaemic.
8. Birth rates fell from the high levels of the 1980s, but not as dramatically as in European transition economies. Soviet policy was pro-natalist; the cost to parents of children was close to zero, and the children were guaranteed jobs once they left school. Since independence some of the services provided freely to parents were reduced, and one consequence of the higher cost of children was increased use of contraceptives (mainly IUDs provided free by the government).
9. This is not due to lack of education. Kandiyoti (in ILO 1996: 138) points out that, although over 50 per cent of university degree holders in Uzbekistan are women, the proportion of women among senior managers is only 17.5 per cent. Within the government there are no women ministers, although there are female deputy ministers. The percentage of members of

parliament who are women fell from 35 per cent in the 1980s to 6 per cent in 1994, although this reflects the end of quotas rather than any change in a continuing low level of acceptance of women's involvement in politics.

10. World Bank estimates imply that the cotton sector provided 13.4 per cent of total government revenue in 1993 (Klugman 1997).
11. Tarr (1994) estimated that Uzbekistan would suffer from a 3 per cent terms-of-trade deterioration following the shift from administered to world prices on intra-USSR/CIS trade. The negative effect was reversed by increases in oil production, which reduced crude oil imports from 9 million tons in 1990 to 0.15 million tons in 1995 (IMF 1996: 8).
12. Other successor states usually included in the category of slow reformers have either been affected by gross mismanagement (Belarus, Ukraine and Turkmenistan) or war (Tajikistan and the Caucasus Republics), which have blown out public expenditures and led to hyperinflation.
13. This Annex draws heavily on Pomfret (1995) and on IMF Staff Country Report No. 96/30 on Turkmenistan (April 1996); all data are from the IMF Report. Turkmenistan has fewer inhabitants than Uzbekistan (its population in mid-1994 was 4.4 million, compared to Uzbekistan's 22.4 million), but started with a higher real GDP in 1991 (3540 PPP$ versus 2790 for Uzbekistan, according to the UNDP (1996) *Human Development Report 1994*). The international agencies stopped giving dollar–GDP estimates for Turkmenistan in the mid-1990s due to the poor data.
14. The contract value of exports enters into the trade account of the balance of payments, while arrears show up in the capital account as an increase in assets abroad. Even though these assets may never be realized, Turkmenistan has little recourse because the direction of gas exports is determined by the pipelines. Plans to build alternative gas pipelines through Iran to Turkey or to the Indian Ocean have been delayed by financing difficulties.

References

Cheasty, Adrienne and Jeffrey Davis (1996), 'Fiscal Transition in Countries of the Former Soviet Union: An Interim Assessment', *IMF Working Paper WP/96/61*, Fiscal Affairs Department, International Monetary Fund, Washington, DC (June) (also in *MOCT-MOST: Economic Policy in Transitional Economies*).

Craumer, Peter (1995), *Rural and Agricultural Development in Uzbekistan*, Former Soviet South Papers, Royal Institute of International Affairs, London.

Horton, Mark (1996), 'Health and Education Expenditure in Russia, the Baltic States and the Other Countries of the Former Soviet Union', *IMF Working Paper WP/96/126*, Washington, DC (November).

ILO (1996), *Social Policy and Economic Transformation in Uzbekistan*, Geneva: ILO.

IMF (1994), *Uzbekistan Economic Review*, Washington, DC: IMF.

IMF (1996), *Uzbekistan – Selected Issues and Statistical Appendix*, IMF Staff Country Report No. 96/73, Washington, DC: IMF (August).

Kaser, Michael (1997), *The Economics of Kazakstan and Uzbekistan*, Former Soviet South Papers, London, Royal Institute of International Affairs.

Klugman, Jeni (1997), 'Uzbekistan: A cautious approach to reform', paper prepared for the United Nations University World Institute for Development Economics Research (UNU/WIDER), Helsinki.

Klugman, Jeni and George Schieber (1996), *A Survey of Health Reform in Central Asia*, Report No. IDP-162, Europe and Central Asia Region Internal Discussion Paper, World Bank, Washington, DC (September).

Lubin, Nancy (1995), 'Central Asians take Stock: Reform, corruption, and identity', *Peaceworks*, No. 2, United States Institute for Peace, Washington, DC.

Pomfret, Richard (1995), *The Economies of Central Asia*, Princeton, NJ: Princeton University Press.

Pomfret, Richard and Kathryn Anderson (1997), 'Uzbekistan: Welfare impact of slow transition', *UNU/WIDER Working Paper*, No. 135, Helsinki: UNU/WIDER.

Popov, Vladimir (1996), 'A Russian Puzzle: What makes the Russian economic transformation a special case?', *Research for Action*, No. 29, Helsinki: UNU/WIDER.

Rashid, Ahmed (1994), *The Resurgence of Central Asia: Islam or Nationalism?*, London: Zed Books.

SCFS (1996), *The Basic Results of Social and Economic Development of the Republic of Uzbekistan, January–June 1996*, Main Computer Center of the State Committee for Forecasting and Statistics of the Republic of Uzbekistan, Tashkent.

Tarr, David (1994), 'How moving to World Prices affects the Terms of Trade of 15 Countries of the Former Soviet Union', *Journal of Comparative Economics*, 18, 1–24.

UNDP (1996), *Human Development Report Uzbekistan 1994*, United Nations Development Programme, Tashkent.

World Bank (1994), *Uzbekistan: Adjusting Social Protection*, Washington, DC: World Bank.

World Bank (1996), *World Development Report 1996: From Plan to Market*, New York: Oxford University Press for the World Bank.

9 Mongolia: The Welfare Impact of Marketization

Sahiya Lhagva

9.1 Introduction

As pointed out by a number of authors, there are two key factors in the former socialist countries that affect the pace and the sequence of transition to a market-based economy: the extent of macroeconomic imbalances, both internal and external; and the degree of centralization of economic management (see, for instance, Fischer and Gelb 1991). Countries with large macroeconomic imbalances and strong centralization need to combine stabilization and structural reforms to transform their economy, while countries closer to macroeconomic equilibrium can concentrate on structural reforms. Hence, for countries with large macroeconomic imbalances the reforms are much more difficult; they must stabilize the economy in a situation where conventional indirect fiscal and monetary policy tools are not available.

Mongolia was one of the countries with large macroeconomic imbalances and strong centralization. The enormous external imbalance caused other domestic ones. For 1985–89, Mongolia's trade deficit averaged 51.1 per cent of the economy's exports. The deficit was financed mostly by grants and conventional loans provided by CMEA partners, which averaged nearly 30 per cent of the country's GDP. The largest imbalance was in trade with the former USSR: for 1985–89 this support averaged 70 per cent of Mongolian exports to the former USSR.

The largest share of grants and loans was in the form of investment goods,[1] the major source of Mongolia's domestic investment. In 1970–90, official aid provided by the former CMEA member countries secured about 85 per cent of annual domestic investment. Mongolia's economic growth was dependent on investment. The share of average annual investment expenditure in GDP was about 50 per cent in 1980–90. Thus the source of the relatively high growth rate (for 1970–90 the average annual growth rate of national income was about 5 per cent) of the Mongolian economy was external aid. Even to maintain zero growth, the economy needed more and more external resources.

The social development of the country also was tied to external aid, as was the economy's growth. Investments made using project loans had created a significant number of jobs in construction, industry and other sectors. The health, education and housing sectors were developed by means of these loans, consistent with a relatively high level of social service development. In the 1980s, nearly 40 per cent of consumer goods sold in the domestic market were imported from the former CMEA countries. Thus, by the end of the 1980s, Mongolia had reached a relatively high level of economic and social development (per capita GDP calculated with the official exchange rate in 1989 amounted to about US$1600, with a literacy rate of about 97 per cent), but with significant and increasing macroeconomic imbalances. With the unexpected termination of aid from the former USSR and other CMEA countries, stabilization and restructuring became inevitable.

The management of the economy was based on strong central planning despite the modest reform steps undertaken in the mid-1980s. The government controlled all prices; five-year and annual plans covered all economic activities. Plan targets determined the distribution of all resources – goods, capital and labour. Liberalization, the development of economic activities based on private ownership and the introduction of a system of macroeconomic regulation with indirect fiscal and monetary tools were needed to transform the economy into a market economy.

It is obvious that these reforms would affect the social welfare system. The impacts would be the stronger, the greater the decline in output of the economy as a result of the reforms and the more centralized the social welfare system.

This chapter aims to assess the impacts of the Mongolian transition on the well-being of the population. The first section describes economic reforms and their impact on social developments; the second section surveys the reforms of the social safety net and social policies during transition. The last section summarizes the changes in well-being during the transition in Mongolia.

9.2 Macro- and microeconomic impacts on welfare changes

Since 1990, economic and social developments in Mongolia have been determined by two factors: external shocks and the transition process. The termination of Soviet aid in 1991 had severe effects on the Mongolian economy, which had been extremely dependent on this aid. Within one year, Mongolian exports to the former USSR declined by a factor of 2.2, imports by a factor of 3, which led to declines by factors of 1.9 and 2.6 in total Mongolian exports and imports respectively. In these circumstances, the coalition government, which was formed as a result of the first democratic elections held in July 1990, initiated reforms to transform the economy from a centrally planned to a market economy. The reform strategy was based on a rapid approach, and the centrally planned system was dismantled, notwithstanding the non-existence of market forces and regulators. Within a short period, five-year and annual plans were abolished, all economic activities were liberalized, control on prices, wages, interest rates and exchange rates were lifted, and a privatization programme was adopted and implemented.

As a result of these developments – in particular, the external shock and the transition process – the economy has experienced a significant contraction. As Table 9.1 shows, after the decline in

Table 9.1 Indices of main indicators of Mongolian economy in 1990–96 (1989 = 100)

	1990	*1991*	*1992*	*1993*	*1994*	*1995*	*1996*
GNP	97.6	94.5	87.1	80.8	83.3	88.7	91.0
Per capita GNP	94.8	84.0	74.2	70.6	71.0	74.3	75.8
Gross industrial output	94.3	80.1	75.6	65.8	67.6	75.6	73.7
Gross agricultural output	96.3	89.1	83.8	80.3	86.0	91.7	93.5
Foreign trade turnover	94.1	42.1	47.9	45.2	36.5	52.7	51.1
Annual inflation rate	–	52.7	325.5	183.0	66.3	53.1	53.2
Unemployment rate (at the end of year)	5.5	6.5	6.3	8.7	8.6	5.4	6.5

Source: Authors' calculations, Mongolian Economy and Society in 1996, 1993 and 1991. State Statistical Office of Mongolia.

1990–94, there is a trend towards stabilization. However, the output of the economy is still less than it was in 1990.

It is obvious that in a declining economy the well-being of people is problematical. In the short run, transitional reforms impose, besides economic decline, changes in the social environment. In pre-reform Mongolia, prices were regulated through subsidies and strong control: children's clothes, electricity and some other prices were subsidized significantly. With the withdrawal of Soviet economic aid, the government lost one of the major sources of its budget revenue and was forced to cut expenditures. And price subsidies were eliminated for two reasons: the budget revenue drop, and price liberalization. By 1992, all price subsidies were eliminated and most prices were 'freed'.

With the lifting of control on prices and the elimination of price subsidies, a rapid increase in prices occured. As shown in Table 9.1, annual inflation peaked in 1992, at 325.5 per cent. Wage control was eliminated early, in July 1991, with the passing by parliament of a new Labour Law. The government was allowed to establish the minimum wage and salaries for civil servants.

With the sharp increase in prices, connected initially with price liberalization and elimination of price subsidies, wages were increasing. Since 1991 the government has increased salaries of public employees several times. In 1996, the average salary of public employees was higher by a factor of approximately 17.7 than in 1991. However, due to high inflation and the policy of salary restraint, which is one of the basic components of a shock approach in transition, real wages have fallen. Between January 1991 and the end of 1996, the difference in public employees' average salary growth and CPI amounted to about 4.2-fold.

There are no data on wages in the private sector and in state-owned enterprises. Estimates given by different sources are unanimous in indicating that wages in the private sector are higher than public sector wages, but not much. Moreover, taking into account the relatively large proportion of civil servants in the total number of employees (in 1990–96, it averaged about 35 per cent, with a gradual decline since 1993), it is likely that there is a notable drop in real wages. The real wage drop is also reflected in household income data. According to a household survey conducted by the State Statistical Office monthly, the share of wages and salaries in total income of urban households declined from 61 per cent in 1992 to 51 per cent in 1996, while that of rural households declined from 39.5 per cent to 27.9 per cent (see Table 9.4).

The another key factor that caused the real wage decline is unemployment. Under the centrally planned system, there was no officially registered unemployment, despite high population growth rate during the 1960–80s. In Mongolia, which had sparse and, more important, declining population the pro-natal policy had been effective. Abortion was illegal, contraceptives were unavailable, the government provided large support for child care, maternity leave, and early retirement for women with more than four children. This resulted in rapid growth of population, at about 2.8 per cent annually in the 1950–80s, and a significant increase in the number of working-age people and children. In the 1970–80s, with the increase of Soviet aid and the associated implementation of large investment projects, the centrally planned system managed to employ a growing labour force. Clearly, cessation of the aid led to significant reductions in employment opportunities.

The cancellation of large investment projects financed with aid caused a notable decline in employment in construction, transport and service sectors. As Table 9.2 shows, from 1990 to 1992 the number of employees in construction declined by 37.3 per cent (or 24 600) and in transport and communication – by 13 per cent (or 7500). The decline was continuing still: in 1996 the total number of employees in construction, transport and communication was nearly half the figure for 1991. Industrial employment has also declined, although some increase was recorded in 1991 and 1992. The decline in industry was caused to a large extent by shortage of critical inputs, spare parts and output marketing, mainly export problems. Only agricultural employment has increased steadily since 1990, due to the privatization of the

Table 9.2 Mongolia: changes in number of employees in 1991–96 (1990 = 100)

	1991	*1992*	*1993*	*1994*	*1995*	*1996*
Total	101.54	102.86	98.62	100.37	101.42	101.05
Industry	100.46	101.75	94.30	76.67	82.14	79.48
Agriculture	106.22	113.68	116.77	130.06	136.9	138.37
Construction	74.85	62.73	50.0	41.36	44.7	45.0
Transport and communication	90.47	87.0	79.72	54.59	54.77	54.77
Trade and service	95.05	98.53	92.49	123.44	118.68	125.46

Source: Authors' calculations, Mongolian Economy and Society in 1996, 1993 and 1991. State Statistical Of°ce of Mongolia.

livestock sector and the increase in the number of private herdsmen. The crop sector has been in continuing decline since 1990; its gross output in 1996 was about 41 per cent of 1990 output; its share in gross output of agriculture declined from 27.1 to 15.3 per cent in corresponding years. The number of employees in trade and services has increased after a decline for three years, which is also connected with the growth of private business activities in the sector. Thus the external shock caused shifts in the composition of employees from the industry, construction, transport and communication sectors, where more skilled labour are employed, towards the livestock sector, where requirements for labour skills are lower. Such a shift will probably encourage a decline in labour skills and the general educational level.

In many other transition cases, the short-run effect of transitional reforms on employment has been negative. However, in the Mongolian case, privatization had a less painful effect on employment, owing to the scheme adopted for its implementation. The Privatization Law, enacted in May 1991, adopted the voucher method of privatization, which permitted each citizen to participate in both the direct sale of small state-owned assets – 'small' privatization – and in 'corporatization' of large enterprises, or in the trading of their shares, which is called 'large' privatization. The privatization programme started in July 1991 with voucher distribution, and the government announced in the middle of 1994 that all small businesses to be privatized under the programme, including livestock, were to be transferred to private hands.

The advantage of the 'small' privatization concerning employment was in opening up more possibilities for self-employment. A herder, previously employed either by a state farm or by an agricultural collective, after privatization of the animals in his charge, becomes a self-employed herder. A worker in a small retail shop, who added his voucher to those of others to privatize the shop, was not fired shortly after privatization. Table 9.2 shows some evidence that, in agriculture, trade and the service sector, employment increased notably during 1991–96, so that the number of employed in agriculture was 38.4 per cent higher than in 1990 and in services and trade the increase was 25.5 per cent. Nevertheless, in two to three years a self-employed herder who lost or sold animals, and a shop worker, who did not care enough to have his name included in a list of co-owners or who simply agreed to exclude his name from the list for a bottle of vodka, became unemployed and poor.

The short-run impact of 'large' privatization on employment was similar. As a result of 'large' privatization state-owned enterprises were transformed into shareholding companies, whose shares were dispersed almost equally among shareholders, because vouchers distributed for large privatization were not allowed to be traded freely and could only be exchanged for shares in another company. Moreover, in many cases the government became the dominant shareholder, having 51 per cent of the shares. For many top executives of such companies, who could not have more shares than other shareholders, waiting for the second stage of privatization when the cash trading of shares would start, was more important than current profit and dividends. They did not fire employees and they paid minimum wages. This was partly due to tradition as well as the anticipated future need for skilled workers. However, during the next stage of privatization, when the new owners of shareholding companies emerge, the situation will change, and hiring will depend more directly on costs.

Liberalization, particularly of domestic and foreign trade, had similar effects on employment. In the early stage of transition, when travel to China and Russia was initially allowed, and when consumer items bought in China could be sold in Mongolia or Russia with 100 per cent profit each week, many Mongols became self-employed traders. In two to three years, when the price differences disappeared, exchange rates became more realistic, and when sanitary requirements and inspections, tax regulations and other controls became stronger, many of the traders became unemployed and poor. Thus unemployment will become a greater problem than it has been so far.

It should be noted that the data on unemployment do not reflect fully the depth and extent of the problem. For instance, as Table 9.3 shows for the six-year period 1991–96, the number of officially unemployed did not increase noticeably; in 1996 the same number as in 1991 was recorded. Also, a more than 50 percentage point decrease in 1995 was caused by a revision of unemployment registration regulations in 1994, under which many of those previously registered were excluded by reason of not having proper documents. There is a generally accepted understanding that unemployment has been increasing since 1991, as well as the unemployment rate, although according to official statistics the number of unemployed and the unemployment rate are relatively low and fell in 1992 and 1995.

Because unemployment is a new phenomenon for Mongolia, the government provided minimum support to the unemployed. However, budget constraints and high inflation significantly reduced the effectiveness of the newly established system, and the real compensation was much lower than minimum living standards.

Table 9.3 Mongolia: number of unemployed

	1991	*1992*	*1993*	*1994*	*1995*	*1996*
Number of officially registered unemployed (000s)	55.4	54.00	71.9	74.9	45.1	55.4
Change, 1991 = 100, %	100.0	97.47	129.78	135.2	81.41	100.0
Calculated number of unemployed (000s)	180.7	221.70	276.9	269.1	271.2	294.9
Change, 1991 = 100, %	100.0	122.69	153.24	148.92	150.08	163.2
Portion of calculated unemployed in potential labour force, %	18.51	21.57	26.38	25.49	25.44	27.13

Source: Authors' calculations, Mongolian Economy and Society in 1996, 1993 and 1991. State Statistical Office of Mongolia.

The decline in the real wage, the increase in unemployment and the absence of an adequate social security system led to a drop in household real income, as well as notable changes in its composition. In the early 1990s, when the transition reforms were in the initial stage and high inflation eroded wages and real incomes, shares of wages in total income of households fell. During 1991, real monetary income of households dropped by nearly half (49.5 per cent) and the share of wages in total monetary income of households fell from 73.5 per cent to 65.3 per cent. Later on, declines in real monetary income of households stopped, even as incomes increased to the 1991 level, while the share of wages in household income remained stable after 1994. However, households' real monetary income still remains less than the pre-reform period level, as well as the share of wages in it (see Figure 9.1.)

As shown in Table 9.4, the share of individual income, or the income from private self-employed business, increased considerably, especially in urban areas. The change is greater when compared with the pre-reform period, although the data for years before 1992 were based on a slightly different system of accounting. For example, the share of wages and monetary income earned from agricultural cooperatives in total monetary income of households averaged about 73 per cent in 1985–89.

The composition of household expenditure has also changed, responding to the decline in real income. The share of food expenditure has increased for both urban and rural households, basically due

Figure 9.1 Mongolia: real income and CPI (1990 = 100)

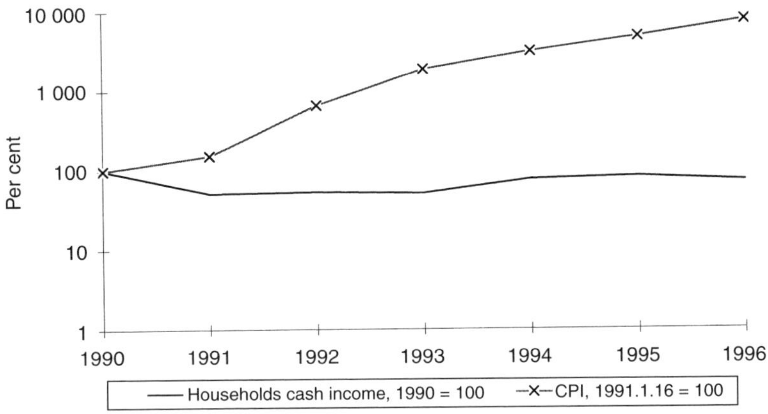

Source: Authors' calculations, Mongolian Economy and Society in 1996, 1993 and 1991. State Statistical Office of Mongolia

Table 9.4 Income and expenditure composition of Mongolian households

	Urban households		*Rural households*	
	1992	*1996*	*1992*	*1996*
Total monetary income	100.0	100.0	100.0	100.0
wages and salaries	61.0	51.0	39.5	27.9
pensions and allowances	8.3	7.8	8.9	5.9
individual income	2.5	9.1	39.2	47.2
Total monetary expenditure	100.0	100.0	100.0	100.0
Expenditure on food – total	49.9	52.7	30.7	45.0
of which, meat and meat products	15.3	14.6	3.5	2.0
flour and bakery products	9.8	17.2	9.2	26.1
vegetables and potatoes	3.2	3.5	0.9	0.8
Non-food expenditure	32.9	25.5	58.9	42.5
Expenditure on services	16.0	21.3	7.5	12.4

Source: Authors' calculations, Mongolian Economy and Society in 1996, 1993 and 1991. State Statistical Office of Mongolia.

to the increase of the share of flour and bakery products. However, this is mostly a result of price increases, since prices for flour increased faster than for other products.

The data in the Appendix table (9A.1) and Figure 9.2 show that in 1989–92 real consumption of almost all food items declined but, after

1992, and for some items after 1993, their consumption tended to increase. Consumption among three groups of food, namely, meat and meat products, milk and dairy products and flour and bakery products, changed more gradually than for other products, remaining the major food items for Mongols. Consumption of some food items changed considerably, but such changes are either due to their own specific reasons, or are not that important for Mongolian food consumption. For instance, annual consumption of butter fell from 3 kg per head in 1989 to 0.6 kg in 1992 and 1993, and then increased to 3 kg in only one year. This became possible because of the receipt in 1992 of butter as food aid from the United States. Fish is a not popular food for Mongols; its major consumers are foreigners, and consumption of fish and fish products per head still is not large: in 1989, it was 1.3 kg. According to statistics in 1996, a Mongolian consumer used 1.4 eggs per year, which is 19 times less than in 1989 and 10 times less than in 1991, although per head production of eggs exceeded consumption in 1996, opposite to the 1989 situation.

The general trend in food consumption and diet after 1990 is a reduction in food diversity which, obviously, indicates a decline in real income. The dynamics of nutritional intake supports this finding. As can be seen in the Appendix table (9A.1), per capita intake of calories, protein and carbohydrates fell in 1991, and although there is a tendency to recover, these are still short of their 1989 levels.

Figure 9.2 Indices of consumption of selected foods in Mongolia

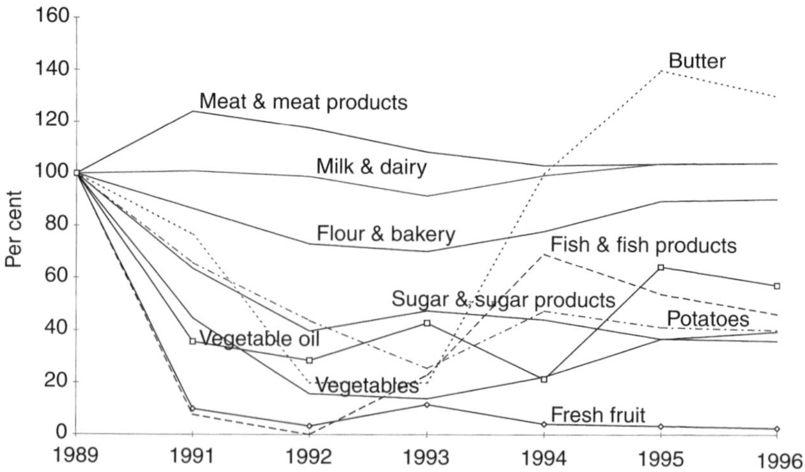

However, real incomes were eroded unequally among all segments of population and, as a result, inequality in wealth and income distribution is growing. In 1995, the income of poor households was less than half the average. Certainly, the transition from a socialist to a market-oriented economy is not possible without removing the equality in living standards of the entire population maintained in a socialist country by repressing incentives. Privatization and liberalization remove the barriers that had reduced incentives, and redistribute wealth accumulated in the past, but fail to consider increasing inequality. In an economy where output and income are in decline, the chance of increasing poverty affecting a larger proportion of population is greater than in an economy where output and income are not in decline. This is one of the reasons why poverty became in a short period of time an acute social and political issue in the Mongolian transition.

One of the priorities of the privatization concept adopted in Mongolia was to provide the most equal opportunity for each citizen to make the process of wealth and income differentiation less painful. However, in reality, the implementation of the privatization programme, based on equal distribution of vouchers, made it inevitable that the process of income differentiation would not be as smooth as expected. Indeed, it became one of the contributing factors to poverty in the country. Livestock privatization contributed to the worsening of welfare conditions of a part of the rural population more directly. In pre-reform Mongolia, about half of total households were engaged in the livestock sector as employees of state farms and members of agricultural collectives.

The privatization programme provided only guidelines for the privatization of animals and other assets of agricultural collectives, and granted to collectives a large degree of discretion. The guidelines included as criteria the number of animals a person contributed from his/her private herd at the time of collectivization and the contribution a person made to the collective. Strict interpretation of these criteria led to an uneven distribution of livestock among herders. For instance, former owners of large herds received animals, even though they had moved to the city after collectivization and were living in the city. In other cases, able-bodied men could receive more animals than single women, on the principle that they had contributed more to the collective.

Moreover, with privatization many herding families received a composition of livestock which had low potential for income generation and future growth. In a pastoral system of herding, the value and function of different types of animals are different, hence households need mixed herds to meet their needs for milk, meat, cash income and growth of number of animals. As a result, many rural households could not receive sufficient assets to maintain their previous living standards.

Privatization, especially livestock privatization, has led to the removal of the limited social services which were previously available within state-owned enterprises and agricultural collectives. Agricultural collectives were responsible for marketing of animal products, supplying basic goods for herdsmen, and providing some additional support for health and educational service units at the level of *som*.[2] With the dissolution of the collectives, herdsmen became responsible for all of that by themselves, which has worsened their living conditions.

Officially there was no poverty in Mongolia before 1990, basic needs were met, and access to a full range of social services was guaranteed. With the economy's decline, a portion of the population became unable to provide for their own basic necessities. In 1992, the government introduced a poverty line (the minimum standard of living) to estimate the poverty situation in the country. The poverty line was calculated on the basis of a minimum basket of goods that should be available to all in accordance with a physiologically adequate food calorie level plus allowance for non-food items such as shelter, clothing and heating, and was set separately for rural and urban areas. Using this measure, the government estimated that about 16 per cent of the population lived below the poverty line.

Since then the government has revised the poverty line several times. The latest revision, made in February 1997, introduced seven separate zones and established different poverty lines for each of them. According to the government estimate, about 20 per cent of the population counted as poor in 1996 (see Table 9.5). However, an alternative assessment of poverty, based on the Living Standards Measurement Survey (LSMS) generated by the World Bank in 1995, indicates the poverty incidence to be 33.1 per cent in the rural areas, 38.5 per cent in the urban areas and 36.3 per cent for Mongolia as a whole.

Members of large and low-income families, female-headed households, disabled people, orphans, children in single-parent households and the elderly with no one to take care of them are the most seriously affected by poverty. Twenty-three per cent of poor families have more than four children, 26 per cent of these families are headed by unemployed, and 21 per cent are female-headed families.

Table 9.5 Poverty incidence in Mongolia

Year	*Rural*	*Urban*	*Overall*
1991	n.a.	n.a.	14.5
1992	n.a.	n.a.	17.7*
1993	19.5	16.5	17.8
1994	26.1	15.1	20.2
1995	16.6	14.7	15.6
1996	19.8	18.7	19.2

* Excluding 7 *aimags* (*Aimags* are administrative areas with population varying from 45 to 120 000. There are 21 *aimags* in Mongolia.)

Source: Authors' calculations, State Statistical Office.

Interestingly, there is a portion of civil servants, whose income per a family member is below the official poverty line. For instance, as was reported recently, about 5 per cent of police staff and 20 per cent of officers in the armed forces had income per a family member below the poverty line. The low salary of civil servants, and unemployment among their family members, especially adult children, are causes of poverty in this group. In the circumstances, public employees naturally seek additional sources of income, but in the current situation there are limited opportunities to employ their education and skills. Most civil servants are engaged in work on the side, not related to their profession, such as self-employment in retail trade, which does not promote the improvement of their skills and, thereby, contributes to the decline in the quality of services they provide.

Furthermore, low wages of civil servants, combined with the rapid differentiation in income and wealth of the population, contributed to the emergence of an environment encouraging corruption and bribery. There are no official statistics on corruption and bribery-related crimes, but the media give plenty of examples. There is no doubt that it has become one of the serious problems of social and economic development of the country. However, no formal study has been carried out on the problem.

Poverty has caused significant changes in human ecology and the human environment. Despite the very few social statistics, the worsening of the human social environment is evident. According to some surveys conducted by non-government organizations, there are about 3000 street children, 800 prostitutes in Ulaanbaatar, the capital city, in contrast with the pre-reform period, when prostitution and homelessness did not exist. The number of crime cases increased by a factor of 2.3 in 1996 compared to 1991. Theft has became so common that there is almost no one who has not been affected. Human relations are worsening: the communist ideology that in the past was a basis of social behaviour of individuals has been destroyed, but new rules that determine social behaviour have not yet developed.

The government policy to alleviate poverty is based on two mutually linked approaches. The first is the promotion of the productive use of the poor's most abundant asset – labour – which means creation of new jobs. The second is the provision of basic social services to the poor: primary health, nutrition and primary education. A National Poverty Alleviation Programme, approved by the government in May 1994, identifies practical actions in accordance with these approaches. In 1992 the government founded a Poverty Fund, which was designated as the major implementation body of the programme. The government is aware that, with its limited resources, programme implementation would be delayed and sought external assistance. At the request of the government, donors are assisting and several projects are being implemented or are in preparation.

New market tools of macroeconomic management, like taxes, still play a limited role in fighting poverty and alleviating income inequality. Theoretically, transitional reforms may be grouped into two different types: liberalizing reforms and establishing reforms. The ultimate goal of the liberalizing reforms is to establish a new economic environment where economic agents are coordinated with the use of indirect tools instead of direct planning. Accordingly, transitional liberalization rejects those macroeconomic tools which were effective in a centrally planned economic system in order to establish a new environment, but this might be done so rapidly that economic agents could not change their behaviour. Moreover, liberalizing reforms should be followed closely with establishing reforms, which means the adoption of new macroeconomic management tools. The time gap between these two reforms could readily lead to a 'macroeconomic management vacuum', or a situation in which tools of the centrally planned system are removed and inactive, but the newly introduced market-based ones cannot function properly due to their incompleteness and the behaviour of economic agents. Poverty in Mongolia is probably partly due to this situation.

The progressive taxation scheme on the personal income which was effective in pre-reform era has not changed except in the details, such as the number of tax brackets. The weak administration of the tax col-

Figure 9.3 Personal income taxes in Mongolia

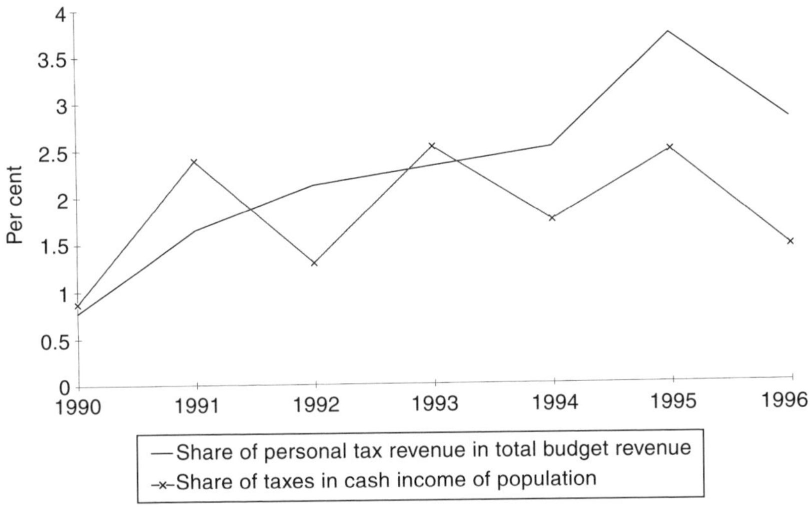

lection and income monitoring system limits the impact of taxes on households' (after-tax) income (Figure 9.3).

Another channel of tax effects on the living conditions of the population is connected with employment opportunities. Progressive taxation with rates of up to 40 per cent on corporate income, combined with import duties, sales taxes and other social taxes made the tax burden for business relatively heavy and did not encourage investment. However, to reduce the tax burden, and thereby to overcome its impacts on budget revenue, it was necessary to complete reforms in the social security system, the institutional structure of the government and other public spheres. Moreover, investment changes are dependent not only on taxes; other factors, such as banking system, insurance and financial market development, are essential for investment.

Figure 9.4 suggests that there is no visible correlation between investment and employment dynamics for 1990–96; investment trends also do not appear to be correlated with the tax reforms of 1991 and 1993.

Substantial increases in social taxes associated with the introduction of the health and social insurance system in 1993 and 1995, which will be described below, increased labour costs and thereby, theoretically, contributed to the increase in unemployment. However, as Table 9.3 shows, the number of officially registered unemployed did not increase

Figure 9.4 Investment and employment in Mongolia

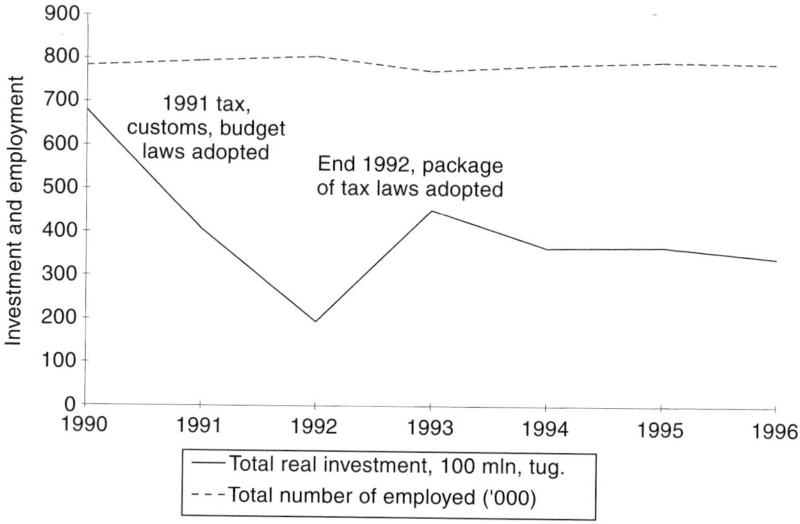

along with the new social taxes; on the contrary, in 1995 the number declined.

The impact of financial sector reforms on welfare changes is difficult to measure. With the establishment of a two-tiered banking system and commercial banks, access to financial sources for private business activities became possible. However, for the majority of the population, especially for the most needy group, commercial loans have not been accessible due to their ability to initiate a profit-making project and the high interest rates caused by inflation. Because of weak management and low discipline in the banking sector, by the end of 1996 bad loans were estimated to be as much as 35 per cent of total outstanding loans; in February 1997, two commercial banks were abolished, one of which was the biggest in the country.

The shortcomings of banking sector reforms, just as reforms in other sectors, hit more seriously the poorer segment of the population. For example, as a result of the bankruptcy announced in 1995, a large number of personal savers in the first 'pure' private commercial bank in Mongolia, established only by private companies and individuals, have lost their deposits. Eighty-five per cent of the depositors/losers are pensioners and low income-people.

9.3 Impact of social policies on welfare changes

In Mongolia, social policies since 1990 have been formulated and implemented under the pressure of a severe resource shortage and transitional reform imperatives. The government budget, the revenue of which for years had been dependent on sources provided by the former USSR, was cut drastically with the termination of aid. In 1996, the budget social expenditures/GDP ratio equalled 15.6 per cent, or less by 10 percentage points than it was in 1989 (see Figure 9.5).

Budget cuts directly affected the delivery of social services and its quality. In the first instance, social programmes such as housing development, construction of schools, hospitals, and cultural centres in rural areas, which had been implemented with Soviet aid, stopped. Houses under construction in 1996 were fewer by nearly 76 per cent of their 1990 figure.[3] Tertiary education was seriously affected with the cessation of full-term scholarship programmes, funded mostly by loans made by the governments of the former socialist countries to the Mongolian government. The programmes had been available for 1000–1500 post-secondary students annually.

A number of primary schools and health posts in centres of the most remote *soms* have closed due to the shortage of financial sources. In 1996, there were 512 primary–secondary schools with 13 155 teachers while, in 1989, the corresponding figures were 615 and 19 800. In total, 1375 medical posts operated in 1990, but in 1996 their number decreased to 917. In most cases, funds allocated to rural schools and medical posts from the budget were sufficient only to pay salaries of personnel. Even in Ulaanbaatar, many cases have been reported in which doctors and hospitals did not provide medicine, syringes and other materials for treatment and patients were required to provide these themselves, including food for their stay in hospital. Debts of hospitals and schools to suppliers of electricity, heating and medicine had been growing until 1995, because of budget funds delay, and the debt problem is still not completely solved .

The education sector in pre-reform Mongolia was relatively well developed: almost all children of primary school age were enrolled. All *som* centres had schools, most of which were junior secondary and boarding schools. In 1990, the education sector employed about 50 000 people, or 6.4 per cent of the total employed in the economy. A figure of 537 000 people or about one-quarter of the total population attended an educational institution, and education accounted for 17.6 per cent of government expenditures and 11.5 per cent of GDP.

Figure 9.5 Budget revenue and expenditure in Mongolia, 1989–96

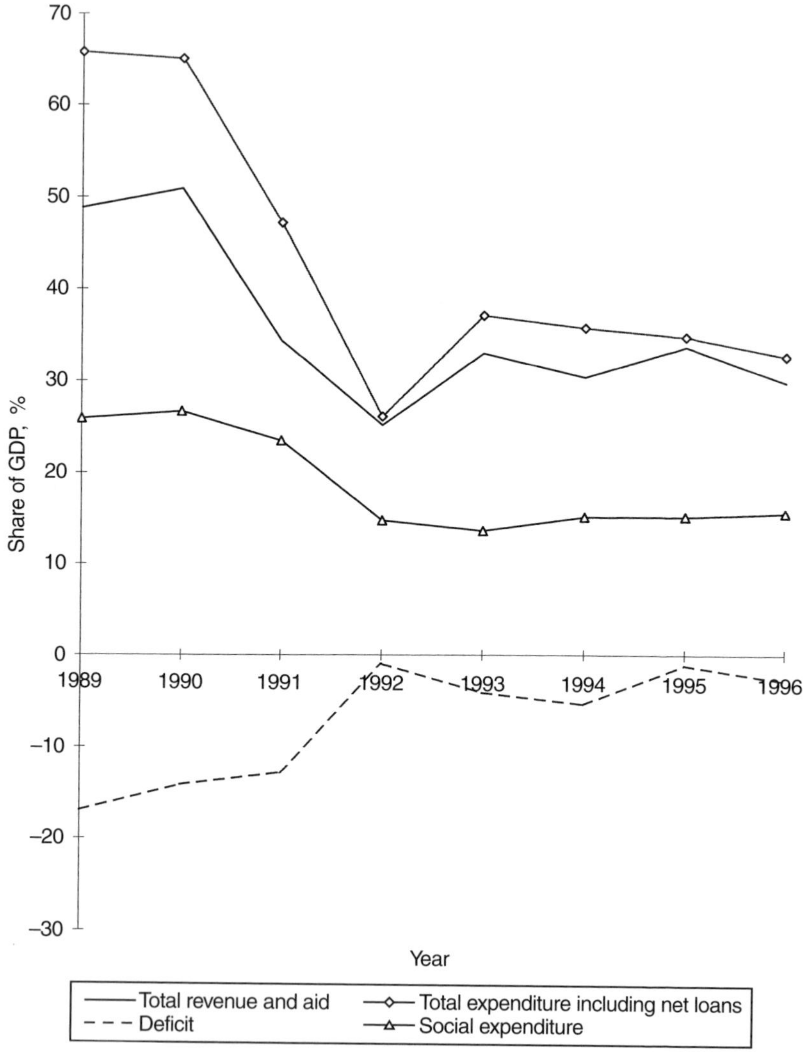

This level of educational spending was very high by international standards, although the percentage of the Mongolian population aged 14 and below was comparable to the average in developing countries, excluding China and India. The gross enrolment ratio was 98 per cent in primary schools, 85 per cent in secondary schools and 15 per cent in tertiary education, which compares favourably with ratios in middle-income countries.

The first radical move to reform the system was undertaken in the middle of 1991, with adoption of a new Education Law, under which general education remained free but higher education became subject to a fee. Private schools and training institutions of any level of education and any field of knowledge were allowed to operate, which in fact was *de facto* legalization of such entities. Primary school education for eight years remained compulsory, though children were allowed to take a break or shift after the eighth grade should they choose to attend specialized classes or vocational courses. To alleviate the burden of post-secondary education fees, a government-financed Fund for Training, which would make loans to students, was established.

As a result of these reforms, private educational institutions have emerged. The number of schools in all categories increased from 782 in 1991 to 930 in 1996, although the total is less than it was in 1989. There were 51 private vocational schools and institutions of higher education in 1996, all established after 1991. However, teaching quality in these schools is not high. Most do not have their own building and library, and only have a few teaching staff. Most of these are part-time teachers from other institutions. There are no special government regulations on private educational institutions, except the need to acquire a licence to establish.

Founders of private schools are free to spend the tuition fee as they wish, running the institutions as profit-making businesses. It is possible that in the future there will be a decline in the number of such institutions, as a consequence of tightening government supervision as well as increased competition among them.

The opening of new private educational institutions caused an increase in the number of schools, but, because of the small size of such institutions, the total number of teachers and students did not increase; on the contrary, these figures decreased. This is also caused by the decrease in average class sizes: traditionally, in rural areas schools were small due to low density, but the intensification of rural migration to urban areas in the last two to three years has led to a further decrease of students there. According to Ministry of Science and Education data, the number of children dropping out before completing secondary school increased from 6133 in 1989 to a peak of 48 446 in 1992, after which the number declined. The combined primary, secondary and tertiary gross enrolment rate was 76 per cent in 1989, 54 per cent in 1992 and 57 per cent in 1995.

Mongolia's health indicators before 1990 were impressive. However, the budgetary constraints caused nearly a 42 per cent decline in real per capita budget expenditure on healthcare in 1990–96. Government expenditure on healthcare as a share of GDP has declined by 40 per cent. The number of hospital beds per 1000 population decreased from 11.8 in 1989 to 9.9 in 1996 and the number of physicians per 10 000 population from 28 to 26.

Nevertheless, basic health indicators have not worsened noticeably; on the contrary, they have improved. Overall life expectancy has increased from 62.6 in 1989 to 63.8 in 1996, infant mortality rate of under 1 year has declined by 44 per cent (see Appendix table 9A.1). This is puzzling in the light of the overall situation in the sector, and most specialists explain it in terms of the fall in records due to the decrease in contact between mothers and health services. It is notable that research conducted for the 1994 and 1996 Demographic Surveys, using birth histories of individual women, found the average infant mortality rate for the period to be as much as 50 per cent greater than the official figures. The figure for maternal deaths increased sharply in 1992, from 93 in 1991 to 129, but after that it decreases consistently, and in 1996 was 90.

Financial constraints have forced reforms in the sector. A Law on Citizens' Health Insurance adopted in 1993 initiated a radical reform of the health sector. The law established a compulsory health insurance system. It was laid down that all segments of the entire population, except a few groups like the unemployed and foreign citizens, would be covered by the insurance system. For these groups, insurance is available. No less than 50 per cent of insurance premiums were stipulated to be paid by the employer, and the rest by the employee. The government was to be responsible for 50 per cent of herdsmen's insurance premium and for 100 per cent of some groups which had low income, such as disabled, pensioners with single pension income and children under 16. The insurance premium rate was to be set by the government, but not to exceed 6 per cent of the salary of the insured. The categories of medical aid free of charge, as well as the health services not covered by insurance, were specified. For other categories, fees were to be paid fully by an insurance fund. Patients now pay more of the cost of medical treatments, supporting the viability of the insurance fund and, as pointed out by the majority in the parliament, 'to make each one more responsible for his/her own health'.

Reforms of the social security system were not simple and straightforward. One of the first laws passed by the interim parliament formed in 1990 by the first multi-party elections in the euphoria of political democratization was the Pension Law. The law was an ambitious one. It widened considerably the coverage of old age pensions by adding to the system agricultural cooperative members who had had a separate system, by lowering minimum pension age and shortening the length of service required to obtain old age pension. Moreover, it became possible to obtain pensions and continue working.

Shortly after the Pension Law was adopted, in April 1991, a Social Benefits Law and a Social Contribution Law were passed. The Social Benefits Law transferred the system of assistance for temporarily disabled persons, which had been managed by labour unions, to government management. The law also introduced a severance payment for released workers. According to these laws, all pensions and benefits except severance payments, were to be paid from the pension fund, the sources of which were contributions by employers and transfers from the government budget. Severance payments were established to be financed from funds which had to be transferred by employers to 'labour markets', a kind of support for the unemployed.

Thus the basic aim of the 1990–91 changes was the improvement of social relief provided by the government; the reform of the social safety net itself was not the goal. As a result, the number of beneficiaries as well as social security expenditure increased significantly. The total number of pensioners increased by approximately 40 per cent in two years – between 1990 and 1992 government pension expenditure increased by nearly 90 per cent in real terms. The burden of the social safety net on the government budget was increasing despite the increase of the employers' contribution rate to the pension fund to 13 per cent of wages and salaries. At the same time, due to inflation, real pensions and benefits were falling rapidly, and living conditions of a large proportion of beneficiaries dependent on the social safety net worsened significantly. This showed the need for reform of the net as a whole.

The social safety net, which was established and functioned in the Mongolian centrally planned economy where income distribution was strongly controlled, did need to make special efforts to identify groups in the population in need of relief. Without strong targeting toward the vulnerable groups of the population, a social safety system becomes ineffective and even a factor that delays growth of the whole economy. With this consideration, the identification of the really needy segment of the population and the targeting of programmes, making current personal contributions to the safety net as the source of future benefits, were laid as the basis of the social policy reforms of the mid-1990s. In January 1995, a package of social insurance laws came into force: in February 1996, the Law on Social Insurance established five separate funds of pensions and benefits, each of which was to be financed according to the different categories of pensions and benefits.

The Law on Social Assistance identified the vulnerable groups as people for whom pensions and benefits from the Social Assistance Fund would be delivered. The sources of the Social Assistance Fund are specified as the central and local government's budget, interest earnings from banks, donations and others.

Thus a social safety net comparable with those functioning in a market economy has been established. However, it is still early to assess the new system because of the short period and insufficient data for comparison.

9.4 Conclusions

Since 1990, Mongolia has been implementing a transition process from a centrally planned economy to a market-based one. The main elements of the transition process, liberalization, privatization and the reform of macroeconomic management, are complicated by the adjustment process, caused by large and deep imbalances exposed by the loss of external assistance which had been available for years previously. The combination of the two processes has had a harsh impact on the well-being of the population. Per capita GDP declined by 25 per cent in 1996 as compared with 1989, unemployment is growing, education and health sectors are in decline, and one-fifth of the entire population lives below the official poverty line. The elderly, disabled, orphans, female-headed households and households with many children are adversely affected by the decline in living conditions.

High inflation, which followed the liberalization, but caused by large imbalances in the economy, was one of the major factors that led to a decline in the real income of the population. The sharp cut in budget expenditures due to cessation of external aid and the rapid decentralization of macroeconomic management led to increased unemployment and to reductions in both delivery and quality of social services.

The impact of privatization on living conditions of the population was complex. On the one hand, it led to a rapid differentiation in income in the population which, in terms of the Mongolian declining economy, inevitably caused an increase in the number of the poorer section of population and a decrease in their average income. On the other hand, privatization and liberalization made labour mobile, opened new opportunities for business and self-employment and, thereby alleviated, to some extent, unemployment growth.

The transition required reforms of the social service sectors, such as education, healthcare and social assistance, which under a centrally planned system were fully provided by the government. A series of reform measures has been undertaken since the transition started, and fundamental changes have been made. A new social insurance system has been introduced, and charges for part of education and healthcare services have been imposed. This has increased incentives for those who provide the services to rationalize their spending and improve the quality of services. Private institutions in the health and education sectors are growing, creating a competitive situation and offering richer choices for people. However, for a proportion of population the reforms caused a decline in living conditions by reducing their access to services available to them before the reform.

To mitigate the adverse effect of the transition on living conditions of a large portion of the population, the government initiated a number of measures, including reforms in the social safety net and a poverty alleviation programme. The reforms of the social safety net were aimed at replacing the previous system by which the goverment provided equally to each with one based on providing assistance to the needy segment and applying the insurance principle.

Thus the basic components of the transformation of the economy have been implemented. However, the final results will be visible only in the future. If the subsequent economic growth made possible by the rapid reforms will prove sufficient to cover the social cost that is now being paid in the short term, it is likely that the impact of the rapid reforms in Mongolia will be assessed as positive.

Appendix

Table 9A.1 Opulence and capability-based indicators, demographic-based and human ecology measures, Mongolia 1989–96

Indicator/measure	*Measuring unit*	*1989*	*1991*	*1992*	*1993*	*1994*	*1995*	*1996*
I Opulence indicators								
1. Per capita income, at 1993 prices	tugrug	106 017	88 938	78 713	74 830	75 273	78 807	79 610
2. Food consumption and diet								
Meat and meat products	kg per head	93.1	115.6	109.6	101	96.1	96.7	97
Milk and dairy products	kg per head	120.7	122	119.5	110.5	120	125.5	125.8
Butter	kg per head	3	2.3	0.6	0.6	3	4.2	3.9
Fish and fish products	kg per head	1.3	0.1		0.3	0.9	0.7	0.6
Sugar and sugar products	kg per head	23.6	15	9.4	11.2	10.4	8.7	8.5
Flour and bakery products	kg per head	105.3	91.2	77	74	82.1	94.3	95.1
Potatoes	kg per head	27.4	18	12	7	13	11.3	11
Vegetables	kg per head	21.5	9.6	3.4	3	4.8	7.9	8.5
Fresh fruit	kg per head	12.1	1.2	0.4	1.4	0.5	0.4	0.3
Vegetable oil	kg per head	1.4	0.5	0.4	0.6	0.3	0.9	0.8
3. Food share in households' total expenditure								
Urban	%	n.a.	n.a.	49.9	61.5	52.7	50.8	52.7
Rural	%	n.a.	n.a.	30.7	49.6	42.6	42.5	45
4. Average savings in households' total expenditure								
Urban	%	n.a.	n.a.	1.2	0.8	0.6	1	0.5
Rural	%	n.a.	n.a.	2.9	5.4	0.8	0.9	0.1

Table 9A.1 (continued)

II Capability-based indicators								
1. Life expectancy at birth, both	year	62.6		62.77				63.78
Male	year	62.2		60.71				52.1
Female	year	62.9		64.9				65.48
2. Infant mortality rates (under 1 year, per 1000 live births)	cases	64.1	62.6	59.5	61.2	48	44.4	40
3. Low birth weight (incidence of birth below 2000 grams)	cases		3 581	4 143	3 105	3 551	3 414	2 843
4. Maternal deaths	cases	n.a.	93	129	124	116	101	90
5. Total morbidity, per 10 000 population	cases		7 871.6	4 143.3	6 752.2	3 856.1	4 105.9	2 583.3
6. Number of hospital beds per 1000 population		11.8	12.1	11	10.4	10.1	9.6	9.9
7. Number of physicians per 10 000 population	number	28	28	28	26	26	25	26
8. Number of educational institutions	number	1 040	782	841	762	819	856	930
General educational	number	615	643	678	663	659	664	658
Private vocational education institutions	number		–	9	25	31	41	51
9. Number of teachers	thousands	24.9	24.2	22.9	22.7	22.5	22.9	24.1
10. Per capita intake of calories	kilocalories	2 621	2 407	1 980.8	1 962.9	2 103.5	2 277	2 278.2
11. Per capita intake of protein	grams	99.6	104.6	94.6	88.6	92	95.5	96.1
12. Per capita intake of nutrients								
Carbohydrates	grams	349	278	213.4	213.8	245.7	262.4	264.5
Fat	grams	84	90.14	77.1	77.6	77.3	86.9	86.1

Table 9A.1 (continued)

Indicator/measure	*Measuring unit*	*1989*	*1991*	*1992*	*1993*	*1994*	*1995*	*1996*
III Demographic-based measures								
1. Marriage rates (per 1000 population over 18)	cases	14.9	19.6	15.7	11.4	12.8	12	10.9
2. Divorce rates (per 1000 population over 18)	cases	1	1	0.9	0.6	0.6	0.7	0.7
3. Total fertility rate		4.6	3.8	2.5	2.5	2.7	2.7	2.5
4. Crude birth rate (per 1000 population)	cases	36.4	32.9	29.1	21.5	23.4	23.7	22.2
5. Crude death rate (per 1000 population)	cases	8.4	8.8	8.4	7.9	7.3	7.3	7.5
6. Natural growth rate of population (per 1000 population)		28	24.1	20.7	13.6	16.1	16.4	14.7
IV Human ecology measures								
1. Abortion rates	cases		31 217	28 103	20 209	17 025	18 335	15 588

Source: Authors' calculation, Mongolian Economy and Society in 1996, 1993 and 1991. State Statistical Office of Mongolia. Center for Welfare Management and Information. Ministry for Health and Social Welfare.

Notes

1. Almost all aid provided by the former CMEA countries to Mongolia was tied aid, and the donors supplied physical goods under aid agreements. Traditionally, there were three types of loans: turnkey project loans; technical assistance project loans; and trade loans.
2. Mongolia is divided administratively into the capital city and the *aimags*, with the further division of *aimags* into *soms*. On average, a *som* has about 3500 people and 800 households.
3. In the former socialist countries, housing was measured by square metre of living area, and statistics do not show the number of constructed houses or apartments. Therefore the figure is calculated by comparing square metres; numbers of houses and apartments are not taken into considerations for the calculation.

Reference

Fischer, Stanley and Alan Gelb (1991), 'The Process of Socialist Economic Transformation', *Journal of Economic Perspectives*, Vol. 5, No. 4, pp. 91–105.

10
Democratic People's Republic of Korea: Structure of the Welfare System and Expected Impact of Marketization

Doowon Lee

10.1 Introduction

Currently, the former socialist economies throughout Europe and Asia are undertaking transformational reform from a centrally planned economy (CPE) system to a market system. Even though the starting years and the initial conditions of these efforts vary from one country to another, there are essential reform measures that every transition economy has to carry out. Also, there are commonly observed side-effects of such reforms,[1] involving not only macroeconomic variables such as loss of output and increased inflation, but also aspects of the deterioration of social welfare. Even though we can classify these transition economies into the Chinese gradualism and the Central European shock therapy models according to the speed and scope of the applied reform measures, almost all transition economies have experienced a certain degree of unintended effects in undertaking their reforms. It is the purpose of this chapter to draw some implications based on previous reform experiences of the transition economies about the expected impacts of the North Korean version of transitional reform on its social welfare indices.

Before further analysis, this chapter is based on two preliminary assumptions. First, it will be assumed that North Korea has not yet initiated true market-oriented reform. Even though North Korea has already tried a restricted open-door policy by introducing the Foreign Joint Venture Law in the mid-1980s, its internal economic system is still operated under the old doctrines of CPE.[2] Therefore, throughout this chapter, North Korea will be regarded as a pre-transition economy, or at best an economy at the very preliminary stage of transitional reform. Second, as the current status of North Korea is defined as at the pre-transition or preliminary early transition stage, it is necessary to predict which transition path North Korea will follow in order to assess the expected impact of its reform on social welfare indices. However, this is not an easy task, given that many North Korean experts are arguing about not only how it will change, but also whether it will change.[3]

Broadly, there are two views about the future of North Korea. One view predicts that, due to its internal dilemma, North Korea will not be able to initiate a true market-oriented reform, and that it will eventually collapse and be absorbed by South Korea, as East Germany was by West Germany. The other group predicts that North Korea has no choice but to follow the precedent of the other CPE countries, and will eventually introduce its own version of reform. In this chapter, conforming to the main theme of the project for which this chapter is written, the second view, which assumes that North Korea will eventually move towards the transition reform while maintaining the current socialist regime, will be taken.[4] Furthermore, it will be assumed that the initial pattern of reform that North Korea will follow will be similar to that of China.

Based on these two assumptions, a brief historical and current overview of North Korean economic and social development will be presented in this section. In Section 10.2, North Korean welfare indicators will be measured by relying on various sources from North Korea, South Korea and international institutions such as the United Nation Development Programme (UNDP). In Section 10.3, based on the second assumption, the expected impact of North Korea's future welfare reforms will be studied. Section 10.4 will introduce several coping mechanisms by households, local communities and the North Korean government to overcome the current welfare deterioration problem of North Korea.

10.1.1 Development strategy and its recent changes

Since independence from Japan, North Korean economic development can be divided into the following four periods: (1) independence and recovery from the Korean war (1945–56); (2) rapid industrialization due to foreign aid and effective resource mobilization (mid-1950s to late 1960s); (3) sluggish growth due to distorted resource allocation towards heavy and chemical industries and accumulated inefficiencies (1970s and 1980s); and (4) negative growth since 1990.

North Korea was able to achieve successful industrialization in the 1950s and 1960s by relying on Soviet-style central planning, nationalization of the means of production, ideological stimuli, and mass mobilization of the labour force. However, these achievements were strongly biased toward heavy industry, especially military-related industries, and neglected light industry and foreign trade, thus creating distorted resource allocation. As a result of inward-oriented industrialization policies, North Korea found itself in short supply of foreign advanced technologies and foreign exchange. In addition to the inefficiency problems of the centrally planned economy, which are present in any socialist economy, the rigid Juche ideology gave domination of the North Korean economic system to the Party. These problems have become visible since the mid-1970s, and by the mid-1980s, North Korea obviously needed to change its economic policies. Even though some material incentives were provided to state enterprises and a foreign joint venture law was enacted to attract foreign capital, these measures have not resulted in a significant improvement in the North Korean economy so far. In addition, the external shock in 1990 caused by the collapse of the Soviet Union and Eastern European countries led the North Korean economy to experience negative growth rates for seven consecutive years.

10.1.2 A brief historical account of the welfare situation

Like the other socialist countries, such as China, North Korea had improved its welfare situation significantly during the recovery from the Korean War. Even though economic growth rates slowed during the 1980s, most social and welfare indices improved until the late 1980s. However, as the economic growth rate turned negative in 1990, most of the welfare indices became stagnant or have since deteriorated. This was particularly the case in food consumption and daily calorie supply, which have fallen drastically since the early 1990s, as we shall see in the next section. However, other social indices, such as life expectancy and fertility rates, remained unchanged, as can be seen in Table 10.1. In particular, the average educational level of North Korea is fairly high, a potential future advantage of the North Korean economy once it initiates a true market-oriented reform. Details of each index are further explained in the following sections.

Table 10.1 Welfare indices of North Korea (1960 and 1990)

Year	Life expectancy at birth	Infant mortality rate per 1000 live births	Daily calorie supply per capita	Number of students (000s)	Adult literacy rate (%)
1960	53.9	85	2000	2528*	
1992	71.1	24	2834	5142**	95
1994	71.4	23			95

* Estimated by Hwang (1994)
** National Statistical Office (1996), p. 309.

Source: UNDP (1997).

10.2 Changes of welfare indicators

10.2.1 Economic indicators

10.2.1.1 Income-based indicators

GNP and per capita income. Estimating North Korean GNP is not an easy task. North Korea does not calculate and report its official GNP according to the United Nations System of National Accounts. The North Korean authority used to calculate its national income according to the gross value of social product (GVSP) method, but now it no longer even publishes these income data. Therefore, estimates of the North Korean GNP variy from one source to the next, depending on the methods and data used. Whatever methods are adopted, however, there are a couple of stylized facts about North Korean GNP estimates. First, North Korean GNP (and also its overall economic performance) reached its peak in 1990, and then declined in absolute terms. Second, even the most generous estimate of North Korean GNP shows that there is a huge gap between the North Korean and the South Korean economy, which may prove a major obstacle should economic integration occur in the future. Third, as the North Korean economy has a highly distorted structure, the imbalance between consumer goods (light) industry and capital goods (heavy and chemical) industry is so severe that the consumption level, especially the food consumption level, of the North Korean people accounts for an abnormally small proportion of the GNP. In this chapter, to maintain the consistency of the argument, the data used are mainly those from the Ministry of National Unification of South Korea.

North Korean GNP and GNP per capita gradually but continuously increased until 1990, as stated above. Table 10.2 shows selected years' per capita GNP and growth rates of North Korean GNP.

As can be seen from Table 10.2, North Korean economic growth slowed down even before the collapse of the Soviet Union. The average growth rate of North Korea during the second seven-year plan (1978–84) was 4.49 per cent, while the average growth rate of the rest of the 1980s (1985–89) was 2.7 per cent. The main reason behind this sluggish growth performance before the collapse of the Soviet Union and the Council for Mutual Economic Assistance (CMEA) was due to inefficient resource allocation in the North Korean economy, which is reflected in the low incremental output–capital ratio (IOCR) of North Korea. According to Lee (1995), from 1971 to 1990, North Korea's IOCR was estimated to be 0.27, while that of South Korea during the same period was 0.52.

Food consumption and production. Among the current economic problems, the most serious one is food shortage. North Korea has rationed food since 1957, and individual farming has not been officially allowed since then. Table 10.3 shows the grain production, demand, North Korean imports as estimated by the South Korean Ministry of National Unification.[5]

The North Korean government is supposed to provide 700 g of food to ordinary workers, and 800 g to heavy labourers and soldiers daily. In order to provide food through this normal ration scheme, North Korea needs approximately 6.7 million tons of grain annually, as shown in Table 10.3. However, as will later be explained, North Korea has been short by more than 2 million tons of grain annually since 1992. In order to overcome this food shortage problem, the North Korean government has confiscated four days' worth of food rations every month since 1973 using the justification of a wartime reserve. Moreover, since 1987, food rations have been reduced by 10 to 22 per cent every month using the excuse of 'food saving'. Also, as grain production began to decrease after the early 1990s, the North Korean government has been running a campaign of 'eating two meals a day', beginning in 1991. Through these methods, it is estimated that about 1 million tons of grain are saved annually.[6] Therefore, the minimum grain demand in 1997 was approximately 5.7 million tons. Even though North Korea could save 1 million tons annually through these measures, it still needed to import approximately 2 million tons of grain per year to meet the minimum grain demand. However, as of

Table 10.2 North Korean GDP (selected years)

Year	*1965*	*1975*	*1985*	*1990*	*1991*	*1992*	*1993*	*1994*	*1995*	*1996*	*1997*	*1998*	*1999*
GNP growth rates (%)	8.5	5.4	2.7	–3.7	–3.5	–6.0	–4.2	–2.1	–4.1	–3.6	–6.3	–1.1	6.2
Per capita income (US$)*	162	342	765	1064	1038	943	904	923	957	910	741	573	

*For 1965–85 data, per capita GDP is used. For 1990–99, per capita GNI is used.

Sources: Bank of Korea (various years); National Statistical Office (various years).

8 July 1997, North Korea has been receiving roughly 1 million tons of grain from international sources such as the Red Cross, World Food Programme (1998) and China.[7] But as North Korea received only 1 million tons of grain as of August 1997 from abroad, its total grain supply could barely meet marginal demand. That is, if the total 4.7 million tons of grain were evenly distributed over the entire North Korean population, each North Korean citizen would be rationed slightly more than 500 g of grain every day, and there would be nothing left for livestock and industrial demand. However, as there are considerable differences in ration amounts across regions and classes, it can easily be predicted that suburban areas will suffer more than urban areas and ordinary citizens more than soldiers and government officials.

Due to the shortage of arable land, North Korea could not achieve self-sufficiency in food and had to rely on imports even when its economy was doing well. In addition to this natural limitation, the food problem of North Korea was aggravated due to the following three reasons: (1) the shortage of fertilizers and farming equipment due to the collapse of industrial production; (2) low labour productivity in cooperative and state farms due to the absence of private incentives; and (3) damage from heavy floods in the two consecutive years of 1995 and 1996.[8]

The North Korean government estimated the 1996 flood damage to have resulted in 116 people killed, 3.3 million people harmed, and 289 000 chungbos' farmland damaged (1 chungbo = 0.99 ha).[9] The flood damage was especially severe due to the excessive cultivation of high-gradient areas in the mountains.

Even though the flood devastated North Korean farmland, the lack of private incentives and industrial failure are the main reasons behind the low productivity of North Korean agriculture. This view has been verified by several anecdotal pieces of information provided by North Korean defectors to South Korea. For example, based on the reports of defectors, Chun (1997: 56) states that labour productivity in private kitchen plots can be twice as large as that of cooperative farms.

Even though the food crisis is an imminent and critical problem for the North Korean economy, it is doubtful whether this food crisis will lead to a regime or system collapse. According to the WFP report cited above, the North Korean economic system, including the distribution of scarce food, did function properly even under the harsh conditions of food shortage. Also, North Korean people have had the experience of undergoing a severe food shortage problem during the Japanese occupation period of 1910–45. Kazuo (1983: 403) shows that the

Table 10.3 Grain demand and production of North Korea (unit: 10 000 tons)

Year	Normal grain demand[a] (A)	Previous year's production (B)	Grain import (C)	Marginal demand	Minimum demand (D)	Absolute shortage (D–B–C)	Population (000s)
1989[a]	600	521.0	69.1	410.0	550.0	–40.1	21 375
1990[a]	620	548.2	86.1	396.4	534.6	–99.7	21 720
1991[b]	647	481.2	129.0	402.0	542.0	–68.2	22 028
1992[b]	650	442.7	83.0	407.6	547.6	21.9	22 336
1993[b]	658	426.8	109.0	413.3	553.3	17.5	22 645
1994[b]	667	388.4	36.0	418.9	558.9	134.5	22 953
1995[b]	672	412.5	96.0[d]	424.9	564.9	56.4	23 282
1996[c]	673	345.0	104.2[d]	431.0	571.0	121.8	23 616
1997[c]	677	369.0	163.0	437.2	577.2	45.2	23 995
1998[f]		349.0	104.0		541.0	88.0	
1999[f]		389.0	101.0		551.0	61.0	

Notes: Grain demand is composed of human, livestock, and industrial demands. Lee (1997b) estimated that North Korea needs at least 4.1 million tons of grain to feed its people and an additional 2.6 million tons for livestock and industrial uses. Population: KDI, North Korea Economic Indices, of 1995–97 is estimated. Minimum/marginal demand: Sejong Institute, 'Realities and Prospect of North Korea'. Marginal demand = 0.5 kg × population × 365. Minimum demand = marginal demand + 1400 thousand tons (minimum industrial and livestock feed demand).

Sources:
[a]Park (1996), p. 195.
[b]MNU (1996a).
[c]MNU (1997).
[d]*North Korea Today* (1997).
[e]*Chosun Ilbo* (13 June 1997) and *Kyunghyang Shinmun* (8 July 1997).
[f]MNU (www.unikorea.go.kr)

average daily consumption of grain from 1931–43 was merely 361 g, which is less than the marginal amount of grain needed to avoid starvation. Even though the experience of the Japanese occupation period is two generations away, the fact that North Korean society has been closed to the rest of the world for the past 50 years makes these past experiences still relevant today. Furthermore, from the Chinese experience of mass starvation in the aftermath of the 'Great Leap Forward' campaign, we can predict that a food crisis alone is not sufficient to lead to a regime collapse in a totalitarian society.[10]

10.2.1.2 Distribution indicators

In order to measure the index of income distribution in North Korea, we need to know the distribution of labour and wealth incomes in North Korea. Even though we can measure the distribution of labour income, as shown in Table 10.4, it is almost impossible to measure the distribution of income from wealth in North Korea. First, as private ownership of wealth assets is not allowed in North Korea, there is no legal source of data for wealth income. Second, even though some privileged people do own considerable wealth income in North Korea, most of this income is earned in the underground economy.[11] The illegal nature of wealth income makes it difficult to estimate. Therefore the distribution of labour income is the only official source for income differences among different types of jobs, as shown in Table 10.4.

As seen from the table, the gap between highest wage level and the lowest wage level is not that large. At most, the highest wage level can be five or six times larger than the lowest wage level. In the case of South Korea, however, this gap can easily exceed ten times.[12] Therefore, given these wage income distribution data, we can say that North Korea has a fairly even distribution of income, especially compared to its southern counterpart.

However, the wage income gap alone does not tell much about the income distribution of North Korea for two reasons. First, there is a huge gap between the official price levels set by the North Korean authorities and price levels in the widespread underground black markets, as we shall see in the next section. When there is a long queue in state stores and the underground black market prices are far higher than the official prices, wage income does not mean much. Second, even though the official wage income differences are small, the existence of a privileged class in North Korea creates class differences. Studying the income distribution problem of the former socialist countries in Eastern Europe, Amsden et al. (1995: 22) stated, 'Yet

Table 10.4 Wage levels of North Korea as of 1992 (unit: North Korean won)

Types of job	*Job ranks*	*Wages (won)*
Party and government officials	Minister level of party and government	300–350
	Provincial chief official	250–300
	Provincial vice-chief official	170–200
Factory and enterprise managers	Manager of special-class enterprises	250–300
	Manager and chief technician of first- and second-class enterprises	150–200
Workers	Heavy worker (miner, steel factory worker)	90–100
	General mechanic and driver	75–80
	Ordinary worker	70–80
Office worker	Office worker	60–70
Service industry	Motels, restaurants, barber shops and stores	20–60
	Doctors	120–250
	Actors	200–500

Sources: National Statistical Office (1996), p. 280.
MNU (1995), p. 286.

despite this overall levelling, income and class differences remained. The major one was the gulf between the nomenclature of party and state officials and the rest of the population'. North Korea is not an exception in this regard. Moreover, it is very likely that the inequality among different classes in North Korea may be more severe than that of the former socialist countries in Eastern Europe.

Because the economic situation (especially the food shortage problem) is getting harsher and harsher, those who have better access to state stores and rationing are doing much better than those who do not have such access. In general, there are three different classes in North Korea: (1) the 'core class', which accounts for 28 per cent of the total population (approximately 6 million people); (2) the 'unstable class', which accounts for 45 per cent of the population (approximately 9.6 million people); and (3) the 'hostile class', which accounts for 27 per cent of the population (approximately 5.8 million people).[13]

Family background is regarded as the most important criterion in determining a person's class. Cadre members of such organizations as the Party, the Administration and the Army are selected solely from the core class, and they represent the ruling class in North Korea. These ruling classes have secure food rationing, and have better access to obtaining goods in state stores. Moreover, rampant bribery is another source of income for this ruling class, as is engaging in 'foreign-exchange-earning businesses'. As the North Korean currency is losing purchasing power continuously, and the gap between the official exchange rate and the black market rate is widening, North Korean society is relying on foreign exchange more and more in preference to its own domestic currency. As Suh (1997) has stated, 'ordinary workers and soldiers are suffering from severe shortages of food and commodities ... North Korea is still a paradise on earth for high-ranking officials and those who know how to do business'.

10.2.2 Capability-based indicators

10.2.2.1 Health

Article 56 of the North Korean Constitution, which was revised in 1992, says, 'The state protects people's lives and enhances workers' health by providing a comprehensive free medical service, reinforcing a "regional responsibility system" of a doctor, and perfecting a precautionary medicine'. According to these principles, North Korea has provided a free medical service since the early 1960s. Also, a doctor is responsible for a certain region, so that the residents can receive systematic and comprehensive medical consultations with a doctor throughout their lifetime. North Korea has emphasized disease prevention rather than treatment.

The overall health level of a country can best be represented by life expectancy at birth. In this measure, North Korea is not very far behind the other developing countries. As seen in Table 10.5, the official life expectancy at birth of North Korea exceeds 70 years, regardless of the various data sources. However, the reliability of these data is highly dubious considering the severity of the food shortage problem and the high infant mortality rate of North Korea. Reflecting these doubts, life expectancy at birth in North Korea was estimated as approximately 63 years, according to *Shin-Dong-Ah* (January 1995: 452), 54 years according to Lee (1990: 17–19), and 64.3 years according to *The Economist* (1997: 33).

10.2.2.2 Education

Education would probably be the area where North Korea has a comparative advantage with respect to other developing countries. Currently, the North Korean education system is composed mainly of four levels: (1) kindergarten (2 years); (2) primary education (4 years); (3) secondary education (6 years); and (4) higher education (2–3 years for vocational college, 4–6 years for university). Eleven years' education from the upper level of kindergarten to secondary school is compulsory. Due to the long compulsory education, the adult literary rate of North Korea is estimated to be 95 per cent (UNDP 1996: 156).

Despite being relatively well established, the North Korean education system has been criticized for emphasizing ideological education excessively. According to the National Statistical Office (1996: 150–52), roughly 10 per cent of total class hours were devoted to ideological education throughout the compulsory education period.[14]

10.2.2.3 Nutrition

As mentioned in the previous section, the severe food shortage problem of North Korea has endangered the nutritional intake of the North Korean people. Even though the North Korean authority reported to the UNDP (1996: 172) that its daily calorie supply per capita as of 1992 is 2834 calories, the real situation seems far different from this official report. According to the WFP report, food rations were reduced to as little as 200 g per day before the harvest season of October, and increased to 450 g shortly after the harvest season in 1996, which implies that the daily calorie intake per capita in 1996 was

Table 10.5 Basic health indices of North Korea

	Life expectancy at birth (years)	*Under-five mortality rate Infant mortality rates (per 1000 live births)*	*Number*	*(per 1000 live births)* *clinics*	*of hospitals*		
NSO	UNDP	Chun	NSO	UNDP	Chun	UNDP	NSO
(95)[a]	(94)[b]	(86)[c]	(95)	(92)	(86)	(93)	(86)
70.3	71.4	67.7	26.8	24	34.6	32	7 172

[a]Data cited from National Statistical Office in (1996).
[b]Data cited from UNDP (1996).
[c]Data cited from Chun (1996).

Sources: UNDP (1996), pp. 156 and 168; National Statistical Office (1996), pp. 127–31; UN (1994).

Table 10.6 Basic demographic profile of North Korea (unit = 1000, %)

Total population (1996)	*Marriage (1987)*	*Divorce (1987)*	*Fertility rate (1992)*	*Crude birth rate (1992)*	*Crude death rate (1992)*	*Population growth rate (1996)*
23 558	188	4.2	2.4	24.1	5.3	1.28

Sources: National Statistical Office (1996) p. 171 and pp. 303–4); UNDP (1995), p. 186.

between 700 and 1500 calories. Even though the food rationing situation varies throughout seasons and regions, it is without doubt that the current nutrition intake situation of North Korea is in its worst ever state.

10.2.3 Demographic-based measures

Table 10.6 summarizes the basic demographic indices of North Korea. In terms of population growth, North Korea still has a relatively high growth rate compared to other industrialized countries. In fact, North Korea had even higher population growth rates previously. During the second seven-year plan period (1978–84), the average population growth rate was approximately 1.9 per cent.[15] Even though the population growth rate has been falling continuously up to 1996, the relatively high population growth rates coupled with sluggish economic growth rates have kept the per capita income of North Korea low.

10.2.4 Environment-based indicators

Most of the former CPEs had pursued an industrialization strategy heavily biased toward heavy and chemical industries. In establishing industrial bases for such heavy and chemical industries, these countries relied on energy-intensive production techniques which were possible due to low energy prices that were arbitrarily set by the central planner. As a result, inefficient use of energy and excessive discharges of pollution were inevitable. The energy-intensive industrial structure coupled with negligence of central planners and factory managers in relation to environmental issues inevitably worsened the environmental problem of the former CPEs.

North Korea is not an exception in this context. Since the early 1980s, environmental problems have arisen in North Korea, and several serious pollution events were reported in the 1990s.[16]

Environmental problems in North Korea arise not only because of its industrial structure, which is biased toward energy-intensive heavy and chemical industries, but also because of its extensive use of coal as the main energy source. As of 1995, coal accounted for 67 per cent of North Korea's energy supply, while oil and hydroelectric power accounted for 6 per cent and 21 per cent respectively.

North Korea began to pay attention to the environmental problem beginning in the early 1970s, as soil and water pollution began to appear as consequences of industrialization. In 1977 North Korea enacted the Land Law to increase arable land and use land more efficiently. In an effort to increase arable land, Kim Il-sung had encouraged the cutting of trees and cultivation of dry fields (so-called *da-rak-bat*) in the mountainous area since 1976. However, due to this measure, forests were devastated, and this eventually compelled Kim Il-sung to acknowledge his own mistake and suspend cultivating mountainous areas in 1980. In 1986, the Environment Protection Law was enacted by Kim Jong-il to seek technical solutions for environmental problems.[17]

10.3 Macro- and microeconomic impact on welfare changes

Because it is assumed that North Korea is currently at the pre-transition stage, it is premature to analyse the impact of transitional reforms on the North Korean welfare system. What we can do now is to analyse the current macroeconomic and microeconomic situation of North Korea, and to predict what might happen once it initiates transitional reforms based on the experiences of the other transition economies, such as China, Russia and Eastern European countries.

Generally speaking, the industrialization level of North Korea is somewhere between the pre-reform Chinese level and the pre-reform Eastern European countries' level. Also, the agricultural population ratio of North Korea is far smaller than that of China, and the significance of state-owned enterprises in North Korea is more dominant than that in China. Furthermore, North Korea has a huge foreign debt problem, and it is also a much more closed economy in terms of its trade volume than almost any other transition economy in the world. Based on these observations, Lee (1997a) and Chun (1996: 34–6) predicted that North Korea would have to initiate agricultural reform first, as was done in China and Vietnam. But the effect of agricultural reform will be limited in North Korea because of its relatively highly industrialized economic structure. Therefore, to yield long-term effects, the rapid privatization of state-owned enterprises and the promotion of export industries are essential to North Korea.

10.3.1 Monetary, fiscal, wage and price liberalization

It is well known that there is hidden and repressed inflation in many CPEs. Hidden inflation is derived from the huge gap between the official prices in state stores and black market prices. Also, there is repressed inflation as long as consumers in a CPE find available supplies and budgets limited.[18] North Korea is not an exception in this matter. A soft-budget problem exists in North Korea, and the resulting budget deficit has to be financed by printing more money. Furthermore, because supplies in state stores are limited, prices in the black market soared in North Korea. Based on the testimony of numerous North Korean defectors, black market prices for various commodities are calculated and shown in Table 10.7.[19]

From Table 10.7 we can see that there is a huge gap between official prices and black market prices. This price gap is particularly large in foodstuffs, which are deemed to have lower price elasticities than luxury goods. In particular, the black market price for rice is extremely high due to the severe shortage of that commodity. From the testimony

Table 10.7 Price levels in North Korea (unit: North Korean won)

	Items	*Unit*	*State store prices*	*1992 black market prices*	*1997 black market prices*	*1999 black market prices*
Food	Rice	1 kg	0.08	20	80–200	64
	Egg	1 piece	0.22	3	17	13
	Pork	1 kg	7.60	60	300	160
Basic necessities	Toothpaste	1 piece	1.70	7		
	Socks	1 pair	1.50	5	100	
	Shoes	1 pair	2.60	35	300–500	
Personal tastes	Soju	1 bottle	2.40	2.40	40	
	Cigarette	1 packet	1.60	1.60	35	
Industrial goods	colour TV	1 set	1 350	20 000	30 000–40 000	
	Radio	1 set	100	750	6000–7000	

Source: National Statistical Office (1996), pp. 267, 269, 271, 273.

of North Korean defectors, it is said that it is virtually impossible for an ordinary citizen to buy rice from the state store, therefore the official price of rice in the state store is meaningless. This kind of hidden inflation can also be found in the foreign exchange market. Although the official exchange rate of the North Korean currency is 2.16 won per US$1, the real exchange rate is far higher than this. In recognition of this gap, the North Korean authorities have depreciated the currency value to as low as 200 won per US$ within the 'Rajin-Sonbong Free Economic and Trade Zone'.[20] In order to soak up this excessive liquidity, the North Korean authorities have carried out currency reform four times.

As we can learn from the experiences of the other socialist economies with liberalized prices, surging inflation after price liberalization is inevitable. Not only is it inevitable, but also necessary. Prices have to rise in order to make the supply side respond to price signals. In the case of Russia, where they experienced overnight price liberalization in January 1992, it took only two weeks for the supply side to respond to the soaring prices.[21] In the case of North Korea, price liberalization can lead to hyperinflation, given the huge gap between official price levels and black market price levels. Moreover, as the production base in both agriculture and industry has deteriorated after seven consecutive years of negative growth rates, it may take a long time for the supply side to respond. Therefore, in the initial stage of reform, the inflow of foreign exchange and foreign goods (especially basic necessities) will be essential to stabilize price levels.

10.3.2 Privatization–marketization–ownership pattern, and the labour market

After the establishment of the North Korean government in 1948, the North Korean regime began to socialize all the means of production. By the end of the 1950s, virtually all agricultural and industrial production was produced either in state-owned or in collectively owned enterprises/farms.

From the experiences of the other socialist economies, we can classify privatization schemes into two main categories: (1) top-down (privatization from above) and (2) bottom-up (privatization from below). The former was used in Eastern European countries such as Russia, Poland, Hungary and the Czech Republic, and the latter was used in China. Furthermore, the so-called top-down privatization can be divided into several patterns: restitution to the original owners; direct sales; public offering; and mass privatization through voucher programmes. Among these alternatives, most studies that have been done so far regarding the privatization of the North Korean economy prefer a mass privatization method to the others.[22]

The reason many North Korean experts prefer a massive and rapid privatization method are as follows. First, the role of state-owned enterprises in North Korea is much more dominant than in China, and the agricultural sector of North Korea is relatively smaller than that of China. Thus the Chinese-style bottom-up privatization, which leaves the state-owned enterprises intact while encouraging the emergence of new enterprises mostly from the rural area, will have limited effect in North Korea. Moreover, since the provision of health and education services is not specific to the enterprises, the possible rise of the unemployment rate due to rapid privatization will produce smaller side-effects than it would in China. Second, the restitution method cannot be applied as it is practically impossible to find out who were the original owners of North Korean properties after 50 years of communism. Third, direct sales of North Korean enterprises is also inappropriate, as private capital accumulation in North Korea is negligible. Fourth, insider-dominated massive privatization through vouchers can provide the North Korean residents with considerable amounts of wealth, and may prevent the massive migration of North Korean residents into neighbouring countries (especially to South Korea) before and after unification.[23]

10.3.3 Trade orientation

Because North Korea has pursued autarkic economic development, emphasizing the importance of self-sufficiency, the role of trade was limited in North Korea. Historically, North Korea followed the path of industrialization with import substitution, while it refused to engage in trade according to the law of comparative advantage. The trade ratio (trade volume/GNP) of North Korea peaked in the mid-1970s, when it reached nearly 30 per cent as North Korea imported massive amounts of capital goods from Western economies such as Japan and West Germany. Since then, the trade ratio has continuously declined to as low as 10 per cent. Not only did the importance of trade decline, but also North Korea experienced chronic trade deficits as its economy could not promote export industries.

Not only has the absolute and relative size of trade declined in North Korea during the last three decades, but the trade structure has also changed significantly. Until the early 1970s, most of North Korean trade was with socialist economies. In particular, trade with the Former

Soviet Union accounted for more than half of all North Korean trade volume.[24] The significance of the Western economies in the North Korean trade structure increased, and peaked in 1974 when trade with these economies accounted for 43 per cent of the total trade volume, but then declined. The Former Soviet Union remained the biggest trading partner with North Korea until 1991, when CMEA was dissolved. Since then, North Korea's trade with Russia has declined drastically, as Russia demanded hard currency in trading transactions with North Korea based on international prices. As of 1995, Japan was the biggest trading partner of North Korea (28.6 per cent), followed by China (26.7 per cent) and South Korea (13.9 per cent).

The importance of South Korea in the North Korean trade structure has increased steadily since the beginning of economic cooperation between North and South Korea in 1988. South Korea is already the third largest trading partner of North Korea, and what is more important, North Korea is enjoying a considerable trade surplus with South Korea. Furthermore, unlike the trade between North Korea and China, where most of transactions are made either in barter trade or at so-called 'friendship prices', South Korea is paying for its imports from North Korea in internationally convertible hard currencies, which is essential to a North Korean economy suffering from foreign exchange shortages.

Even though North Korea has a highly closed and distorted economy, we can predict how the North Korean economy might look if it behaved like a 'normal' one. Noland et al. (1996) used gravity model regression to generate North Korea's 'natural' pattern of trade. The result of this regression can be interpreted as a prediction of the post-reform trade pattern of North Korea. According to this study, North Korea's natural trade partners would be Korea, Japan, China and the United States with trade shares of 35, 30, 13 and 7 per cent respectively. The share of total trade in GDP will dramatically increase from the current level of 10 per cent to 71 per cent, according to this model. Also, the export and import structures of North Korea will be changed. Exports will be concentrated in light manufactures and mining, and imports will be concentrated in food and capital goods. This reflects the comparative advantage of North Korea, which has relatively abundant natural resources and cheap labour. Furthermore, this study stresses that the static income gain measured by increased real GDP that can be obtained by reallocating resources, may be as large as 30 per cent. That is, by liberalizing trade and reallocating resources following the law of comparative advantage, North Korea will have a different trade structure, changed trading partners, increased share of trade in its GDP, and 30 per cent higher real GDP.

10.4 Responses to shock or gradual changes

As Kornai (1980) stated, a CPE system inevitably creates shortage problems. As has been stated, North Korea has had severe shortage problems in food, consumer goods, energy and foreign exchange. In order to overcome these shortage problems, several notable measures were taken both by individual households and by government. However, these measures were introduced to complement and perfect the central planning mechanisms rather than to move towards a market economy (Andress 1989). Due to these measures, it is deemed that there exists a significant non-state sector economy (some activities are legal, and some are illegal) functioning in North Korea as of today. The non-state sector economy, or the so-called 'second economy', helps the North Korean economy in dealing with the shortage problems, but at the same time creates some side-effects as well.

10.4.1 Private plots: kitchen plots and petty plots

Facing a gradual decline in agricultural productivity during the 1960s, the North Korean government allowed each farm household privately to cultivate a small 'kitchen plot' (*tut-bat* in Korean), and to sell the crops and livestock they raised there in the 'peasant market', where prices were determined by market forces. Cultivation of kitchen plots was regarded as a necessary evil, and was implicitly tolerated by the North Korean government until it was finally permitted in the mid-1960s.[25] From the very beginning, the approved size of kitchen gardens was very small because Kim Il-sung feared that the farmers might be more interested in profit-making than in participating in cooperative farms.[26] Based on the experience of China, we can presume that the productivity of these kitchen plots would be higher than that of the cooperative farm. Though the absolute and relative size of this privately cultivated land is small compared to cooperative farm size, the existence of a private ownership system and a free market for the privately produced crops can be viewed as evidence that a market exists in North Korea.[27] In addition to the kitchen plots officially allowed to individuals, there are also kitchen plots that are allowed to workers in a firm. According to Chun (1997: 55–6), each worker is allowed to cultivate 165 m^2 (50 *pyong*) in mountainous areas designated by North Korean authorities. According to the testimony of defectors, the labour productivity in these kitchen plots is two to three times higher than that in cooperative farms.[28]

In addition to these official kitchen plots for farmers and workers, there are also private 'petty plots' (*duigi-bat* in Korean) that are officially illegal but tolerated by the North Korean authorities. These petty plots are usually located in mountainous areas, and crops such as corn and beans are cultivated. Cultivating petty plots has been in fashion since 1986, and there was a report that grain prices in the underground peasant market decreased by 30 per cent as grains produced in these petty plots were sold in the market.[29]

10.4.2 The peasant market

The peasant market was established in 1958, replacing the traditional rural market. Originally it was open every ten days, and major grains such as rice and corn were not allowed to be traded. However, since 1993, peasant markets open every day, and the trade of rice and corn is allowed.[30] Originally, peasant markets were established in the rural areas, and small amounts of grain produced in kitchen plots were traded. However, as the food and consumer goods shortage problems persisted, peasant markets began to emerge in urban areas, and the goods traded were also diversified. According to a study by Samsung Economics Institute, farmers purchase 95 per cent of industrial goods in peasant markets, and workers in urban areas purchase 40–50 per cent of food in peasant markets.[31]

10.4.3 Border trade

China has been the most important trading partner of North Korea during the last several years. In 1995, the official trade volume between China and North Korea was 550 million dollars, and most of this trade took place in the Sino-Korean border area. In addition to the official trade, however, a considerable amount of unofficial trade is going on between the two countries. According to the study by Lee, Jong-Seok (1996: 29), the unofficial trade volume is estimated to be as large as 300 million dollars in 1995. Most of this trade is done either in dollars or as barter trade. Furthermore, as all the goods traded are basic necessities, it helps to assuage the shortage problem of North Korea, and it also helps to stabilize black market prices in North Korea.

10.4.4 The 1984 8.3 Production of People's Consumer Goods Programme

The year 1984 was one of partial reform of the North Korean economy. In August 1984, 'The August Third (8.3) Programme', which allows a certain amount of consumer goods' production outside the confines of central planning, was announced. The 8.3 Production of People's Consumer Goods Programme can be termed as a partial reform in two respects: it allowed the production of consumer goods outside the planned economy; and these products were allowed to be sold in the market rather than in state stores. In addition, this programme had two more distinctive features. One is that most of the products produced under this programme were basic necessities made using scrap from state enterprises and locally available resources and waste. The other is that production decisions were made by local authorities, and products were produced and sold inside local provinces. According to a January 1990 article by Choe In-Duk, in *Kulloja*, sales of those products produced under the 8.3 Programme accounted for 9.5 per cent of total consumer goods sales.

10.4.5 The subwork team management system

The subwork team management system was first proposed by Kim Il-sung in 1965, and applied to cooperative farms nationwide in North Korea in 1966. It divided the labour force of a cooperative farm into several subwork teams, each composed of 10–25 people. At the end of the year, each subwork team's production was evaluated and distributed to subwork team members according to their achievement. However, due to the so-called 'ratchet effect', production was under reported due to the fear that the next year's production target would be set at a higher level than the current year's.

In order to remove this unintended effect, and to provide more production incentives, the North Korean authorities modified the subwork team management system on 24 October 1996.[32] According to this revision, the size of a subwork team was reduced to seven to eight people, and the production target was reduced as well. Furthermore, any surplus production was allowed to be freely disposed of by each subwork team, thus officially allowing the transaction of major grains. Even though the North Korean authorities stated that this measure did not imply that the country was moving toward an individual farming system, this measure can be interpreted as an experimental step towards a Chinese-style contract farming system.

10.4.6 Restricted open-door policy

More visible changes are observed in the North Korean open-door policy. North Korea enacted the Foreign Joint Venture Law in 1984 in the expectation of inviting foreign (especially Western) capital and technology. However, by the early 1990s, the result of this open-door policy proved unsatisfactory. Most of the investors were pro-North Korea Korean–Japanese, and the invested amounts were minimal. In an effort to attract more capital, North Korea established a Free Economic and Trade Zone (FETZ) in the Rajin-Sonbong area in 1991. However, the poor infrastructure of the region and the uncertainty about the future of the North Korean regime made foreign investors hesitant to invest.[33]

Recently, a more active version of North Korea's open-door policy was implemented. As a result of the Geneva Accord of 1994 between North Korea and the US, the Korea Energy Development Organization (KEDO) was established to build two light-water nuclear reactors in the Shinpo area of North Korea in return for North Korea's abolition of its nuclear programme.

10.5 Conclusions

10.5.1 Assessment

This chapter has examined extensively the historical and current status of North Korean economic and social development. As noted in the previous sections, the North Korean economy, as well as its societal indicators, gradually and consistently improved until the late 1980s, but has deteriorated since then. After seven consecutive years of negative growth rates, it is generally believed that North Korea is currently having its worst time in dealing with its economic and social difficulties. However, North Korea can enjoy the so-called 'advantage of backwardness' by initiating transitional reform later than the others.

First, North Korea can learn lessons from the experiences of the other transition economies. Second, as the current economic and welfare status of North Korea is at its worst level, it may be relatively easy for North Korea to produce an initial visible success, by creating popular support for further reform measures. Even though the international community has begun to deliver aid to North Korea, the aid can only be temporary relief if North Korea adheres to its current economic system. Among many difficulties, the food crisis is the most urgent and serious that North Korea is facing. However, according to many witnesses, the social order remains stable.[34]

10.5.2 Tendencies of future changes

Even though the collapse of the North Korean economic system may not be imminent, it is clear that North Korea must initiate internal and external economic reforms to avoid the eventual breakdown of its system. To a certain extent, North Korea has already initiated a Chinese version of economic reform; declaring the Rajin-Sonbong area as a Free Economic and Trade Zone, North Korea has tried to attract foreign capital into these regions, as China did in the late 1970s after it designated its offshore cities as special economic zone. Based on the Chinese experience, it is clear that an open-door policy such as FETA will eventually move North Korean leaders to introduce internal economic reform.

Notes

1. For detailed explanation of these essential reform measures and macroeconomic side-effects, see Lee (1997).
2. For further references to the North Korean Foreign Joint Venture Law, see Lee (1993).
3. On 11 December 1996, the outgoing director of America's Central Intelligence Agency, John Deutch, told the Senate intelligence committee that within the next two or three years, North Korea would either make war, make peace, or implode (*The Economist* 1997: 33).
4. Whether North Korea can maintain the current regime or not after it initiates its own version of reform is one of the heated debates among the country's experts. However, as regime change can be different from the leadership change, it will be assumed that the current socialist regime will maintain its power despite a possible leadership change. Recently, the special report of the World Food Programme (WFP) stated that the North Korean socialist system continued to function even with harsh food shortage problems (*Sisa Journal* 1996).
5. There are a couple of other estimates of North Korea agricultural product and demand. For example, Quinones (1997) has estimated grain production and consumption based on the officially published data of North Korea and the special report of the WFP.
6. Ministry of National Unification, *Weekly Report on North Korea*, Vol. 312 (1997) p. 20.
7. China provided 0.54 million tons of grain to North Korea in 1996. Half of this was given for free, and the other half was sold at a friendship price. (*Jung-Ang Ilbo* 1997a).
8. The Economist Intelligence Unit (EIU, *Country Report: South Korea, North Korea*, 2nd quarter, 1997: 52–3) pointed out the following as the reasons for the crisis in North Korean agriculture: (1) unfavourable mountainous terrain, with only around 20 per cent of the land cultivable; (2) collectivization: incentives would produce higher yields if contract farming or private ownership were introduced; (3) mono-cropping: Kim Il-sung's insistence on rice and (mainly) maize as priorities has been harmful in several ways; (4) fertilizer: one version is that overuse of inorganic fertilizers has exhausted the soil and caused yields to decline; the alternative view is that shortage of fertilizer is the problem, due to the virtual shutdown of factories; (5) the industrial crisis has had other knock-on effects on farming; and

(6) ecologically, terracing high up on the hills to grow more maize has proved a double disaster.

9. See *Country Report: South Korea, North Korea* (EIU, 4th quarter, 1996: 50). Also note that the total arable land of North Korea is approximately 2 million chungbo (Lee 1996: 14).
10. It is estimated that as many as 30 million Chinese died of hunger between 1959 and 1961 during the 'Great Leap Forward' campaign. See Becker (1997).
11. Chun (1997: 58) states that there is even an underground curb market in North Korea, where 10 to 20 per cent interest rates are charged.
12. According to a 1994 survey in South Korea, the lowest labour income per month was 247 600 won, while the highest labour income level was 2 755 200 won (National Statistical Office 1995: 96–7).
13. See *A Handbook on North Korea* (Seoul: Korea Herald, 1996). See also Institute of Political Education for National Unification (1996: 172).
14. In kindergarten, 160 out of 1200 class hours were spent on ideological education in 1992. The respective figures in primary school and secondary school were 308 out of 3570 hours, and 669 out of 6538.5 hours.
15. Ministry of National Unification (1994: 23).
16. Ministry of National Unification (1995: 25).
17. Associated Press (1995: 252–65).
18. Amsden, et al. (1995: 24).
19. As of 1990, there were 20 380 retail stores in North Korea. A total of 98 per cent of these stores are state stores, and the rest are collectively owned. See Kim et al. (1995: 24).
20. Hyundai Research Institute (1997b: 40).
21. Kim (1997: 6).
22. Chung (1996) and Park (1997); see also Yoon (1996).
23. In the case of emergency or sudden unification, massive migration from North to South Korea is possible. Hyundai Research Institute (1997a: 9) predicted that approximately 4 million people (mostly from the hostile class) may defect to South Korea. Also, Koo (1996: 138) estimated that about 1.4 million North Korean labourers will migrate into South Korea if Korea is unified with the current income gap maintained.
24. In 1970, 42 per cent of North Korean exports and 61 per cent of North Korean imports were made with the Soviet Union (Korea Development Institute 1994: 110).
25. Kim Il-sung stated that in the socialist stage the 'peasant market' cannot be abolished completely. He suggested that the 'peasant market will disappear when the country becomes industrialized and there are plenty of consumer goods available to the people'. See Park and Park (1990: 116–17).
26. Initially, each farm household could own as much as 260 m^2. However, as the grain shortage problem became worse, the size has shrunk to 66–99 m^2 in 1977. More recently, according to an interview with Min-Bok Lee, a North Korean defector, the officially allowed size of kitchen plot is 99 m^2 (30 *pyong*). See *Monthly Chosun* (1995: 321–39).
27. When the average amount of land cultivated by each farm household is 1.34 ha (see Kim 1992: 13), the existence of kitchen plots of approximately 100 m^2 implies that as much as 0.75 per cent of all cultivated land is privately owned kitchen plots.

28. Lee, Keun (1997: 13).
29. *Monthly Chosun* (July 1995: 336).
30. Chun (1997: 53–4).
31. *Jung-Ang Ilbo* (1997b).
32. Ministry of National Unification, *Weekly Report on North Korea*, Vol. 303 (1996) pp. 7–12.
33. After visiting the Rajin-Sonbong International Investment and Business Forum, 13–15 September 1996, Noland and Flake (1996a: 2) pointed out that the lack of infrastructure is the major obstacle to investment in this zone. Also, noting that the South Korean delegation did not attend the forum, Noland and Flake (1996b: 4) stated: 'Western participants ... argued that South Korea must invest first, not only in order to lay the basic infrastructure, but also to give Western firms a green light'.
34. The WFP report (1998) says: 'even when the daily rationing fell to the worst level of 200 gram per person, the North Korean economic system was still functioning'.

References

Amsden, Alice, Jacek Kochanowicz and Lance Taylor (1995) *The Market Meets its Match: Restructuring the Economies of Eastern Europe*, Cambridge, MA: Harvard University Press.

Andress, Wladimir (1989), 'Economic Reforms in North Korea and Viet Nam', *Seoul Journal of Economics*, Vol. 2, No. 1, pp. 87–107.

Associated Press (1995), *50 Years of North Korea*, Associated Press (December) (in Korean).

Becker, Jasper (1997), *Hungry Ghosts*, New York: The Free Press.

Chun, Hong-Taek (1996), 'The System Transformation of North Korea and the Main Problems of Economic Integration of South and North Korea', *Policy Study Series 96-01*, Korea Development Institute (in Korean).

Chun, Hong-Taek (1997), 'Features and Function of the Second Economy of North Korea', *The Reunified Korea Economy*, Hyundai Research Institute (February) (in Korean).

Chung, Hyung-Gon (1996), 'Exploring Ways of Privatization in Reunified Korea', *The Reunified Korea Economy*, Hyundai Research Institute (October) (in Korean).

The Economist (1997), Korea's twin crises, 22 February pp. 72–3.

Hwang, Eui-Gak (1994), 'North and South Korean Economics Compared', *Pacific Focus*, Vol. IX, No. 1 (Spring).

Hyundai Research Institute (1997a), 'Increasing North Korean Refugees and Countermeasures', *VIP Report* (February) (in Korean).

Hyundai Research Institute (1997b), (21 June) (in Korean).

Institute of Political Education for National Unification (1996), *Understanding North Korea*, Seoul (in Korean).

Jung-Ang Ilbo (1997a), 17 January (in Korean).

Jung-Ang Ilbo (1997b), 25 April (in Korean).

Kazuo, Kawai (1983), *A Study on Korean Modern Economic History*, Seoul: Sagyejol Press (in Korean).

Kim, Dong-Joe (1997), *The Russian Economic Reform and Labor Market Structure*, Masrer's Thesis of Economics Department, Yonsei University (June) (in Korean).
Kim, Woon-Keun (1992), 'The North Korean Economic Policy and Prospect as well as Status of Agriculture, Forestries, and Fisheries', presented at the Conference on Agriculture of North Korea and Agricultural Reform of Socialist State, Seoul: Korea Rural Economic Institute (in Korean).
Kim, Young-Tae, Dae-Sik Kim and Jong-Chul Lee (1995), 'A Study on the Privatization of the North Korean Economy Following the Inter-Korean Integration', *International Economic Journal*, Vol. I, No. 2 (December) (in Korean).
Koo, Sung-Yeol (1996), 'Problem of Migration, Employment and Building Social Safety Net of North Korean Population', Economic Integration Strategy under Radical Unification, Institute for Unification Studies of Yonsei University (September) (in Korean).
Korea Development Institute (1994), *A Tendency of North Korean Economy: The First Half of 1994* (August) (in Korean).
Kornai, Janos (1980), *Economics of Shortage*, Amsterdam: North-Holland.
Lee, Doowon (1993), 'Assessing North Korean Economic Reform: Historical Trajectory, Opportunities, and Constraints', *Pacific Focus*, Vol. 8, No. 2 (Fall).
Lee, Doowon (1995), 'Inter-Korean Economic Relations: Rivaled Past, Unbalanced Present, and Integrated Future', *Yonsei Economic Studies*, Vol. II, No. 1 (March).
Lee, Doowon (1997a), 'Lessons of Transition Economies' Reform for North Korea', *The System Transformation of the Transition Economies: Europe, Asia and North Korea*, Seoul: Yonsei University Press.
Lee, Doowon (1997b), 'Economic Crisis of North Korea and the Limitation of Open Door Policy", *The Journal of Social Science*, Vol. 13, No. I., Seoul, Myungji University (November) (in Korean).
Lee, Jong-Seok (1996), 'Realities and Prospects of North Korea's Economic Difficulty', Policy Report 96-01, Sejong Institute (in Korean).
Lee, Keun (1997), 'Between Collapse and Survival in North Korea: An Economic Assessment of the Dilemma', *MOCT–MOST Economic Policy in Transitional Economies* Vol. 7, No. 4, pp. 155–72 (July).
Lee, Woo-Hong (1990), *Republic of Poverty*, Seoul: Tongil Ilbo (in Korean).
MNU (Ministry of National Unification) (1994), *Overall Evaluation on the 3rd Seven-Year Plan of North Korea* (in Korean).
MNU (Ministry of National Unification) (1995) *Weekly Report on North Korea*, serial no. 174 (in Korean).
MNU (Ministry of National Unification) (1996) *Weekly Report on North Korea*, serial no. 219 (in Korean).
MNU (Ministry of National Unification) (1997) *Weekly Report on North Korea*, serial no. 312 (in Korean).
Monthly Chosun (1995), July (in Korean).
National Statistical Office (1995), *1994 Annual Report on the Family Income and Expenditure Survey* (June).
National Statistical Office (1996), *Comparative Socio-Economic Features of South and North Korea* (November) (in Korean).
Noland, Marcus and L. Gordon Flake (1996a), 'Evaluation of the Rajin-Sonbong Free Economic and Trade Zone', Institute for International Economics.

Noland, Marcus and L. Gordon Flake (1996b), 'Assessment of the Rajin-Sonbong International Investment and Business Forum', Institute for International Economics.

Noland, Marcus, Sherman Robinson and Monica Scatasta (1996), 'Modeling Economic Reform in North Korea', Institute for International Economics (June).

North Korea Today (1997) 'Democratic Peaceful Unification Advisory', February, p. 127.

Park, Han-Shik and Kyung-Ae Park (1990), *China and North Korea: Politics of Integration and Modernization, Asian Studies Monograph Series,* Hong Kong: Asian Research Service.

Park, Jehoon (1997), 'Prospect for the Privatization of the North Korean Economy: Implications from the Experiences of Transitional Economies', *The System Transformation of the Transition Economies: Europe, Asia and North Korea,* Seoul: Yonsei University Press.

Park, Jung-Dong (1996), *Economic Special District of North Korea,* Korea Development Institute (in Korean).

Quinones, C. Kenneth (1997), 'Food and Political Stability in North Korea', *Korea's Economy 1997,* Vol. 13, a publication of the Korea Economic Institute of America and the Korea Institute of International Economic Policy.

Shin-Dong-Ah (1995), January (in Korean).

Sisa Journal (1996), 18 December (in Korean).

Suh, Jae-Jin (1997), 'Causes of Class Split in North Korean Society', *Vantage Point,* Vol. XX, No. 2 (February).

UN (United Nations) (1994), *World Population Prospects 1950–2050,* New York: United Nations.

UNDP (United Nations Development Programme) (1996), *Human Development Report 1995,* New York: Oxford University Press.

World Food Programme (WFP) (1998) Special Report FAO/WFP Crop and Food Supply Assessment Mission to the Democratic People's Republic of Korea 12 November (http://www.fao.org/WAICENT/faoinfo/economic/giews/english/alerts/1998/srdrk981.htm).

Yoon, Gun-Young (1996), 'Privatization of North Korean Economy', *The Economic Integration Strategies Following Radical Unification,* Institute for Korean Unification Studies, Yonsei University (September) (in Korean).

IV Policy Conclusions and Recommendations

11
Sustaining Welfare During the Transition: Lessons from Asia

Aiguo Lu and Manuel F. Montes

The studies in this volume amply demonstrate that the diversity in the approaches to transition and the wide range of experiences in the Asian transition economies provide a rich source of insights into welfare policy in these countries.

Economic growth or the lack of it has been a decisive factor in changes in basic welfare indicators such as average income, nutrition and level of poverty. In China and Vietnam, rapid economic growth has resulted in higher household incomes, greater access to consumer goods, improvements in diet, and rising living standards, as well as sharp reductions in poverty. In these economies, the initial achievements in poverty alleviation are indeed remarkable, underlining the fact that reform-induced growth has benefited the most disadvantaged in the population.

In those countries which have suffered through economic recession, little hope of such improvement has been available to the majority, and poverty has increased. However, economic performance has not represented a clear dividing line between countries which have gained from the transition and those which have been the losers. Many other social indicators, such as life expectancy at birth, school enrolment and health conditions, are showing trends which do not depend merely on economic growth. Furthermore, in terms of social cohesion, relative economic performance appears to be even less relevant, since in this respect there seems to have been deterioration everywhere in the Asian transition economies. The transition shows once again that economic growth alone is insufficient to produce human betterment in all its facets.

Welfare performance during the transition has frequently been measured against the record of the socialist past. This comparison is made not to argue against reform, but to demonstrate the direction and the degree of welfare changes and to highlight the importance of non-economic factors in welfare provision and development.

In the next sections, we shall juxtapose outcomes and policy responses, organizing the discussion around issues of poverty, income inequality, employment and labour markets, human development, crime and social cohesion, and the status of women.

11.1 Poverty incidence

Poverty takes many forms and is determined not only by low per capita income. In analysing its impact on transition, we have utilized a broader conception of poverty in the form of 'inadequate access to and control over basic social and economic resources and opportunities that can develop human capabilities necessary to participate in and contribute to society' (UNDP 1996: 3). In this conception, to eradicate poverty is to establish access to basic resources for all. To alleviate poverty requires not only economic growth, but also a wide participation by the population in the benefits of this growth.

The Asian transition economies have had a range of experiences with poverty during transition. The negative growth which occurred in the Central Asian Republics (CARs) and Mongolia has contributed to a rise in the incidence of poverty in those countries. As output has shrunk, general income levels have dropped, and people at the low end of the income scale have slipped into poverty. Moreover, as might have been expected, because of the declines in state revenue following economic contractions, governments have faced greater pressure to cut public spending on social provisions, which have usually helped those people most in need. This sudden, widespread, but relatively shallow poverty emerging in transitional economies has been labelled 'transitional poverty'.

'Shallow' poverty is the type in which people move easily back and forth, into and out of poverty. The creation of new avenues of employment and the return to growth can reduce the incidence of this kind of poverty. In addition, cutbacks in social security systems can push people into the poverty category. In Uzbekistan, the generous pension entitlements initially cushioned the fall into poverty of the elderly, but the programme claimed 11.4 per cent of GDP. In 1994, the government reformed the indexation system and halved the pension cost as a percentage of GDP (Pomfret and Anderson, Chapter 8, this volume).

In transitional economies such as China and Vietnam, where growth has been rapid and broadly based, poverty has declined substantially. These countries have managed to reduce poverty at the very beginning and throughout the early years of reform. However, the process of poverty reduction even in countries in which economic growth has been sustained and rapid has not been widespread and has created the risk of leaving some sectors of the populace in a permanent state of poverty (Lu, Zhu, and Jansen, Chapters 4, 5 and 6, this volume).

In China and Vietnam, the risk of creating a permanent poverty class as part of the marketization process is real. Most of the remaining poor in China are concentrated in remote, resource-deficient areas, which are usually populated disproportionately by minorities. The Chinese government failed to achieve its goal of eliminating poverty by the year 2000. In Vietnam, the same kind of considerations apply to the tribal minorities and subsistence farmers.

For people with limited education and skills, for the aged and for children without sufficient family support, economic growth is even less an immediate solution. Social interventions in the form of government programmes and public assistance need to be strengthened to help the particularly vulnerable. In the long run, a combination of sustained, broadly based economic growth and social and government support measures is necessary for the elimination of poverty and the improvement of living standards so that an entire population can live decent lives with dignity.

11.2 Income inequality

Between the 'Asian model' (China and Vietnam), which had positive growth, and the 'East European path' of transition (the CARs and Mongolia), which experienced output declines, the contrast in overall economic performance is very sharp. Nevertheless, irrespective of whether overall economic performance was positive or negative, the Asian transition economies shared a common feature during transition: income inequality increased significantly. The only differences are in the degree and speed of such growth.

China's experience is instructive. On the eve of the reforms, a characteristic of income distribution in China was the coexistence of a wide income inequality gap between urban and rural areas and highly egalitarian income distribution within each area. Largely due to the conspicuous rural–urban income gap, the overall Gini coefficient in China was higher than in other centrally planned economies of the Former

Soviet Union and Eastern Europe, even though it was lower than in developing market economies.

Chinese economic reforms induced a further increase in income inequality. However, the source of the inequality shifted from being mainly due to differences between rural and urban areas to being driven primarily by a widening gulf between the rich and the poor within each of the areas, a marked divide in income between coastal and inland regions and an even more extended chasm in living standards between rural and urban populations (Ahmad and Wang 1991; Griffin and Zhao 1993; Wei 1996, Lu, Chapter 4, this volume).

Based on the first Vietnam Living Standards Survey (VLSS), Jansen (Chapter 6, this volume) reports a still-unelevated Gini coefficient of 34.8 for Vietnam in 1998 and only a mild increase from the 1993 level of 33. However, other studies, using indirect indicators, and current trends suggest that, amid the substantial improvement in overall standards of living, income gaps since the reforms have been widening in Vietnam.

In the Asian transition economies which have experienced economic recession, economic decline has meant a substantial deterioration in the living standards of large portions of populations and shattered the sense of income safety for all. But a class of the newly rich has also emerged and income inequality has become more severe.

Pomfret (1996: 97) associates the drastic fall in the protein component in the caloric intake, accompanied by an increase in the consumption of potatoes and bakery products in the CARs after 1992, with a rapid increase in income inequality. According to a World Bank estimate, the Gini coefficient increased from 9.33 in 1987–88 to about 50 in 1993 in the Kyrgyz Republic (World Bank 1996: 69). Even when the economic situation in some CARs began to improve in the mid-1990s, income inequality continued to rise.

Rising income inequality was also the pattern in the CEECs (World Bank 1996: 68–70). An increase in income inequality following economic transition had been widely expected in the transition economies as a result of wage decompression associated with wage liberalization and the increase in the incomes earned from private enterprise and mounting individual wealth. In this framework, income inequality is a necessary consequence of the transition, and in transitional economies the current level of income inequality has been viewed as tolerable or reasonable. Inequality is said to be good for economic efficiency, since 'greater disparity of wages, income, and wealth is – up to a point – a necessary part of transition, because allowing wages to be determined by the market creates transitions incentives for efficiency that are essential for successful reform' (World Bank 1996: 66).[1]

This approach suggests that policies to deal with income problems should focus mainly on the issue of poverty. According to this mainstream thinking, as long as the economy is growing and as long as governments are able to restructure social safety nets to provide effective poverty relief, the issue of inequality should not be a particular concern. There is, however, a growing body of economic literature which argues that equality is not only morally desirable and a necessary condition for the maintenance of social stability, but also actually good for economic growth (Birdsall et al. 1995; Alesina and Perotti 1996). Between these two opposing positions, others have tried to look for a balance (for example, see Fforde and de Vylder 1996).

The experiences of the Asian transition economies suggest that rising income inequality has had little to do with macroeconomic performance. Depending on the extent and speed of the rise in income inequality, the social character of the transitional economies is being reshaped. The drastic growth in income inequality has transformed some of the formerly centrally planned economies from relatively egalitarian into highly polarized societies.

11.3 Employment

Under central planning, full employment and life-long job security were the key features of social safety nets. In Asia, however, full employment under the centrally planned systems cannot be taken at face value. In almost all the Asian transition economies, the underutilization of the labour force, or disguised unemployment, was a serious problem in the pre-reform era. In the case of China and Vietnam, in which rural residents represented the vast majority, full employment did not mean that welfare conditions were the same between rural and urban areas. Significant job shortages existed in the CARs for years before the onset of the transition. Related problems, such as low labour force efficiency and the lack of labour mobility, were endemic. As a general rule, the work-related benefits for rural populations remained definitely inferior to those available in the state sector or in larger towns and cities.

In the CARs and Mongolia, unemployment mounted steadily during the early years of the transition. Serious economic recessions have usually been blamed for this trend. When there is a sharp decline in output, job opportunities shrink. It was thus anticipated that, when the economic situation improved, job opportunities would appear, thereby easing the pressure of unemployment. However, this has not occurred. In Kyrgyzstan in 1995, for example, although the declining trend in GDP that had been evident between 1992 and 1994 was significantly slowed, the labour market did not rebound accordingly, and unemployment continued to rise (Interfax 1995: 22).

Normally, growing unemployment is most closely associated with economic distress. However, in the Asian transition economies, unemployment has been climbing without exception and regardless of economic performance. It has already become an important component of economic and social life and is having a marked effect on the well-being of entire populations, not just the unemployed.

Economic transition entails a repositioning of the state and private sectors, adjustments in the industrial sector, outward reorientation of the economy, and so forth. Problems such as overemployment or hidden unemployment under socialist full employment come to the fore, and a large portion of the labour force becomes redundant, along with the shrinking of the state sector. The state is constrained in its ability to create new employment because the overall output reduction is reducing its revenues or because of intended reductions in state participation in the economy. A solution to transitional unemployment therefore depends not only on renewed and sustained economic growth, but also on the capacity of the non-state sector to absorb the labour force which the state sector has been shedding.

Thus, in the CARs, rising unemployment has as much to do with economic transition as with economic recession. The growing unemployment in these countries has everywhere been created also by restructuring and company shutdowns. In Kyrgyzstan, almost 80 per cent of industrial enterprises surveyed in late 1995 had sent workers home on extended leave during the first nine months of the year, and over 50 per cent of these workers had been sent home for more than 15 weeks (Interfax 1995: 22). In general, labour demand remains low, and the gap between supply and demand appears to be wide. A similar situation has been observed in Mongolia, where, according to official figures, unemployment rose from 3.2 per cent to 3.6 per cent in 1990–91 (Kim 1996).

Despite its record-breaking economic growth, China has also been facing mounting pressure from unemployment. Between 1983 and 1992 the official unemployment rate fluctuated between 1.8 per cent and 2.5 per cent, except in 1989, when it reached 2.6 per cent. Then, in 1992, it began a steady climb, from 2.5 per cent in that year to 2.9 per cent in 1995, and 3.1 per cent in 1998.

In Vietnam, as in China, dynamic economic growth has not prevented a rise in unemployment. The adoption of a more market-oriented system has been accompanied by mounting unemployment, as well as increasing domestic and international migration.

Although growing unemployment is a universal phenomenon in the Asian transitions, economic performance and the nature of reform policies are playing an important role in the speed, scale and character of the unemployment in each country.

While the economies of the Central Asian Republics and Mongolia have declined sharply, the rise in unemployment has been much less dramatic. That is, compared with the severity of the drop in output, unemployment in the Asian transition economies has remained low. The governments in these countries have been reluctant to resort to mass layoffs, and state firms have been encouraged to maintain the labour force. The financial difficulties involved in this effort have been limited because the methods used to achieve this goal have consisted of reducing or even eliminating wage payments, while continuing to provide certain job-related benefits. In this way workers have remained formally employed, although they are working less or not at all. Many workers have taken jobs in the non-state sector in order to earn cash. At the same time, because the expansion of the non-state sector in these countries has been relatively slow, workers have generally lost income, living standards have deteriorated, and poverty has increased.

In China, the dynamics of the rise in unemployment have been different. Indeed, state sector employment continued to grow until 1993, stagnated during 1994–97, and began to decline only thereafter. However, the ability of the state sector to provide employment has weakened considerably. Thus, while the state sector accounted for about 70 per cent of all new jobs in urban areas during the first phase of urban reform in 1985–90, by 1993 it was providing only 9 per cent of the new urban jobs. The engine of employment growth had become the non-state sector, particularly the township and village enterprises, among which employment levels were climbing ten times more quickly than they were in the public sector.

Changing patterns in employment and unemployment in the Asian transition economies have been brought about by the restructuring of state-owned enterprises, by the dynamics of the non-state sector and by greater labour mobility. As long as the industrial restructuring process is unfinished, transitional unemployment will be a significant problem. As labour markets adjust to the emerging economic structures, unemployment benefits and social security programmes will have to be modified.

In China, for instance, increased labour mobility has rendered enterprise-based social security systems problematic. This will mean that the eligibility requirements for employment-related benefits, unemployment compensation, insurance and retirement pensions will have to be reexamined.

11.4 Human development

Education, health and long life are essential if people are to be able to participate fully and meaningfully in the economy and society. In this sense, the initial outcomes of the reform process in the Asian transition economies have been mixed at best. In those Asian countries in the throes of economic recession, the effort at human development has weakened, and, if declining economies continue to impose resource constraints, there may be long-term effects on populations. In others experiencing economic growth, progress in human development has been uneven or non-existent.

Before the reforms, the record of the Asian transitions in human development was relatively good, given their low levels of income. This can be largely attributed to government investments in social programmes to promote human capacity building. However, with the transition, these programmes have met with many difficulties, which progressive social policies alone, even those that consistently emphasize equitable access to welfare provision, have not been able to overcome.

Reforms in these Asian countries have necessitated changes in the institutional framework of welfare provision. In China and Vietnam, as pre-reform institutions such as rural collectives and state-owned enterprises have collapsed or been restructured, responsibility for the management of welfare provision has shifted to emerging market-oriented institutions, while users are being required to cover the service costs.

Therefore, in China and Vietnam, the concentration in reform-induced economic growth is constraining broad access for the great majority of the population to adequate social services. Some key health status indicators in China such as life expectancy at birth and maternal mortality continue to improve. However, one must bear in mind that some of these indicators measure long-term cumulative trends, which might not be reversed even by rather dramatic economic or social changes over the short term (Preston 1975; Rodgers 1979; Murray and Chen 1992). Moreover, the improvements in certain indicators mask the fact that rural populations are not benefiting in equal measure.

In education, a modest degree of improvement in China has been achieved since the onset of the reforms. Between 1982 and 1990, the illiteracy rate declined from 21 per cent to 13 per cent for men and from 49 per cent to 32 per cent for women. In 1999, illiteracy fell again to 15 per cent of the total population aged 15 and over, with 9 per cent for men and 22 per cent for women. On the other hand, if women's education can be viewed as a gauge of general educational achievements, then China's record is disturbing. The ratio of illiteracy among women in total illiteracy actually increased slightly during 1982–90, from 69 per cent to 70 per cent. The illiterate population is overwhelmingly concentrated in rural areas. In some of the poorest rural villages, half the boys and in some minority areas nearly all the girls are not attending school and will not become literate.

To be sure, unequal capability attainment among rural and urban populations has historical roots to the extent that the situation was not essentially different before the reforms. However, based on the resource allocation mechanism of the collective farming system in China, great progress was made in the countryside during the central planning period in both Vietnam and China. The collapse of the commune system eliminated in some regions and fundamentally weakened in others the financial ability of rural communities to provide public goods. A system of cost recovery rapidly replaced collective safety nets, creating problems of access for the large majority among rural populations, particularly the poor. Attempts to establish alternative mechanisms were so slow in coming that some of the previous gains were not maintained.

The experience in Vietnam has been similar to that in China. Before the reforms, Vietnam established a universal educational framework despite the poverty of the country. The health status of the population improved significantly, due to these social interventions. Life expectancy at birth rose from 42 years in 1960 to 59 years in 1983, and the infant mortality rate declined from 165 per 1000 live births in 1960 to somewhere between 35 and 64 per 1000 in the mid-1980s (Fforde and de Vylder 1996: 234). This achievement can to a large extent be attributed to the existence of a nationwide primary healthcare network, which linked communal healthcare centres.

On the eve of the reforms, the most serious health-related problem in Vietnam was the lack of adequate food supplies. More than half of all children were affected by malnutrition to varying degrees, and the estimated calorie intake per capita was 20 per cent short of the recommended daily level (Fforde and de Vylder 1996: 233). To boost food production and consumption was therefore essential in Vietnam, and, indeed, the country has made remarkable progress in these areas during the reform period. Agricultural production has been climbing at an annual rate of between 2 and 4 per cent. Within a rather short time after market reform began, Vietnam emerged as an important rice exporter. The jump in food supplies has led to better, more adequate diets and created conditions favourable to a general rise in health status.

None the less, the reforms in Vietnam suggest once again that economic growth does not automatically translate into enhanced welfare and human capability. There have been worrying signs of deterioration in social development. The dismantling of the collective social security system has affected a large swath of the population, especially the vulnerable. There have been ups and downs in public expenditure on healthcare and education. User fees have become common at healthcare centres and primary schools. By 1991 education in Vietnam could no longer be called 'free', because the families of pupils were being required to support schools by paying various fees. Due to state budget constraints and the lower salaries offered to teachers, staff shortages became a problem in many places.

Regional gaps in access to education and healthcare and in service quality have been widening. If this trend continues, the admirable progress achieved in basic education and health status in the country will be endangered. As in some of the other Asian transitions, but especially China, one might call the reforms a success in terms of economic growth, but not in terms of social development. The lesson is that advances in social development in parallel with economic growth will require focused efforts and appropriate investment.

In the case of the Central Asian Republics, several indicators improved during the economically difficult period of transition. This has been the case for life expectancy in Uzbekistan and Turkmenistan, and infant mortality in all the Central Asian Republics except Turkmenistan between 1991 and 1994 (World Bank 1996: 172; Pomfret and Anderson 1997). In the Kyrgyz Republic, the death rate began to fall in 1995, largely as a result of declining infant mortality and fewer deaths from circulatory diseases.

However, in general, while the lack of information makes it hard to assess the overall situation in Central Asia and Mongolia, it is none the less clear that all these countries have experienced deterioration in human development since the onset of the transition. Large-scale emigration has represented a further hazard for the health status and education of populations, but especially the migrants.

Table 11.1 The registered unemployed as a percentage of the labour force in the CARs

Country	*1992*	*1993*	*1994*	*1995*	*June 1996*
Kazakhstan	0.4	0.5	0.8	1.5	3.7
Kyrgyz Republic	0.1	0.2	0.4	1.9	4.6
Uzbekistan	0.1	0.2	0.2	0.3	0.4

Sources: For 1992, OECD (1994); for 1993–96, OECD (1996), p. 26.

In Central Asia, the deterioration in maternal mortality has been dramatic. The immediate causes include lack of contraceptives and the high rates of abortion. However, the much larger background cause is the deterioration in socioeconomic conditions which has weakened the provision of healthcare services.

In Mongolia the rise in maternal mortality rates has been rapid, and the overall health status of women, particularly mothers, has been especially affected by the collapse of the healthcare system. The maternal mortality rate jumped from 120 deaths per 100 000 live births in 1991 to 200 in 1992 and 240 in 1993.

Compared to China and Vietnam, the Central Asian Republics and Mongolia had more extensive state-financed welfare systems during the socialist period. This high level of state support rendered the systems more vulnerable to sudden economic changes. In the worsening macroeconomic situation and the financial crisis linked to the transition, social programmes have usually been among the first casualties of budget cuts.

By the mid-1990s, many indicators of human development in Central Asia and Mongolia were no longer more favourable than those in China and Vietnam, although these two countries had much lower per capita incomes (Table 11.1).

11.5 Crime

Rising crime has been a common feature during the transition. Rapidly growing crime rates during the early stages of transition and the maintenance thereafter of the relatively higher levels have been a general tendency in the Asian experience.

In China, crime rates have been climbing since the onset of reform (Lu, Chapter 4, this volume). Crime surged in Central Asia during the transition. In the Kyrgyz Republic 50 per cent more crimes were reported during the first nine months of 1992 than during the corresponding period in 1991. In 1993 the increase was even more striking, and in 1994 the number of crimes was still going up by 32 per cent. More of these crimes involved weapons or violence, including homicide, assault and rape, and there was more organized crime.

In 1996, as in the Commonwealth of Independent States (CIS) countries, the number of registered crimes declined in Kazakhstan, the Kyrgyz Republic and Uzbekistan, although the number continued to rise in Turkmenistan. Meanwhile, certain types of crime were becoming still more frequent. In 1996, Turkmenistan recorded a 10 per cent increase in first-degree murder. The number of rapes went up by 18 per cent in Kazakhstan, 13 per cent in the Kyrgyz Republic and 23 per cent in Uzbekistan. The number of muggings and armed robberies soared by 23 per cent in Kazakhstan and 30 per cent in Turkmenistan, and drug-related crimes were becoming more common in almost all these countries (Interfax 1996: 15).

The causes of the rise in crime in the Asian transition economies are complicated. One of the most direct and common contributors has been the weakening ability of the state apparatus to fight crime. Virtually all governments in the Asian transition economies faced financial constraints on police enforcement. Sharp economic decline in Central Asia and Mongolia created difficulties in maintaining and strengthening law enforcement. In economically booming countries such as China, problems with decentralization and inadequate tax collection contributed to the financial constraints. Corruption is another factor. Government responses to the crime wave have been hobbled not only by a lack of resources, but also because of corruption among law enforcement officials.

Higher crime rates reflect the growing tensions created by the broader social outcomes of the transition, including the widening income gap, rising unemployment and the acceleration in social stratification in all the Asian transition economies. These causes have been exacerbated in some countries by ethnic conflict and large-scale migrations. The rise in crime, like the renewed outbreaks of communicable disease, is a further symptom of the social disruption which has augmented the sense of insecurity in these Asian countries.

11.6 The status of women

Gender equality is as an important indicator of overall well-being. Women almost everywhere experience discrimination. Health indicators, adult literacy rates, school enrolment ratios, and the percentage share of earned income are consistently lower among women than they are among men in most countries. Political representation and participation, legal rights, and access to and control over economic resources are all fields in which gender equality has yet to be achieved. Empirical evidence shows that in countries where there is greater gender equality, welfare in general is likely to be better.

Women fared far better under the socialist systems than they have under the market economies in the region. Under socialism, gender equality was considered a development priority, and policies were implemented to improve the access of women to education, maternal and child healthcare, political life and employment. Women, like men, were expected to work full time, and for this to become a reality, public or enterprise-based childcare and healthcare services were commonly developed, at least in urban areas. The conditions among rural women were generally less favourable. Even here, efforts to draw large numbers of rural women into the labour force in the formal sector of the economy produced remarkable results in the enhancement of women's position in the workplace and in the home.

The transition has affected women differently than it has men in a number of ways. It appears that in countries where the transition has been accompanied by growth, the welfare of women has improved in some respects, but worsened in others, whereas in countries experiencing sharp economic decline, the adverse effects have been more pronounced among women than among men. In general, it is likely that the transition has had a negative impact on the economic independence and political representation of women.

One of the most important areas in women's welfare is employment. Unemployment has risen in virtually all the Asian transition economies, and this has meant that increasing numbers of women have dropped out of the labour force. Women have accounted for a larger share of the layoffs linked to economic restructuring, especially in state-owned enterprises.

In China and Vietnam, rapid economic growth has led to the creation of new jobs, which has somewhat offset the job losses among both men and women in the state sector. Women have begun to enjoy greater freedom of choice in employment, as the transition has introduced a wider variety of income-earning opportunities, such as self-employment and employment in the rapidly expanding non-state sector.

Despite the fact that women have lost ground to men in employment and in some other areas, female labour participation in the Asian transitions has generally remained high.

A high female labour participation rate is generally considered a positive sign of gender equality. In the case of transitional economies, however, the 'rewards' of women's employment should also be measured. For rural women in China and Vietnam, the return to family-based production has created greater workloads for women without producing a corresponding improvement in their welfare. In urban areas wage differentials between women and men have persisted.[2] In some of the Central Asian Republics, income trends among women have become more unfavourable (ADB 1996: 29).

The economic decline in Central Asia and Mongolia has meant special hardship for women. Employment and income have dropped off among women more than they have among men. Government expenditure cuts in social programmes have had a doubly adverse effect on women. First, they have boosted female unemployment, since women hold a majority of jobs in the social services whose expenditures have been cut most severely. Second, the reduction in the provision of social services has hurt women more than it has hurt men, since women have the primary responsibility in childbearing and in the care of the young, the sick and the elderly that these services help provide. The closure of kindergartens, day-care centres and clinics has increased the work of women in the home, and this burden has in turn reduced women's prospects for employment (ADB 1996: 28).

Education has become less readily accessible to many women during the transition. Women's education has been more adversely affected by the rising cost of schools than has education among men. In China and Vietnam, girls outnumber boys among school dropouts in rural areas. Educational attainment has remained high in Central Asia and Mongolia, but it has become more difficult to maintain this achievement because education in these countries is confronted by financial constraints, and alternative sources of non-state financing have not emerged or are very inadequate in a situation of serious economic recession.

11.7 Social policies and institutions

Economic reform unavoidably entails social changes, which government policies are designed, belatedly or in advance, either to encourage or to counteract. During the central planning period, the governments placed high priority on the provision of social services, offering generous benefits to populations. The relatively high welfare standards in the pre-reform era are testimony to the support-led approach. This record stands in contrast to the reform policies focusing on growth that are believed by many to be the only source of welfare improvements.

The social policies implemented during the transition in the CARs have, in a broad sense, been adopted to overcome problems inherited from the socialist welfare systems, such as low efficiency, and to accommodate emerging market-oriented economic structures. Governments in economic recession have often been forced to undertake temporary measures to deal with the urgent pressure of shrinking resources.

In all the Asian transition economies, policy-makers have made great efforts to evaluate and adjust the provision of services in education, healthcare and social welfare. The role of the public and private sectors in supplying these services has been constantly redefined with respect to organizational structure and financing mechanisms. Various cost recovery schemes and methods to encourage the participation of the non-state sector in social services and social insurance have been tried. In the course of this process, the slowly evolving market structures have become intermingled with the old welfare systems.

One clear tendency has been a retreat of the state from welfare obligations. Governments everywhere are reducing their role in the administration and coordination not only of the economy, but also in social welfare and protection measures. The character and speed of this retreat are being affected by the overall approach to transition. The most significant retreat seems to have taken place where the approach has been most radical.

In the provision of social services, one common step has involved adjustments in the budget allocations to, for example, education and healthcare. The governments in Central Asia and Mongolia have been financially squeezed because of economic recession, but also because, following the collapse of the Soviet Union, outside assistance dried up.

It has frequently been said that the economic difficulties in these countries have rendered generous social welfare provisions no longer affordable. However, cuts in social spending, especially during the early stages of the transition, have been engineered even in those countries in which the economy has been growing. Therefore, the financial constraint cannot be the sole explanation.

In China and Vietnam, where there has been strong economic growth, budget expenditure in specific areas of social provision has sometimes either stagnated or been reduced as a proportion of GNP (Yu 1997, Jansen, Chapter 6, this volume).

The retreat of the state from the social sector has led to a chain reaction. Schools, medical centres and other welfare institutions which depended entirely on state financing now face great difficulties. Salaries in the social sector were already generally low, and the retreat has meant that they are falling further behind the pay being offered in the non-state sector or in other professional areas. There has therefore been an exodus of welfare personnel. In Vietnam and Central Asia, a considerable number of educators and medical personnel have left their low-paying jobs in the social sector or left the country altogether (ADB 1996: 27–8).

Insufficient state funds have created difficulties in the maintenance and improvement of healthcare and educational facilities, and this has contributed to the collapse of services in some places and to a decline in service quality in others. Service providers from the non-state sector have sometimes emerged, but usually they have been too limited in number and in coverage to replace state services, and they have often been too expensive for ordinary citizens. In response to the financial difficulties, public sector schools and healthcare institutions have begun to charge fees. Student expenses have become substantially higher.

The welfare impact of budget cuts depends on a number of factors, including the scale and speed of the cuts. In general, the more reliant social services were on state financing, the more severely they are likely to be affected. Economic growth has raised individual incomes and the purchasing power of the population. However, the experience of the Asian transitions suggest that, while the role of the state undoubtedly needs to be modified, the state cannot afford simply to remain passive if past gains in human development are to be maintained and strengthened. Reforms in public financing in the social sector should aim at enhancing rather than weakening the role of the state in social provisions, if not as a direct provider, then at least as a key promoter and regulator.

Another common feature of the Asian transition economies is that social policies are frequently out of step with economic and institutional changes, and this tends to create additional hardships for populations. In China and Vietnam, the collapse of the rural collective system and social safety nets took place long before alternative mechanisms for welfare provision were identified. This left the vast rural population without organized social welfare coverage and protection, and may have been responsible for the stagnation or the worsening in a number of human development indicators during the early reform period.

In contrast, there has been no sudden and thorough destruction of welfare institutions in Central Asia or Mongolia or in the urban sector in China and Vietnam, largely because of the fear of the social unrest which could arise due to welfare losses. The gradual approach to reform in social welfare systems has probably helped prevent further deterioration in human conditions in the face of drastic socioeconomic changes.

In Central Asia and Mongolia, where welfare systems reached universal coverage long before the transition, the problem is to maintain social provisions at levels consistent at least with their externality costs while making adjustments consistent with the new role of the market as a dominant mechanism for resource allocation. Facing economic difficulties, governments have cut social expenditures so as to bring budgets under control and achieve macroeconomic stability. For instance, Kazakhstan eliminated the indexing of social benefits to cost-of-living increases and tightened eligibility requirements in order to reduce the government fiscal deficit. While these measures have allowed the government to achieve some control over the budget, the process has left gaping holes in the social safety nets (ADB 1996: 28).

In general, it would be a disaster for the well-being of populations if the focus of social policies during the reform process were simply towards the reduction of welfare provisions and social protection, instead of the construction of systems which are more efficient, but which enhance welfare.

11.8 Balancing well-being and economic transition

Few expected the transition to be smooth, without cost, or painless. Such a large-scale socioeconomic transformation was bound to cause discomfort, disruptions, even breakdowns. The transition process has entailed the reorientation of external economic relationships and changes in trade regimes. This process has been especially costly for those countries which were tightly integrated into the CMEA trading system. The collapse of this trading system has had a very severe impact on the Central Asian Republics, Mongolia and, to a lesser extent, Vietnam. The sudden collapse of CMEA trade and the end of transfer payments have been particularly devastating for Mongolia and extremely painful for Uzbekistan and the Kyrgyz Republic. China was the least affected by this event, because the initial success in rural reform and the reorientation of trade have tended to promote growth. In contrast, similar efforts in Central Asia and Mongolia have been of little help in preventing economic recession. A sharp economic decline during the early stages of transition was not an unusual experience among the transition economies. Immediate and sustained economic growth on the heels of reform has occurred in only a very few countries.

It had been anticipated that the well-being of populations would suffer during the transition. The transition had also been expected to lead to an increase in inequality. From an economic point of view, it has been argued that greater income inequality would represent an incentive to output and competition, thereby contributing to productivity and overall economic efficiency. In the long run, although some may become richer than others, all would be better off, according to this view.

Economic and welfare losses were expected to be recovered rather quickly, because the transition process was not expected to last long. It followed that a more radical transformation, although causing greater pain, would shorten the duration of the transition.

It appears, however, that whatever the actual strategy chosen, the transition is turning out to be a more torturous process than expected, and it is apparent that it is likely to last a long time. Political regimes can be changed quite quickly. Reform measures such as privatization can be carried out in a short time (as in the case of Mongolia, for instance). It did not take long to do away even with certain established institutions. In China and Vietnam, the shift from the rural collective system to family farming was accomplished within a couple of years, and in Vietnam many state enterprises were shut down or merged with others very rapidly. None the less, in all these countries, the economic and social transformation – understood as the establishment of a well-functioning socioeconomic structure – seems to be far from over.

Outside of East Asia, the Kyrgyz Republic and Kazakhstan have pursued, or have been forced to pursue, a more radical type of transition. The economic results have remained far less benign than anticipated. One obvious lesson is that the process of transition and its consequences are not entirely subject to the control of policy-makers. The transition outcomes are not merely the end products of government policy inputs. Markets are not created in a vacuum, and changes occurring in socioeconomic conditions are the result of the constant give and take of various social forces.

By now it ought to be clear that there are no quick fixes. Anyone who still expects private markets to solve all economic and social problems is likely to be very disappointed. Dealing with current social problems will require the constant reassessment of policy priorities and, perhaps more importantly, a rethinking of some of the guiding principles behind the transitional and social development initiatives.

China and Vietnam and in a passive sense Uzbekistan have exhibited exceptionally good economic performance, but even where per capita income has grown substantially, the welfare achievements have been neither even nor consistent.

In view of the welfare changes in Asian countries during the transition, a new pattern of development seems to have emerged. Under the central planning system, the achievements in human development were greater than the level of economic development might indicate. Now, the focus has shifted, and human development has suffered. However, simply shifting the ideology to free-market doctrines has not proven conducive both to economic growth and human welfare. The market will not produce all the answers and the ability of markets to work their beneficial effects depends on institutional features that are being dismantled as part of the transition to the market. Efforts to maintain welfare gains are critical, and policy-makers should abandon the idea that they can afford to wait because economic growth will automatically generate solutions to welfare problems.

Governments should make greater administrative and organizational efforts to improve the well-being of people. Uzbekistan resorted to a traditional system of community welfare as a key welfare delivery system. China has a relatively efficient relief system which has been employed successfully to distribute grain during periods of extreme shortage, thereby preventing starvation. This system and similar institutional networks should not be abandoned because of economic reform. The effective organizational abilities and extensive administrative frameworks which governments have inherited from the central planning era can play an important role in facilitating social development. Social support networks and the non-state sector should be encouraged to participate more energetically in welfare provision. Likewise, governments should support mass participation in the establishment of people-based, welfare-oriented institutions. This could be achieved, for example, by mobilizing families, communities and cooperatives and other organizations to join together to form an integrated welfare system, by creating among people a higher level of awareness of the importance of well-being, by putting people first, and by emphasizing that well-being is the ultimate goal of economic development.

There is really only one fundamental issue: the purpose of economic transition. As increasingly recognized in development theory, economic development can have significance only if it leads to improvements in human welfare. This concept should be applied to the economic transition. The transition is not an end in itself. Its success will be judged only on the basis of the outcomes for human development.

Notes

1. The problem with the analysis of the World Bank (1996) is that it treats inequality in the same way as it does poverty, thus creating considerable confusion. While it may be correct to say that 'The key to containing and reducing poverty, therefore, is resumed growth' (World Bank 1996: 67), the same cannot be said of inequality. The World Bank concedes that 'income inequality is not out of line with that in comparator market economies and therefore may not fall significantly' (ibid.).
2. Survey data in 1988 in China show that the wage gap between men and women in the urban sector and the per capita income gap between men and women in rural areas were not substantial. Moreover, no severe poverty differences were observed between men and women in either the 1988 or 1995 surveys (Knight and Song 1993; Gustafsson and Li 1993; Li 1996).

References

ADB (Asian Development Bank) (1996), *Annual Report, 1995*, Manila: Asian Development Bank.

Ahmad, Ehtisham and Wang Yan (1991), *Inequality and Poverty in China: Institutional Change and Public Policy 1978–88*, Development Economic Research Programme, STICERD (Suntory-Toyota International Centre for Economics and Related Disciplines), CP/14, London: London School of Economics (July).

Alesina, Alberto and Roberto Perotti (1996), 'Income Distribution, Political Instability and Investment', *European Economic Review*, Vol. 40, No. 6, pp. 1203–28.

Birdsall, Nancy, David Ross and Richard Sabot (1995), 'Inequality and Growth Reconsidered: Lessons from East Asia', *World Bank Economic Review*, Vol. 9, No. 3, pp. 477–508.

Fforde, Adam and Stefan de Vylder (1996), *From Plan to Market, The Economic Transition in Vietnam*, Boulder, CO: Westview Press.

Griffin, Keith and Zhao Renwei (eds) (1993), *The Distribution of Income in China*, London: Macmillan.

Gustafsson, B. and Li Shi (1993), 'Inequality of Well-being in China at the End of the 1980s' (mimeo).

Interfax (1995), 'Statistical Report', Denver, CO: Interfax-America (19–26 April).

Interfax (1996), 'Statistical Report', Denver, CO: Interfax-America (11–18 October).

Kim, Young C. (1996), 'Mongolia', pp. 295–425 in Pradumna B. Rana and Naved Hamid (eds), *From Centrally Planned to Market Economies: The Asian Approach*, Vol. 2, *People's Republic of China and Mongolia*, Hong Kong: Oxford University Press.

Knight, John and Song Lina (1993), 'Why Urban Wages Differ in China', pp. 216–84 in Keith Griffin and Zhao Renwei (eds), *The Distribution of Income in China*, London: Macmillan.

Li Shi (1996), 'Changes in Poverty Reduction in China' (mimeo), Helsinki: UNU/WIDER.

Murray, Christopher and Lincoln C. Chen (1992), 'Understanding Morbidity Change', *Population and Development Review*, Vol. 18, No. 3, pp. 481–503.

OECD (1996), *Short-term Economic Indicators: Transition Economies*, Paris, Organization for Economic Cooperation and Development (Paris: OECD).

Pomfret, Richard (1996), *Asian Economies in Transition: Reforming Centrally Planned Economies*, Cheltenham, UK: Edward Elgar.

Pomfret, Richard and Kathryn H. Anderson (1997), 'Uzbekistan: Welfare Impact of Slow Transition' (mimeo), Helsinki: UNU/WIDER.

Preston, Samuel H. (1975), 'The Changing Relation between Mortality and Level of Economic Development', *Population Studies*, Vol. 29, No. 2, pp. 231–48.

Rodgers, G. B. (1979), 'Income and Inequality as Determinants of Mortality: An International Cross-section Analysis', *Population Studies*, Vol. 33, No. 2, pp. 343–51.

UNDP (1996), 'Regional Cooperation Framework for the Asia-Pacific Region (1997–2001)' (mimeo) (27 November).

Wei Ying (1996), 'Woguo xianyou gelei weishing chouzi moshi jieshao' ('An Introduction to Financing Models for Health Care in China'), pp. 16–24 in Centre for Health and Economic Training of China (1996), *Zhongguo weishing chouzi yanjiu baogao* (Report of Research on Health Care Financing in China), Beijing, Centre for Helth and Economic Training of China.

World Bank (1996), *From Plan to Market: World Development Report, 1996*, New York: Oxford University Press.

Yu Dezhi (1997), 'Decentralization of Finance System, Price Reform and Commune System Disintegration: The Changes in China's Healthcare System' (mimeo).

Index